# THE LIMITS OF LEVIATHAN

Much of international law, like much of contract, is enforced not by independent sanctions but rather through cooperative interaction among the parties, with repeat dealings, reputation, and a preference for reciprocity doing most of the enforcement work. *The Limits of Leviathan* identifies the areas in international law where formal enforcement provides the most promising means of promoting cooperation and where it does not. In particular, it looks at the International Criminal Court, the rules for world trade, efforts to enlist domestic courts to enforce orders of the International Court of Justice, domestic judicial enforcement of the Geneva Convention, the domain of international commercial agreements, and the question of odious debt incurred by sovereigns. This book explains how international law, like contract, depends largely on the willingness of responsible parties to make commitments.

Robert E. Scott is a nationally recognized scholar and teacher in the fields of contracts, commercial transactions, and bankruptcy. He was the inaugural Lewis F. Powell Jr. Professor of Law at the University of Virginia School of Law from 1982 to 2003 and William L. Matheson & Robert M. Morgenthau Distinguished Professor from 2001 to 2003. In 2003 he was named an inaugural recipient of the David and Mary Harrison Distinguished Professorship. He has delivered numerous papers and published extensively in law journals. He has coauthored four books on contracts and commercial transactions. Among his many articles are six that he coauthored with Professor Charles Goetz that set the standard for the economic analysis of the law of contracts.

Paul B. Stephan is an expert on international business and Soviet and post-Soviet legal systems who has spent his career studying and writing about the globalization of the world economy and the transition away from Soviet-style socialism. He joined the Virginia faculty in 1979 and was the Percy Brown Jr. Professor of Law from 1991 to 2003. In 2003, he succeeded Scott as the Lewis F. Powell Jr. Professor of Law. He has written extensively on international law, corruption, and the history of the Cold War, as well as on taxation and constitutional law. He has worked in Russia, Georgia, Ukraine, Albania, and Slovakia on behalf of the U.S. Treasury and in Kazakhstan and Azerbaijan on behalf of the International Monetary Fund.

# THE LIMITS OF LEVIATHAN

## Contract Theory and the Enforcement of International Law

**ROBERT E. SCOTT**

David and Mary Harrison Distinguished Professor of Law, University of Virginia

**PAUL B. STEPHAN**

Lewis F. Powell Jr. Professor of Law and Hunton & Williams Research Professor, University of Virginia

**CAMBRIDGE**
UNIVERSITY PRESS

CAMBRIDGE UNIVERSITY PRESS
Cambridge, New York, Melbourne, Madrid, Cape Town, Singapore, São Paulo

Cambridge University Press
32 Avenue of the Americas, New York, NY 10013-2473, USA

www.cambridge.org
Information on this title: www.cambridge.org/9780521858465

First published 2006

Printed in the United States of America

*A catalog record for this publication is available from the British Library.*

*Library of Congress Cataloging in Publication Data*

Scott, Robert E., 1994–
The limits of Leviathan : contract theory and the enforcement of International
Law / Robert E. Scott, Paul B. Stephan.
    p.   cm.
Includes index.
ISBN 0-521-85846-1 (hardback : alk. paper)
1. Execution (Law)   2. International and municipal law.   3. Treaties.
4. Breach of contract.   I. Stephan, Paul B.   II. Title.
K2330.S26   2006
341–dc22        2006004854

ISBN-13   978-0-521-85846-5 hardback
ISBN-10   0-521-85846-1 hardback

# CONTENTS

# FOREWORD

This book has its origins in work we presented at a conference on Freedom From Contract, organized by Omri Ben-Shahar of the University of Michigan and hosted by the University of Wisconsin Law School. That conference reinforced two impressions that had motivated our collaboration: Contracts scholars and international lawyers have not made much of an investment in learning what each field has to offer the other, and the possibilities for mutual enrichment are great. This extension of that project represents our effort to demonstrate both that problems in international relations illuminate some of the most challenging issues in contract theory today, and that international law takes on great theoretical richness and rigor when it employs the insights of contract theory.

For the most part, our theoretical claims in this book are positive and descriptive rather than normative. We believe that contract theory (an umbrella phrase that we use to describe both the law and economics of contracts as well as the separate discipline of the economics of contract) explains much of current practice regarding the enforcement of international law. Seeking to understand why we see the legal institutions we do, as opposed to describing and defending a better world in which we might live, is more familiar to contracts scholars than to international lawyers. One of the exciting challenges of international law and international relations theory, however, is to give a convincing account of the world as we find it, and for this purpose contract theory does important work. We will be happy if this book challenges both contracts scholars and international lawyers to rethink what their disciplines do.

We could not leave the subject, however, without showing some of the normative implications that contract theory has for current controversies in international law and its enforcement. The final chapter of this book considers some of these questions. We recognize that not everyone will appreciate the normative implications of our theory and that some will resist them. We welcome the challenge of this criticism, as our primary purpose is to open a conversation. Where this leads us is less important than that we start down the path.

We recognize that an attempt to marry widely divergent scholarly traditions, with distinct methodological approaches and normative commitments, presents great obstacles. We have learned from our collaboration that scholars in one field tend to regard those in the other as speaking a separate language. One modest contribution that we make toward overcoming these barriers is the glossary at the back of the book, which is meant to help the reader negotiate through the terminological hurdles that interdisciplinary work necessarily erects. More generally, we believe that this book demonstrates how scholars from different traditions can craft a joint research agenda of general interest.

Our paper for the Freedom From Contract conference and the subsequent book manuscript has received careful comments from many colleagues. We benefited from comments of the conference participants, in addition to insights derived from workshops at the University of Chicago Law School, Georgetown University Law Center, Case Western Reserve Law School, Vanderbilt Law School, Washington and Lee Law School, and the University of Virginia School of Law. In addition, a number of colleagues have shared with us both their criticism and wisdom. Jody Kraus and Ted White in particular gave valuable guidance at a time when we were considering what this book should look like. Other attentive and helpful readers included Karen Alter, George Bermann, Curtis Bradley, Rachel Brewster, Jack Goldsmith, Andrew Guzman, Julian Ku, Allen Lynch, John Setear, Dan Tarullo, Joel Trachtman, George Triantis, John Yoo, and four anonymous referees. The staff of the Arthur J. Morris Law Library at the University of Virginia, and in particular Xinh Luu, were always at our beck and call and never let us down. Jeremy Weinberg provided invaluable research assistance, and Aaron Mahler displayed great skill as an editor. Our Dean, dear friend and colleague John C. Jeffries Jr., ensured that we never lacked for support. John Berger persuaded us to undertake this project, and we remain in his debt. Laura Lawrie was an excellent copy editor. Last, but far from least, Pamela Clark and Elizabeth Scott gave us the right mix of uncritical acceptance and coruscating insight.

# 1 INTRODUCTION

If a covenant be made, wherein neither of the parties perform presently, but trust one another; in the condition of mere nature, which is a condition of war of every man against every man, upon any reasonable suspicion, it is void: but if there be a common power set over them both, with right and force sufficient to compel performance, it is not void. For he that performeth first, has no assurance the other will perform after; because the bonds of words are too weak to bridle men's ambition, avarice, anger, and other passions, without the fear of some coercive power.

Thomas Hobbes, LEVIATHAN (1651)

We are determined to work at all levels to tackle global terrorism and stem the weapons of mass destruction. To this end, we will promote relentlessly the dialogue among civilizations and contribute uncompromisingly to strengthening the institutions of global governance and expanding the reach of international law.

Athens Declaration on the Signing of the Treaty of Accession on the Enlargement of the European Union, April 16, 2003

RECENTLY, A CANADIAN COMPANY AND ITS PRINCIPAL STOCKHOLDER put the civil justice system of the United States on trial. Outraged by a huge punitive damages award that drove the company into bankruptcy, they claimed that a Mississippi lawsuit violated their fundamental rights. Remarkably, the victims based their suit on international law, and brought it before an international tribunal empowered to issue a monetary award against the United States. [1]

---

[1] The Loewen Group, Inc. v. United States, Final Award (Jun. 26, 2003) (egregious misconduct in civil trial leading to enormous damages manifestly a denial of justice subject to Chapter 11; no relief available because victim failed to seek appellate review). The United States is a party to the Convention on the Settlement of Investment Disputes Between States and Nationals of Other States, Mar. 18, 1965, art. 52, 17 U.S.T. 1270, 575 U.N.T.S. 159 (1985), which obligates it to respect the awards

In Europe, vindicating rights derived from international law through an international tribunal is nothing new, as the language of the Athens Declaration quoted earlier suggests. Anyone who believes someone has infringed an interest protected by the European Community's Treaty of Rome, to which twenty-five states now adhere, can both demand that domestic courts hear the claim and obtain review of these decisions in the European Court of Justice in Luxembourg. Using these tools, women in Northern Ireland have forced the British government to hire them as police officers; foreign beer producers have overturned Germany's restrictions on their sales; and professional soccer players have obtained free agency.[2] A victim of human rights violations by any of forty-five European states can sue in the European Court of Human Rights, based in Strasbourg, and obtain both a determination of the rights in question and a damages award. In recent years, the Strasbourg court has confronted issues that, in the U.S. context, provoke great passion. It has, for example, vindicated the right to die, forbidden discrimination against the transgendered, and mandated the inclusion of homosexuals in the armed forces.[3] Many European states also authorize their domestic courts to enforce the same body of human rights law. The statute empowering British courts to do so functions something like a Bill of Rights, the first in British history.

In the United States, the Supreme Court in *Sosa v. Alvarez-Machain* recently endorsed the idea that federal courts can entertain suits under international law, even in the absence of a treaty or statute explicitly authorizing the litigation.[4] For nearly a quarter-century in advance of this decision, some lower courts had been doing this. Federal litigation based on international law has challenged the employment policies, environmental records, and mining and drilling

of these tribunals. *See* 22 U.S.C. §§1650, 1650a (2001). *Cf.* 28 U.S.C. §2414 (2001) (obligating Secretary of Treasury to pay awarded after confirmation by federal court pursuant to 22 U.S.C. §1650a). For a general discussion, see Guillermo Aguilar Alvarez & William W. Park, *The New Face of Investment Arbitration: NAFTA Chapter 11*, 28 YALE J. INT'L L. 365 (2003).

[2] Union Royale Belges des Sociétés de Football Association v. Bosman (Case C-415/93), [1995] E.C.R.-I 4921 (soccer free agency); Commission v. Germany (Case 178/84), [1987] E.C.R. 1227 (beer purity standards); Johnston v. Chief Constable (Case 222/84), [1986] E.C.R. 1651 (sex discrimination).

[3] For representative cases, see Lopez Ostra v. Spain, 20 Eur. H.R. Rep. 277 (1994) (solid waste treatment plant located near home violates right to privacy); Maria Guerra v. Italy, 26 Eur. H.R. Rep. 357 (1998) (serious environmental pollution violates right to privacy); Jordan v. United Kingdom, 37 Eur. H.R. Rep. (2001) (deficiencies in police investigation of homicide constitute a violation of European Convention's right to life); Pretty v. United Kingdom, 35 Eur. H.R. Rep. 1 (2002) (right to die); I. v. United Kingdom, 36 Eur. H.R. Rep. 53 (2002) (failure to give legal recognition to sex change violates right to privacy); E. v. United Kingdom, 36 Eur. H.R. Rep. 31 (2002) (failure by social services to exercise due diligence in supervising children endangered by home environment violates European Convention).

[4] 542 U.S. 692 (2004) (dismissing claim that arbitrary arrest of Mexican national by Mexican police constituted a violation of international law for which a damages remedy was available).

practices of a host of prominent multinational firms.[5] A recent spate of litigation has asserted the obligation of U.S. courts to obey a decision of the International Court of Justice regarding the rights of aliens arrested in the United States, a position that a majority of the Supreme Court did not reject and that four justices seemed to embrace.[6] Legislation in the United Kingdom, Canada, and other large and important jurisdictions has opened up domestic courts to claims based on international law. Finally, in *Roper v. Simmons* the Supreme Court, hesitantly and controversially, seems to have embraced international law as a tool for interpreting the more elastic clauses of the Constitution.[7]

What these phenomena embody is a new approach to the enforcement of international law. Traditionally, states contracted for obligations, which they undertook to enforce through methods ranging from diplomatic protests to economic pressure to armed attack. Informal sanctions, largely involving effects on reputation and threats of retaliation, did most of the day-to-day work of ensuring compliance. International law was soft, in the sense that there existed no Hobbesian Leviathan to sanction default. The new approach, in contrast, allows private enforcement, employs independent tribunals and courts to do the enforcing, and empowers those tribunals and courts to wield the same array of tools that domestic courts traditionally use to compel compliance with their decisions. International law has become hard law, with its own Leviathan.

---

[5] For a representative sample of the cases, see Aldana v. Del Monte Fresh Produce, N.A., Inc., 416 F. 3rd 1242 (11th Cir. 2005) (lawsuit by Guatemalan trade unionists against plantation owner for physical abuse); Alperin v. Vatican Bank 410 F.3d 532 (9th Cir. 2005) (lawsuit against bank for assisting in human rights violations during World War II); Ungaro-Benages v. Dresdner Bank AG, 379 F.3rd 1227 (11th Cir. 2004) (lawsuit against banks for assisting Nazi takeover of Jewish-owned companies); Flores v. Southern Peru Copper Corp., 343 F.3rd 140 (2nd Cir. 2003) (lawsuit against mining company for pollution-related injuries); Doe v. Unocal, 395 F.3rd 932 (9th Cir. 2002) (lawsuit against energy company for slave labor compelled by local military on behalf of company); Aguinda v. Texaco, Inc., 303 F.3rd 470 (2nd Cir. 2002) (lawsuit against energy company for environmental damage); Bano v. Union Carbide Corp., 273 F.3rd 370 (2nd Cir. 2001) (lawsuit against chemical company for release of toxic gas); Bigio v. Coca-Cola Co., 239 F.3rd 440 (2nd Cir. 2000) (lawsuit against companies that rented or purchased property that had been seized by Egypt from Jewish owners); Wiwa v. Royal Dutch Shell Corp., 226 F.3rd 88 (2nd Cir. 2000) (lawsuit against energy company for complicity in suppression of critics of its relations with Nigerian government); Beanal v. Freeport-McMoran, Inc., 197 F.3rd 161 (5th Cir. 1999) (lawsuit against mining company for environmental abuses and genocide); Hamid v. Price Waterhouse, 51 F.3rd 1411 (9th Cir. 1995) (lawsuit by depositors in collapsed bank against business associates of bank). According to press reports, the Unocal lawsuit resulted in a substantial settlement in 2004, after the Supreme Court decided *Sosa*, although the amount of the defendant's payment remains undisclosed.

[6] Medellin v. Dretke, 544 U.S. 660 (2005) (dismissing lawsuit in light of presidential order seeking to implement ICJ decision); *id.* at 672 (O'Connor, J., dissenting) (asserting jurisdiction to hear suit).

[7] 543 U.S. 551 (2005). The Supreme Court currently has before it a joined case that might allow it to address these issues yet again. Sanchez-Llamas v. Oregon, No. 04-10566, and Bustillo v. Johnson, No. 05-51, argued March 29, 2006. One of us (Stephan) filed a brief *amicus curiae* in support of the respondents in those cases.

In the case of the dispute over civil justice in Mississippi, for example, the tribunal had the authority to issue an award of damages against the United States, which U.S. law required the government to honor.

Throughout this book, we will use the term *formal enforcement* to distinguish legalized, institutionally based, privately initiated mechanisms from the traditional informal means of enforcement that remain subject to state control. The key characteristics of the formal enforcement process are the promulgation of nondiscretionary rules governing the behavior of affected parties and the existence of a body with both the authority and the capacity to consider claims brought by a representative range of interested parties and to grant relief through direct imposition of preannounced and salient sanctions for noncompliance. When we say "a representative range of interested parties," we do not mean that standing to initiate proceedings has to extend to all interested persons, but only that it is not limited solely to states. When we talk about "direct imposition" of sanctions, we mean to exclude cases where a body can only call on states to carry out its judgment. Throughout, our focus is on the formality of enforcement and not the formality of dispute resolution. International law has many tribunals with the capacity to hear complaints and deliver pronouncements. We are concerned with the limited (but growing) number of cases in which a disinterested dispute resolver (not necessarily exercising state power) has the capability directly to impose costs on rule breakers.

Formal enforcement, in sum, is more than a centralized system of dispute resolution: It entails independent authority by a legal body to take up a matter and the capacity directly to impose meaningful sanctions. As we explain more fully in this book, our concept of formal enforcement embraces private commercial arbitration and a private group's centralized enforcement of its membership rules as well as state-created adjudicative bodies. The key distinction is not between private and public adjudication but between, on the one hand, ex ante legalization with centralized enforcement and, on the other hand, informal sanctions for noncompliance imposed ex post without much coordination.

A long-standing conversation among international legal scholars involves the distinction between hard and soft law. Hard law creates a clear obligation, although these scholars rarely specify what kinds of enforcement mechanisms are entailed. The model, however, is domestic law, which courts enforce with a variety of sanctions at their direct disposal. Soft law expresses hopes rather than commitment, and by its terms entails no direct enforcement. Without taking sides in the debate about the definition and significance of hard and soft law, we will appropriate the term for our discussion of enforcement. We regard international law that is enforced formally to be hard law, and the growth of formal enforcement constitutes a hardening of international law. We recognize that for some specialists the hard/soft distinction refers only to the content of an obligation, and not the enforcement mechanisms attached to it.[8] We are persuaded, however, that a functional analysis of any set of legal rules, international law most of all, must give a central role to enforcement mechanisms.

Elements of our argument challenge conventional understandings about the enforcement of international law. First, the significance of formal enforcement of international law by independent courts and tribunals remains controversial. Mainstream international law scholars mostly see international law as, at best, weakly enforced, and discount the power and influence of the enforcement institutions that do exist.[9] A widespread, and in our view erroneous, belief holds that international law enjoys no formal enforcement. Accordingly, many scholars bemoan the ability of individual states, first and foremost the United States, to frustrate the enforcement of international law and call for strengthening existing formal mechanisms and adding new ones. In particular, those who aspire to more hardening of international law dominate the legal academy.

A dissident strain of scholarship argues that the already existing institutions represent an intolerable threat to national sovereignty. Critics on the left attack the tribunals that enforce investment protection treaties as illegitimate impediments to necessary national environmental, labor, cultural, and social regulation. Critics on the right complain that the International Criminal Court, the European economic and human rights courts, and the increasing willingness of domestic courts to fashion rights and remedies based on international law all represent a threat to liberty and democratic self-governance.

Both the mainstream scholarship and the dissident strands miss crucial points. The mainstream scholars do not appreciate how much formal enforcement already exists in the international system and how it has become more significant in recent years. Its expansion undermines concerns about its weakness: The trend is clearly away from impotence. International law, because of the growth of formal enforcement, has become a real force with direct and material consequences for a wide range of actors. The institution may not wield

---

[8] Kenneth W. Abbott & Duncan Snidal, *Hard and Soft Law in International Governance* in LEGALIZATION AND WORLD POLITICS 37 (Judith L. Goldstein, Miles Kahler, Robert O. Keohane, & Anne-Marie Slaughter, eds. 2001). For a recent discussion of these concepts that proposes to substitute "legal" and "nonlegal" for "hard" and "soft," see JACK L. GOLDSMITH & ERIC A. POSNER, THE LIMITS OF INTERNATIONAL LAW 81–100 (2005).

[9] For recent instances, see Anupam Chander, *Globalization and Distrust*, 114 YALE L.J. 1193 (2005); Allison Marston Danner, *Enhancing the Legitimacy and Accountability of Prosecutorial Discretion at the International Criminal Court*, 97 AM. J. INT'L L. 510 (2003).

the full extent of power associated with Hobbes's Leviathan, but its capabilities are considerable and growing.

The dissidents, in contrast, do not overstate the extent of formal enforcement so much as draw the wrong inferences about what it does. It is not plausible that a phenomenon of sufficient breadth to alarm both the left and the right results from a covert and illegitimate usurpation of national sovereignty. Formal enforcement has grown because it bolsters otherwise valuable cooperation, not because it represents a power grab by unaccountable actors.

## METHODOLOGY

This book draws on several scholarly discourses in the course of establishing its claims. We recognize that the switching among fields required by inter-disciplinary work makes demands on our readers, but we try to lighten that burden by providing sufficient background for each. We of course address international lawyers, both scholars and other policy makers, who continue to search for ways of grounding their discipline in robust theory and convincing empirical analysis.[10] We hope to persuade them that modern contract theory provides an important new perspective for understanding both what international law does and what society should ask it to do. We also draw heavily on the work of political scientists who specialize in international relations and seek to extend their insights. Our core methodological commitment, however, remains with law and economics, the discipline that has most influenced contract theory over the last three decades. Our underlying purpose is to convince international lawyers and international relations experts of the value of this methodology as a tool for understanding their fields.

A related goal is to normalize international law scholarship. In spite of the rise of formal enforcement and the consequent intrusion of international law claims into a growing number of domestic public policy debates, international law specialists tend not to engage much with other members of the legal academy. Some of the traditional barriers between the discipline and other approaches to law have begun to come down, partly as a result of a growing collaboration between international lawyers and political scientists, partly because the public policy issues have attracted the interest of leading public law scholars, and partly

[10] When we speak of "other" policy makers, we mean to suggest that, for international lawyers, scholars count as policy makers. For insiders to international law, the term "publicist" does this work. It refers to persons who propound international law in an authoritative manner. For example, Article 38(1)(d) of the Statute of the International Court of Justice refers to "the teachings of the most highly qualified publicists of the various nations, as subsidiary means for the determination of rules of law."

because a handful of private law scholars with an interdisciplinary bent have become interested in the subject.[11] We seek to build on these developments by demonstrating that insights originally developed to elucidate a core legal subject – contract law – also extend our understanding of the function of international law.

We will spell out our informal model of optimal enforcement later in this book, but a few general methodological observations are necessary here. The foundation of our model comes from contract theory, which draws on economic science for its key assumptions and methodology. In particular, because the enforcement of international law entails costs, both directly through the monitoring of behavior and the imposition of sanctions and indirectly through the opportunities foreclosed to actors seeking compliance with the rules, we assume that states seek to attain a level of enforcement that maximizes the benefits from compliance net of enforcement and compliance costs. Again, we recognize that ascribing to states the same welfare maximizing motivations that are assumed to apply to private firms requires some justification. We will seek to persuade the reader that the similarities between the behavior of states and that of private entities are sufficient to make this analytical exercise worthwhile.

It should be obvious in any case that optimal enforcement is not maximum enforcement. To take a hypothetical example inspired by the dispute between the United States and the European Community (EC) over genetically modified food, suppose that multinational enterprises had the right to sue states for injuries to their business caused by food safety restrictions that lack a sound scientific basis and therefore violate an international agreement on trade barriers. Further suppose that the rule of compensation requires states to pay some multiple of actual injury to increase deterrence against wrongful regulation. It seems plausible that, for a sufficiently large multiplier and a sufficiently high level of controversy about the science underlying a potential health threat, the supercompensation mechanism will deter states from implementing objectively desirable regulation. Overdeterrence of the proscribed

---

[11] On collaboration between political scientists and international law scholars, see Anne-Marie Slaughter, Andrew S. Tulumello, & Stepan Wood, *International Law and International Relations Theory: A New Generation of Interdisciplinary Scholarship*, 92 AM. J. INT'L L. 367 (1998). For representative work by public law scholars, see Bruce Ackerman, *The Rise of World Constitutionalism*, 83 VA. L. REV. 771 (1997); Curtis A. Bradley & Jack L. Goldsmith, *Customary International Law as Federal Law: A Critique of the Modern Position*, 110 HARV. L. REV. 815 (1997); Laurence H. Tribe, *Taking Text and Structure Seriously: Reflections on Free-Form Method in Constitutional Interpretation*, 108 HARV. L. REV. 1221 (1995). For a recent review of the impact of law and economics scholarship on international law, see Alan O. Sykes, *International Law*, in HANDBOOK OF LAW AND ECONOMICS (Mitchell Polinsky & Steven Shavell eds. 2006).

behavior – here spurious regulation designed to protect domestic producers from import competition – can deter valuable conduct – here beneficial health and safety rules – that might be mistaken for the proscribed behavior.

Isolating the issue of optimal enforcement might strike some as ignoring the elephant in the room. Not all international cooperation is beneficial. A producer cartel such as the Organization of the Petroleum Exporting Countries, for example, benefits its members by restricting the supply of its product at a low level to attain monopoly rents. Under most conventional analyses, the loss to consumers from the high prices more than exceeds the producers' excess profits. Is it possible to talk about optimal enforcement without considering the optimality of the underlying cooperative project?

We acknowledge that there exist many perspectives from which one might launch indictments of some or all of international law. Critics on the left argue that international economic law reflects the interests of multinational firms to the detriment of workers and consumers; voices from the developing world argue that international law constitutes an extension of the colonialist project intended to redistribute wealth and power from the third world to the first; and some on the right contend that much of international law represents an effort to perpetuate socialist and statist programs that have largely failed on the national level.[12] But we do not think it necessary to grapple with these critiques to expound a model of optimal enforcement.

It is enough to show that the analysis of optimal enforcement can be independent of the assessment of the underlying objectives of a cooperative product. If this is true, and if it is conceivable that some instances of international cooperation can be valuable, even if the cases we see in the present world incite controversy, then a model of optimal enforcement has value. The large body of scholarship devoted to the theory of the firm, for example, focuses on the agency costs associated with particular forms of organization and does not consider the underlying social costs or benefits produced by particular enterprises.[13] Analytically, we do exactly the same thing: We consider only the question of how to optimize the value of a given cooperative project under conditions of costly enforcement.

---

[12]  From the left, see Chantal Thomas, *Globalization and the Reproduction of Hierarchy*, 33 U.C. DAVIS L. REV. 1451 (2000). For the perspective of third world scholars, see Makau Mutua, *Savages, Victims, and Saviors: The Metaphor of Human Rights*, 42 HARV. J. INT'L L. 201 (2001). From the right, see ROBERT H. BORK, COERCING VIRTUE: THE WORLDWIDE RULE OF JUDGES (2003); Jeremy Rabkin, *Is EU Policy Eroding the Sovereignty of Non-Member States?* 1 CHI. J. INT'L L. 273 (2000).

[13]  The seminal works include R. H. Coase, *The Nature of the Firm*, 4 ECONOMICA 386 (1937); Michael C. Jensen & William H. Meckling, *Theory of the Firm: Managerial Behavior, Agency Costs and Ownership Structure*, 3 J. FIN. ECON. 305 (1976); OLIVER E. WILLIAMSON, THE ECONOMIC INSTITUTIONS OF CAPITALISM: FIRMS, MARKETS, AND RELATIONAL CONTRACTING (1985).

Our model for the enforcement of international law rests on several assumptions that we will specify and support later in the book. We assume that people who represent states in the making of international law – principally, but not exclusively, the architects of international agreements – act rationally, in the sense that they seek to optimize certain values based on preferences that remain consistent. We further assume that a process of natural selection operates, at least weakly, so that over time representatives who make wrong guesses about what choices will maximize their preferred values, or whose preferences undermine their capacity to act as an agent of a state, will be replaced by representatives who guess better and whose preferences bolster their capacity to act as an agent. The analysis, in other words, is at some level Darwinian, although certainly not social Darwinist. We further believe that these selective pressures operate to some degree on all kinds of representative structures, dictatorships as well as democracies, although we concede that different structures may respond to these pressures with various degrees of immediacy and rapidity. These assumptions suggest that the long-term trend in the enforcement of international law may be in the direction of optimality, and also that there exist conditions under which short-term trends might lead to reduced welfare.

The remainder of our model draws on the economics of information, in particular the analysis of private knowledge and obstacles to verifying certain states of the world, and on theories of informal enforcement of obligations based on reputational effects and the threat of retaliation. We link this literature to the work of experimental economists who have uncovered evidence of a widely held but not universal preference for reciprocity on the part of individuals. The results of this research is consistent with the work of experimental anthropologists and evolutionary theorists who find substantial evidence for a theory of cultural selection of norms of reciprocity. These allied methodologies provide the basis for our prediction that formal and informal enforcement often operate as rivals rather than as complements and that, within its separate domain, each one dominates the other in motivating socially beneficial cooperation.

## Formal and Informal Enforcement of International Law

We can illustrate formal enforcement of international law by both what it is and what it is not. For much of the twentieth century, states have had the ability to invite international tribunals to resolve their disputes. The League of Nations had its Permanent Court of International Justice, the United Nations has its International Court of Justice (ICJ), the General Agreement of Tariffs and Trade (GATT) facilitated arbitration of trade disputes, and the World Trade Organization (WTO) has its Dispute Settlement Body (DSB). But though their

proceedings are legalized and thus represent instances of formal dispute settlement, these institutions do not involve formal enforcement as we understand
the concept. First, only interested states have the capability to initiate proceedings, which means that states control access to the process and can exercise
this power for reasons besides vindication of particular legal interests. Second,
none of these bodies has the authority to impose sanctions directly on those
who violate international law obligations. At most, they can invite others to
impose sanctions, as the WTO does when it authorizes an aggrieved member
to retaliate against a transgressor.[14]

Informal enforcement, as in the case of the ICJ and the WTO DSB, is by
no means nonenforcement. Informal enforcement occurs when one or more
actors (perhaps states, but also firms, nongovernmental organizations, political
parties, and others) imposes costs on a rulebreaker in the absence of centralized
coordination and control. A regime responsible for torture and repression at
home and terrorism abroad, for example, can become an international pariah
and thus lose valuable opportunities to transact with other states, even if no
central authority brands the regime as outlaw. Informal enforcement employs
informal sanctions, namely *retaliation* (as in trade disputes), *diminished reputation* (which affects the propensity of other actors to transact with the violator),
and *manifestations of reciprocity* (a preference for rewarding law abiders and
punishing law breakers, which can exist independently of whatever direct payoffs an actor can get for dishing out rewards and punishments).[15]

The conventional wisdom holds that *only* informal enforcement applies in
international law. Because international bodies lack armies or other traditional
means of coercion, scholars have thought that law enforcement necessarily has
depended on the uncoordinated cooperation of influential actors, principally
states. As a result, contemporary discussion of the legalization of international
law neglects the question of enforcement. The conventional definition of international law focuses on *opinio juris*, the idea that a practice arises from a sense
of legal obligation rather than as a matter of naked preference.[16] So framed, the

---

[14] For a fuller discussion of the WTO DSB as an informal enforcement mechanism, see KYLE BAGWELL
& ROBERT W. STAIGER, THE ECONOMICS OF THE WORLD TRADING SYSTEM 95–110 (2002).

[15] The economist Thomas Schelling and the political scientist Robert Axelrod pioneered the study of
informal enforcement mechanisms in international relations. THOMAS C. SCHELLING, THE STRAT-
EGY OF CONFLICT (1963); ROBERT AXELROD, THE EVOLUTION OF COOPERATION (1984). Regime
theorists also explore the incentives for international cooperation in the presence of exclusively
informal enforcement. *E.g.*, STEPHEN D. KRASNER, INTERNATIONAL REGIMES (1983); ROBERT O.
KEOHANE, AFTER HEGEMONY: COOPERATION AND DISCORD IN THE WORLD POLITICAL ECONOMY
(1984); ROBERT O. KEOHANE, INTERNATIONAL INSTITUTIONS AND STATE POWER: ESSAYS IN INTER-
NATIONAL RELATIONS THEORY (1989).

[16] AMERICAN LAW INSTITUTE, RESTATEMENT (THIRD) OF THE FOREIGN RELATIONS LAW OF THE UNITED
STATES §102(2) (1987).

debate revolves around what constitutes a legal obligation, rather than about what follows from noncompliance. A widely cited definition of legalization, which attempts to wrestle with the self-evident circularity of deriving legality from legal obligation, offers a more elaborate, but fundamentally no more satisfying, approach: Legalization, it asserts, refers to *obligation, precision*, and *delegation*.[17] The enforcement process, and in particular whether a delegation comprises enforcement power (as distinguished from responsibility for implementation), is not part of the definition. Unfortunately, this means that current analysis neglects the instrumental consequences of noncompliance. We seek to correct this shortcoming.

The gap in the literature reflects in part the newness of formal enforcement of international law. When we say that this is new, however, we do not mean that it is unprecedented. Common law courts always have had some latitude to refer to international law for rules of decision to apply to cases over which they otherwise have jurisdiction. Some civil law jurisdictions also authorize their judiciary to take account of certain international obligations. On occasion, states have established tribunals to which private persons can take claims for compensation based on interests protected by international law. But the frequency and scope of private access to courts (and to tribunals that in most respects mimic domestic courts) in order to vindicate international law claims has grown enormously in recent years.

Consider a few examples:

- *International criminal law*. International tribunals to punish war criminals go back to the Nuremberg proceedings after World War II, but the International Criminal Court (ICC), established in 2002, is the first to have the discretion to determine its own jurisdiction and consequently to prosecute at the behest of private persons. The ICC's future remains uncertain, as the United States and most other great powers have not accepted it, but the mere creation of this tribunal already has had ramifications in some domestic legal orders. Building on the ICC model, several European states have authorized independent prosecutors to conduct their own prosecutions of international criminals.

[17] Kenneth W. Abbot, Robert O. Keohane, Andrew Moravcsik, Anne-Marie Slaughter, & Duncan Snidal, *The Concept of Legalization*, in LEGALIZATION AND WORLD POLITICS, note 8 *supra*, at 17. *See also* JACK L. GOLDSMITH & ERIC A. POSNER, note 8 *supra*, at 91–100 (distinguishing legal from nonlegal obligations in international law without reference to enforcement mechanisms). For a cursory discussion of enforcement mechanisms in the context of control over formal implementation, see Robert O. Keohane, Andrew Moravcsik, & Anne-Marie Slaughter, *Legalized Dispute Resolution: Interstate and Transnational*, in LEGALIZATION AND WORLD POLITICS, *supra*, at 82–84. For a recent work expanding on the topic but not drawing on any theoretical perspectives, see MATH NOORTMAN, ENFORCING INTERNATIONAL LAW – FROM SELF-HELP TO SELF-CONTAINED REGIMES (2005).

- *Investment protection.* Treaties that allow foreign investors to seek monetary awards from independent tribunals as compensation for unjustified expropriations have been around for decades, but building this institution into the 1993 North American Free Trade Agreement (NAFTA) led to a new era of international litigation challenging regulation in the United States, Canada, and Mexico. The three states professed surprise at these challenges and sought to redefine the scope of their commitment, but the litigation continues apace. When it came time to extend this regime through the Central American Free Trade Agreement (CAFTA), the participating states designed a virtually identical enforcement mechanism to protect investors.
- *International intellectual property.* The Internet has increased the global value of brands by making worldwide access to products easier. One valuable component of a brand is the ability to use a Web site "domain name" that invokes the producer's identity. Since 1998, a private tribunal, operating with the cooperation of the world's domain name registrars, has decided when first-in-line registrants have improperly appropriated someone else's brand. Its decisions are ruthlessly enforced through the simple expedient of deregistration.
- *Private arbitration.* The practice of using specialist arbiters to resolve private commercial disputes is older than most countries' judicial systems. The principal multilateral treaty that reinforces contemporary arbitration practice dates back to 1958, almost the dark ages of our transformed international legal environment. But the post–Cold War period has opened up new fields for international commercial arbitration, and the United States in particular has allowed an extension of this process to regulatory fields, such as antitrust and securities regulation.
- *European integration.* Direct judicial enforcement of the treaties creating the European Community goes back to the 1960s, but a deepening and an expansion of the treaties in the 1990s increased the significance of this mechanism. Formal enforcement of the European Convention on Human Rights was transformed by a 1998 protocol that opened up the European Court to a wide range of private claims. European integration to some extent looks at the creation of the United States as a model for its future, and visionaries in Latin America, Africa, and Asia in turn watch the European project with interest. In particular, states in Africa and Central and South America have established putative common markets and created regional courts modeled closely on the European Court of Justice, although the effectiveness of these organs remains unproved.

- *Civil litigation.* Only in 1980 did a U.S. court discover a general power
  for federal judges to enforce international law, and the Supreme Court
  did not endorse this claim until 2004. But the world's most plaintiff-
  friendly legal system now is open for private enforcement of international
  law claims, with only the courts responsible for setting limits to these
  lawsuits. Already one suit against a major oil company has resulted in a
  substantial cash settlement for the plaintiffs. The British Human Rights
  Act, which took effect in 2000, authorized British courts to implement
  directly the jurisprudence of the European Court of Human Rights. They
  have embraced this new power with gusto, famously invalidating portions
  of the United Kingdom's post-9/11 antiterrorist legislation because of
  what they regarded as discriminatory use of pretrial detention.[18] Canada
  in 1982 enacted analogous legislation authorizing domestic courts to hear
  private suits based on international human rights law, with New Zealand
  following in 1990 and the capital territory of Australia in 2004. In none of
  these commonwealth countries did courts previously have the authority
  to invoke "higher" law to invalidate legislative acts: International law
  enforcement now performs this function.

Formal enforcement is a central element of our positive theory about the
emergence of enforcement mechanisms in international law, which we develop
in Chapters 3 through 6, and our normative arguments about the desirabil-
ity of various proposed changes, which we address in Chapter 7. We should
emphasize several points about our theory. At the outset, one must distinguish
enforcement from compliance. In the last decade, a substantial literature has
emerged explaining why states comply with international law. As some critics
have pointed out, this body of work pays insufficient attention to the distinction between costly and cheap compliance, that is between rules that simply
describe the behavioral preferences of states in the absence of any collective
agreement and those rules that require states not to do what they otherwise
would prefer.[19] Although both kinds of rules might be interesting, only rules
that prevent states from doing what they otherwise would do implicate the
question of enforcement. Only these rules require some mechanism to alter
state preferences. Put simply, what is it about a rule of international law that
induces a state to change its conduct?

Enforcement, we argue, involves the commitment of resources by various
actors, both states and private persons, to induce compliance with a rule.
Enforcement is necessarily costly, in that it requires the diversion of time,

[18] A. v. Secretary of State, [2005] 2 W.L.R. 87 (H.L.).
[19] The criticism is developed in JACK L. GOLDSMITH & ERIC A. POSNER, note 8 *supra*, at 27–28.

energy, and both human and financial capital from other possible uses. These costs fall on actors that wish to induce the subject of the rule to comply with it. In contrast, compliance with a rule may or may not be costly, depending on what alternative conduct a state might undertake. Compliance thus involves the subject's *opportunity costs*, while enforcement entails an array of other investments to detect and sanction noncompliance. We seek, first and foremost, to illuminate the connection between enforcement and compliance, that is the link between investments to induce compliance and the willingness of actors to absorb the opportunity costs associated with compliance. As part of our explanation, we seek to identify the factors that lead actors to select particular enforcement strategies, including the fundamental choice between formal and informal enforcement mechanisms.

All the instances of formal enforcement that we describe here have different instrumental consequences from the more widely studied type of international adjudication, where states and only states bring claims before international tribunals that have no independent power to impose sanctions. A recent literature exploring the "legalization" and "judicialization" of international relations looks at these institutions, sometimes also including the two European courts. These studies, either implicitly or explicitly, regard the establishment of international courts and the role of the international judge as the most significant developments, and pay little or no attention to the linked questions of *standing* and *control over sanctions*.[20]

Standing, that is, deciding who has the capability to engage a tribunal's jurisdiction, is a critical determinant of the array of disputes that a tribunal can affect. If governments can control which disputes go to a tribunal, they can sacrifice interests subject to legal vindication for other considerations. During the period of superpower competition, for example, the United States did not always challenge the human rights practices of governments that sided with the West. Strategic and political interests might have justified this reluctance, but it certainly resulted in less enforcement of these rights, and arguably in less compliance with basic human rights obligations, than an alternative regime based on formal enforcement. When the Carter Administration decided to change the U.S. approach to international human rights enforcement, it focused largely on informal enforcement, but it also encouraged the U.S. courts to interpret old, seemingly irrelevant legislation as providing for formal enforcement of this body of law.[21]

---

[20] For a sample of this literature, see LEGALIZATION AND WORLD POLITICS, note 8 *supra*; KAREN J. ALTER, ESTABLISHING THE SUPREMACY OF EUROPEAN LAW (2001); Laurence R. Helfer & Anne-Marie Slaughter, *Toward a Theory of Effective Supranational Adjudication*, 107 YALE L.J. 272 (1997).

[21] *See* Memorandum for the United States as Amicus Curiae, Filartiga v. Peña-Irala, 630 F.2d 876 (2d Cir. 1980), reprinted in 19 I.L.M. 585 (1980).

We recognize that standing seldom is absolute. In the world of private law, for example, shareholders normally have only limited rights to overturn the decision of a firm's managers not to bring a lawsuit on behalf of the firm. In the international context, what is crucial for enforcement to have greater salience is that national governments not monopolize the decision whether to seek redress before a tribunal. The question of choosing which nongovernmental actors to endow with standing is secondary.

The ability of a tribunal to mete out its own sanctions also affects the instrumental force of the tribunal's decision. We concede that mapping out the instrumental effects is tricky, particularly when a tribunal imposes sanctions on a state rather than a private person. Government officials may not regard the payment of a money judgment, which presents budgetary issues, with quite the same perspective as a private person, who experiences possession and ownership more directly.[22] But the ability directly to levy a sanction has at least two important consequences. Because the tribunal's authority is not limitless, the expenditure of its prestige and power on the outcome reinforces the signal that the tribunal is serious about its decision. Because submission to a sanction generally is easier to observe than compliance with an advisory opinion that delineates rights and responsibilities, the question of whether a party has complied with its obligations becomes starker, and the reputational consequences of noncompliance greater.

As we noted earlier, our definition of formal enforcement reflects our focus on the behavioral effect of incentives. We are interested in the instrumental consequences of enforcement mechanisms, rather than their symbolic or cultural importance. We regard the independent determination of a tribunal's caseload and the direct consequences of a tribunal's decisions as more significant than whether the tribunal members are called judges, wear special costumes, and otherwise follow procedures and write opinions of the sort associated with domestic courts.[23]

What does the growth of formal enforcement of international law mean? For many observers, these developments are the leading edge of a transformation in the global environment. Jürgen Habermas has spoken of "an enormous advance in the rights revolution" that, among other things, would end the

---

[22] Daryl J. Levinson, *Making Government Pay: Markets, Politics, and the Allocation of Constitutional Costs*, 67 CHI. L. REV. 345 (2000).

[23] A recent debate over the significance and influence of permanent international courts has suffered, in our view, from a failure to distinguish between legalized dispute resolution, on the one hand, and formal enforcement power, on the other. Compare Eric A. Posner & John C. Yoo, *Judicial Independence in International Tribunals*, 93 CALIF. L. REV. 1 (2005), and Eric A. Posner & John C. Yoo, *Reply to Helfer and Slaughter*, 93 CALIF. L. REV. 957 (2005), with Laurence R. Helfer & Anne-Marie Slaughter, *Why States Create International Tribunals: A Response To Professors Posner and Yoo*, 93 CALIF. L. REV. 899 (2005).

capacity of states to judge their own conduct in matters of the greatest national interest:

> But why should the impartial adjudication of conflicts within the medium of law be assured only within states? Why should not the same be brought to bear, judicially, on international conflicts? This is not trivial. Who is to determine, on the supranational level, if "our" values truly merit universal acceptance, or if we are truly exercising universally recognized principles, or whether we are perceiving a conflict situation truly non-selectively, for example, or whether, instead, we are taking into consideration only what is relevant to us? This is the whole point of inclusive legal procedures which condition supra-national decision-making upon the adoption of reciprocating points of view and consideration of reciprocal interests.[24]

Others would take the hardening project, based on formal enforcement, beyond questions of war and human rights to matters such as general economic rights. Many commentators, for example, envision a day when private persons bypass governments to prosecute complaints before the World Trade Organization. Some, to complete the analogy with a domestic court, have proposed giving that body the power to assess damages.[25] These authorities see the world as embracing an international civil society that would propagate its norms and rules through institutions that operate both above and below the level of state-to-state relations.[26]

In sum, formal enforcement of international law has become more salient, and respected authorities would like to see even more of it. The interesting question, however, is why we have seen such a growth of formal enforcement, and whether the explanations we can come up with for the phenomenon can justify the calls for its expansion. To addresses these two challenges, we turn to contract theory.

## CONTRACT THEORY AND INTERNATIONAL LAW ENFORCEMENT

This book addresses the question of international law enforcement instrumentally rather than historically. We look at how it has changed, and explore what it accomplishes. We consider two overlapping questions: Why has formal enforcement of international law become so significant? What is the particular

---

[24] *America and the World – A Conversation with Jürgen Habermas, with Eduardo Mendieta*, LOGOS: A JOURNAL OF MODERN SOCIETY & CULTURE 3.3 (Summer 2004).

[25] GREGORY SHAFFER, DEFENDING INTERESTS: PUBLIC-PRIVATE PARTNERSHIPS IN WTO LITIGATION (2003); Andrew T. Guzman, *A Compliance-Based Theory of International Law*, 90 CALIF. L. REV. 1823, 1872–75 (2002); Joel P. Trachtman & Philip M. Moremen, *Costs and Benefits of Private Participation in WTO Dispute Settlement: Whose Right Is It Anyway?* 44 HARV. INT'L L.J. 221 (2003).

[26] For a recent synthesis and defense of this account of international law, see ANNE-MARIE SLAUGHTER, A NEW WORLD ORDER (2004).

function of formal enforcement in a world where other, informal enforcement mechanisms exist?

Both questions invite a positive inquiry. We use an informal model of optimal international law enforcement that draws on recent work in contract theory to explain the particular benefits of different methods of enforcing international law. Our model begins with the observation that international law enforcement, like contract enforcement, is a mixed system. It consists of a combination of formal sanctions imposed by independent enforcement bodies and informal sanctions that, as we noted earlier, affect parties' reputation, or their prospects of future relations, or otherwise punish their failure to behave reciprocally. All of these forces motivate parties to comply with the obligations of international law, just as they provide persons who make contracts an incentive to honor them.

In the field of contract law, the literature long has embraced two complementary perspectives on enforcement. On the one hand, private lawsuits brought by parties dissatisfied with a contract or its performance encourage compliance with bargains struck. These lawsuits have salience because their outcomes produce meaningful consequences: The loser faces a judgment for damages that fairly automatically leads to a payment of money, and perhaps other sanctions that also have real purchase.[27] On the other hand, parties face an array of informal sanctions as well if they fail to cooperate. In many cases, especially the open-ended arrangements called relational contracts, informal sanctions may do much of the enforcement work.[28]

We argue that essentially the same is true with respect to the enforcement of international law. To be sure, informal enforcement has been the norm historically. States that violated a norm invited retaliation by other states and also developed a bad reputation; states that adhered to their commitments both avoided retaliation and built up a reputation as a successful cooperative party. War, trade sanctions, diplomatic reprisals, the seizure of property and hostages all operated as forms of retaliation; states with reputations as effective cooperators were rewarded with more opportunities to engage in beneficial cooperation.[29] From time to time, states turned to third parties to adjudicate their disputes, but instances where third parties had the power to compel

---

[27] *E.g.*, to 22 U.S.C. §1650a (2001) (allowing claimant of an ICSID arbitral award to bring enforcement action in federal district court); 28 U.S.C. §2414 (2001) (obligating Secretary of Treasury to pay federal district court awards against United States).

[28] *See* Robert E. Scott, *A Theory of Self-Enforcing Indefinite Agreements*, 103 COLUM. L. REV. 1641 (2003); Robert E. Scott, *The Case for Formalism in Relational Contract*, 94 Nw. U. L. REV. 847 (2000); Robert E. Scott, *Conflict and Cooperation in Long-Term Contracts*, 75 CALIF. L. REV. 2000 (1987); Charles J. Goetz & Robert E. Scott, *Principles of Relational Contracts*, 67 VA. L. REV. 1089 (1981).

[29] *See generally* Andrew T. Guzman, note 25 *supra*.

compliance with these determinations were rare. However, that has changed in recent times, making the analogy to contract enforcement apt.

To be sure, the precise way in which sanctions influence states is more complicated than the effect of a money judgment for breach of contract on the behavior of private parties. We are sensitive to these distinctions and explore them in detail in subsequent chapters. Nevertheless, the fundamental question remains the same. The question is whether changes in the relative roles of formal and informal mechanisms will produce greater or less compliance as well as more or fewer commitments in the future. Both contracts and international law have at their core voluntary adoption of obligations, and in both cases a change in the method of enforcement can have an effect on *activity levels*, namely the willingness of individuals, firms, and states to invest in cooperative activity that enhances the collective welfare of the group.

Contract theory suggests that formal and informal enforcement represent distinct, and to a considerable extent mutually exclusive, responses to particular problems inherent in cooperative relationships. When parties (or states) voluntarily commit to invest in a collective activity that is mutually beneficial, there exists an inevitable separation between the costs of the activity, which the parties bear individually, and the benefits, which they share. This tension creates a moral hazard: Each participant has the perverse incentive to shirk on its obligations so as to capture a larger share of the surplus benefits. But if everyone shirks, the benefits from cooperation vanish. Thus, the agreement must embody a method of enforcing each party's commitment to invest in the collective enterprise. And, when each of the affected parties has *private information*, the resulting asymmetries further complicate efforts to ensure compliance with the respective commitments.

As we have observed, what distinguishes formal from informal enforcement mechanisms is a system of ex ante rules (either promulgated by a centralized lawgiver or evolving over time as in the common law process) and the centralized coordination and control of the sanctioning process. Contrast such a system with an ongoing relationship that enables each party to respond to the other's behavior, whether good or bad. For example, consider the "code of honor" that exists in various sports, which requires one team to inflict a punishing foul (e.g., a hard fastball to the ribs) on the other team if the latter has fouled excessively. Indeed, a current partner need not be the only agent to impose informal sanctions. Members of a community may take reputation into account when deciding whether (or to what extent) to enter into future relations with a person. In cases of compact and homogenous communities, such as the ethnic-minority middlemen that Janet Landa and others have studied, community members in extreme cases can ostracize a malefactor, cutting off not just business ties but all the benefits of belonging to the group.[30]

The preference for reciprocity provides one explanation for how and why informal sanctioning works. Absent such a preference, it may be irrational for individuals to absorb the costs of shaming, boycotting, and ostracizing. Why not free-ride on the expectation that others in the community will impose these sanctions, and pursue advantageous transactional opportunities with bad actors? Experimental evidence indicates that there exists a widespread, but not universal, preference for cooperation among individual actors, which leads them to reward cooperators and punish opportunists even when they derive no direct and particular benefits from doing so. This preference can reinforce a desire to preserve a good reputation and to maintain the prospect of gain from further transactions with a particular party.

Formal enforcement, by contrast, involves some centralized mechanism that both declares whether rule compliance has occurred or not and imposes sanctions on rule breakers. To continue with the sports metaphor, an umpire or referee provides formal enforcement, with authority grounded on the capacity to throw players out of the game. Ultimately the sanction is exclusion, just as in a community boycott, but the mechanism involves a central decision maker endowed with certain powers, rather than uncoordinated (if perhaps predictable) action by members of a group.

We argue that the dramatic hardening of international law enforcement in recent years can best be understood as a response to the limitations of informal means of ensuring compliance with international law commitments. Reputational sanctions such as boycotts and expulsion work well only when other parties can conveniently observe which of the parties in a dispute was responsible for the breakdown in cooperation and are able effectively to disseminate this information to others. The prospect of a withdrawal of future beneficial relations disciplines a party who otherwise is inclined to shirk only so long as the benefits from future dealings outweigh the costs of compliance. A preference for reciprocity may extend the reach of informal sanctions to one-shot agreements between individuals with neither a previous history nor any prospect of future relations. Nevertheless, even assuming that such a preference exists among states and between private parties and states, all informal sanctions are

[30] JANET TAI LANDA, TRUST, ETHNICITY, AND IDENTITY: BEYOND THE NEW INSTITUTIONAL ECONOMICS OF ETHNIC TRADING NETWORKS, CONTRACT LAW, AND GIFT EXCHANGE 112 (2001); Lisa Bernstein, *Merchant Law in a Merchant Court: Rethinking the Code's Search for Immanent Business Norms*, 144 U. PA. L. REV. 1765 (1996); Lan Cao, *Looking at Communities and Markets*, 74 NOTRE DAME L. REV. 841 (1999); Avner Greif, *Reputation and Coalitions in Medieval Trade: Evidence on the Maghribi Traders*, 49 J. ECON. HIST. 857 (1989); Eric A. Posner, *The Regulation of Groups: The Influence of Legal and Nonlegal Sanctions on Collective Action*, 63 U. CHI. L. REV. 133 (1996).

subject to an inherent limitation: They depend on transparent interactions so that an unjustified noncooperative response by one party can be distinguished from justifiable retaliation for a wrongful defection by the other party. Thus, when transactions are complex and the interactions occur simultaneously, parties may require an authoritative referee to police the interactions according to a previously announced set of rules. Moreover, unlike a sports referee who can observe the interactions directly and then declare "fouls," a legal arbiter must extract essential information known only to the disputants to reach an optimal outcome. The capability to impose sanctions makes such extraction possible. This is the unique function served by formal enforcement.

Explaining the increase in formal enforcement as a response to the limitations of informal mechanisms does not imply that more formal enforcement is always desirable. There is evidence that, in private contracting, formal enforcement can interfere with the informal mechanisms that sometimes can induce even better compliance at less cost. What we call the optimal enforcement model juxtaposes formal enforcement against the informal mechanisms that still operate alongside it. Under some conditions, the costs of formal enforcement, including the reduction in effectiveness of these informal mechanisms, may exceed the benefits. We argue, therefore, that some of the proposals for expanding formal enforcement of international law may be counterproductive, in the sense that they may actually reduce beneficial international cooperation.

What goes into the trade-off between formal and informal enforcement? Here studies of private contracting behavior are illuminating. In experimental settings, formal enforcement by independent actors wielding sanctioning powers has been shown to undermine informal norms. This research has demonstrated that, in many instances, informal mechanisms operate as complements for each other but as substitutes for formal enforcement.[31] Moreover, the informal mechanisms that a system of formal enforcement would displace are in some cases less costly and more effective than the formal alternative. In particular, informal mechanisms for inducing cooperation in contractual relations are likely to be optimal whenever key conditions are *observable* but not *verifiable*: The parties themselves may be able to detect the existence or nonexistence of the condition, but the costs of proving this to a disinterested third party may exceed the gains from enforcement.

We do not mean to suggest here that a sharp dichotomy exists between verifiable and nonverifiable conditions. As we discuss in detail in the chapters that

---

[31] Robert E. Scott, *A Theory of Self-Enforcing Indefinite Agreements*, note 28 *supra*; Alan Schwartz & Robert E. Scott, *Contract Theory and the Limits of Contract Law*, 113 YALE L.J. 541 (2003). For our earlier work applying this research to international law, see Robert E. Scott & Paul B. Stephan, *Self-Enforcing International Agreements and The Limits of Coercion*, 2004 WISC. L. REV. 551.

follow, the question is whether the benefits of using informal norms to enforce a difficult-to-prove condition (such as the level of effort needed to comply with a contractual commitment) are greater than the alternative of verifying compliance with a less accurate but more easily established proxy for the condition in question.[32] The important point, however, is that informal enforcement mechanisms can take into account conditions that are hard to verify even when formal mechanisms cannot. For example, parties to an agreement often can observe whether one has exercised "best efforts" to perform its obligation, but it would be very costly to marshal the evidence necessary to demonstrate this fact to a disinterested third party. Where this is true, a move toward formal enforcement can deprive cooperating parties of mechanisms that can promote better compliance at a lower cost.

That formal and informal means of enforcing private contracts are potentially rivalrous does not mean that one is consistently inferior to the other. The complexity of particular transactions may make it difficult for either the parties or casual observers confidently to determine whether one has departed from the agreed course of conduct or not, but the information necessary to make that decision may be accessible at a reasonable cost to a neutral observer. The imposition of sanctions by an authoritative third party might both deter opportunistic behavior and clarify the parties' behavior by substituting compliance with the sanction for compliance with the agreement. In these circumstances, formal contract enforcement may be optimal even though it undermines informal enforcement.

The same factors that motivate contract compliance, we argue, operate at a fundamental level in international law: Formal enforcement by independent bodies with the capacity to impose material sanctions for international law violations can help states maintain complex cooperative relationships, but also may diminish the effectiveness of informal incentives that motivate compliance. Of course, we recognize that states may differ from private firms in the ways that they react to incentives. Nevertheless, we will argue that the differences are matters of degree and not of kind. The tension between formal and informal enforcement is a product of the difference in the timing and flexibility of the sanctions that are imposed. So long as states respond to incentives in some measure (and most deterrence theories certainly assume that they do), the imposition of (relatively) inflexible sanctions ex ante may undermine the efficacy of the more flexible informal sanctions that are imposed ex post.

---

[32] For a discussion of how parties can cope with the problems of verifiability by anticipating in their contract the expected path of litigation, see Robert E. Scott & George G. Triantis, *Anticipating Litigation by Contract Design*, 115 YALE L. J. 814 (2006).

As an example, when states agree to cooperate through an express treaty or comply with unwritten cooperative norms characterized as customary international law, they often want to condition their obligation on circumstances that may be observed by others but not easily proved to a disinterested third party. In areas as diverse as trade and human rights, commitments are conditioned on circumstances – the state of the economy, the existence of civil peace – that cannot reliably be determined by an independent decision maker at an acceptable cost. Rather than stipulate proxies for these conditions that can be verified but do not fully capture the relevant circumstances, contemporary practice allows the parties to rely on informal mechanisms – reputation, future interactions, and a preference for reciprocity – to induce compliance.

In cases such as this, where verifiability remains a legitimate concern, a move toward greater formal enforcement of international obligations may have negative effects. In Chapter 6, we discuss three instances in U.S. law, involving the 1945 UN Charter, the 1947 GATT, and the enforceability of ICJ orders by domestic courts, as well as the proposed adoption of a constitution for the EU, where the threat of hardened legal enforcement may have undermined important legal commitments. This substitution of a formal for an informal sanction may yield *both* higher enforcement costs and reduced compliance – less bang for more buck, as it were.

Few observers see any tension between formal enforcement of international law and the traditional means of obtaining compliance. The conventional scholarly position takes for granted that any increase in the capacity of independent bodies to induce compliance is desirable. Several younger scholars have challenged this assumption, but their arguments differ from ours.[33] We assume that states create international obligations mostly to induce valuable cooperation in situations where individual interests depart from collective interest. But the hardening of these obligations through formal, third-party enforcement may deny states the opportunity to demonstrate that they have the capacity and desire to cooperate, and in effect restricts cooperation to those subjects where independent observers can verify the conditions for cooperation and sanction defections. In this way, formal enforcement can impede rather than promote valuable cooperation. Here again, the U.S. experience with both international human rights law and trade obligations and the debacle of the EU constitutional treaty are instructive.

---

[33] For examples of recent scholarship that has questioned the traditional legal maximalism of international lawyers, see JACK L. GOLDSMITH & ERIC A. POSNER, note 8 *supra*; Ryan Goodman & Derek Jinks, *How to Influence States: Socialization and International Human Rights Law*, 54 DUKE L.J. 621 (2004); Laurence R. Helfer, *Overlegalizing Human Rights: International Relations Theory and the Commonwealth Caribbean Backlash Against Human Rights Regimes*, 102 COLUM. L. REV. 1832 (2002).

In a nutshell, therefore, our model of optimal international law enforcement supports the following claims: (1) the domain of informal enforcement of international law is likely to be considerably larger than has been conventionally understood. Moreover, informal enforcement where it is effective is both *cheaper* and *better* than formal enforcement. It permits parties to make credible promises at less cost regarding nonverifiable measures of performance, thus increasing joint surplus. (2) To the extent that informal enforcement of international law is linked to reciprocity, it depends significantly on the transparency of the responses to uncooperative behavior. Informal enforcement thus has some significant limitations. (3) Formal enforcement can complement and support informal enforcement when it is deployed as a supplement rather than as a replacement. Thus, when legal enforcement is invoked only to enforce the verifiable conditions of a complex agreement, and when there is some prospect of an ongoing relationship, formal enforcement may stimulate norms of trust and reciprocity, thereby enabling parties better to enforce those portions of the relationship that are not verifiable. (4) But once the entire relationship, including its informal aspects, is subject to formal enforcement, voluntary reciprocity will decline along with the overall level of cooperation. In plain language, therefore, our model predicts both the conditions under which the hardening of international law is optimal and the conditions under which it is not.

Our argument is not simply a matter of theory and methodology. Our claims bear directly on hotly contested contemporary issues. The International Criminal Court, opposed by the United States to the great dismay of many, constitutes an extension of direct and powerful third-party enforcement of international criminal law. The struggle over a constitution for the European Union revisits the question of how much power should the Union's institutions have and the extent to which interested parties may bypass national governments in the formation and enforcement of EU public policy. The European human rights regime remains a work in progress, as evidenced by spirited debates over national implementation of the jurisprudence of the European Court of Human Rights. In the United States, the recent Supreme Court decisions endorsing, in principle, international law litigation in federal courts and international-law-based constitutional interpretation has left unresolved almost every conceivable question about the content and scope of these functions. Much of the academic community envisions rapid growth in the internationalization of domestic law, although the U.S. government at present does not.

In each of these cases, we ask whether more formal enforcement of the relevant body of international law will come at too great a cost. Too often, the architects of these proposals do not consider whether hardening of the law will diminish informal incentives to comply. That formal enforcement can bolster cooperation does not mean that it inevitably does, or that the growth we have seen in the recent past is a precursor of what is to come. What is needed, and what we seek to provide, is an analytic perspective for assessing when greater formal enforcement is desirable, and when it is not. What is crucial for optimal enforcement, therefore, is understanding how formal enforcement interacts with informal incentives.

## THE STRUCTURE OF THE ARGUMENT

Chapter 2 begins by demonstrating how international law resembles contract law. Both result from the repeated efforts of people and organizations to discover and improve mechanisms that support cooperative behavior, what contract theorists call the *joint production of social welfare*.[34] Because the efforts involve repetition, the processes that lead to the formation of contracts and international obligations present opportunities for learning through trial and error and selective pressure in favor of optimal mechanisms. Both subjects, in short, provide an opportunity for exploring how the creation and enforcement of obligations reflect the search for welfare-maximizing solutions to problems that accompany cooperative projects.

This chapter also addresses arguments against comparing the enforcement of contracts and of international law. We anticipate objections based on several distinct claims. First, one might argue that states generally respond to different incentives and face different constraints on their decision making than do private actors. In particular, states do not confront the same kinds of risks of failure and dissolution that constrain private persons, and may derive less benefit from interstate cooperation than individuals and firms do from cooperating with each other. Second, many scholars maintain that much contemporary international law has little to do with state-level decision making, but instead reflects the actions and preferences of discrete groups operating both inside and across national boundaries. If this is true, then an analogy between firms and states is beside the point. Third, some scholars strongly contest the claim that actors, whether firms, individuals, or states, seek to maximize welfare. They argue that cultural limitations on beliefs, expectations, and perceptions play a far greater role in constraining state behavior than does the search for welfare-maximizing outcomes. This argument, to the extent it is true, undermines the validity of any positive account of legal institutions based on an assumed effort to optimize social interactions.

---

[34] Robert E. Scott & Paul B. Stephan, note 31 *supra*, at 552 & n.4.

Chapter 2 explains why each of the objections is either mistaken or overstated. Evolutionary pressure works on both firms and states, not so much at the level of the entity but rather on their management. Bad choices result, not inevitably but frequently, in new leaders. The collapse of the Soviet system from internal pressures as well as the external removal of the Ba'athist regime in Iraq illustrate in particular how this process can apply to undemocratic regimes. In both contracts and international law, we can see an effort by decision makers to optimize their prospects, a quest that has some relationship to the search for ways of optimizing the value of transactions in which they engage.

Next, the death of the state in international relations and international law has been much reported but insufficiently analyzed. Changes in communications, transportation, migration patterns, and the technology of destruction have increased the possible benefits from international cooperation, but this cooperation requires responsible actors that can make credible commitments. States need not be the source of these commitments as a matter of logic, but rarely do alternative actors exist. Although observers have proclaimed the irrelevance of the state in international relations for more than a century, it remains the locus of deliberative decision making about international commitments and thus is still an essential part of the creation of international law.

Finally, the presence of cultural limits on both private and public decision making does not negate the value of the evolutionary perspective, which, unlike cultural explanations, generates predictions that admit of empirical falsification. We do not reject deep description as a method for understanding any human institution, including international law enforcement, but we do believe that an effort to ground a positive account of social behavior in a theory susceptible of generalization and validation has its uses. We do not argue that our approach is the only way to understand international law enforcement, but we do believe that our model is sufficiently plausible, and our (admittedly anecdotal, rather than quantitative) empirical support is sufficiently persuasive, to justify our inquiry. We also hope that others will respond to our work with rigorous quantitative analysis that will either validate or falsify our main claims.

Chapter 3 introduces the reader to the main insights of contemporary contract theory. We explain why individual actors want to make their promises enforceable and how they achieve this goal. In particular, private parties wish to make credible (i.e., enforceable) promises to motivate their contracting partners to invest in jointly profitable activities. But the uncertain future and problems of private information present substantial obstacles to the accomplishment of these goals. As a result of uncertainty, parties cannot easily design contracts that maximize jointly beneficial investments *and also* respond appropriately to changing conditions. And even if parties can describe fully all future conditions, they may not be able easily to verify the conditions of performance that they can observe. Although economists have designed contractual mechanisms that can work to maximize joint welfare both ex ante and ex post, these mechanisms depend on the assumption of a perfectly functioning and costless system of enforcement. In the real world, parties must expend substantial resources to enforce commitments legally and, in many cases, courts will lack the information needed to assess the parties' actions under the disputed agreement.

The lesson from contract theory, therefore, is that legal enforcement alone cannot ensure the full realization of jointly beneficial cooperative ventures. Instead, legal enforcement, supported by the coercive power of the state or some other coordinated group, is only one mechanism for inducing cooperation, and in long-term relationships it typically has only a limited role to play. Depending on the degree of uncertainty about the future and the relative costs of contracting, parties can (and do) choose between, on the one hand, writing simple contracts that look to renegotiation once the future is known and, on the other hand, complex, highly structured contracts that are designed to discourage subsequent attempts to renegotiate. Although complex contracts can specify proxies for performance that reduce the wedge between observable and verifiable conditions, the costs of writing such complex agreements may overwhelm the benefits. In that case, if the parties could rely only on formal agreement backed up by legal enforcement, they would be unable to derive all the potential benefits from cooperation. Although many complex contracts lend themselves to effective formal enforcement, simple contracts require informal mechanisms if the parties are to realize both beneficial investment and adjustment.

In Chapter 4, we evaluate the informal (or nonlegal) methods of enforcing promises that are available to individual actors. We begin by asking whether informal mechanisms can substitute for the deficiencies in formal enforcement. In many instances, informal sanctions are *both* cheaper and better than formal enforcement in the sense that they can motivate higher levels of compliance at less cost. The conventional understanding, however, holds that informal sanctions – such as loss of reputation and withdrawal of future dealings – are only effective in limited environments such as closely knit communities with common interests. But recent experimental evidence, supported by evolutionary theory, suggests that the powerful norm of reciprocity (the willingness to reward cooperation and punish defection) is sufficiently widespread to support effective cooperation even among strangers dealing with each other for the first time.

We review these studies and draw out their implications for the enforcement of contractual obligations. One dimension of the information problem embedded in cooperative ventures is the need for parties to signal a preference for reciprocal treatment, which can exist in the absence of any history of interaction between the parties. Informal enforcement can facilitate this kind of signaling, whereas formal enforcement appears to suppress this information.

Even assuming widespread preferences for reciprocity, however, there exist inherent limitations on the effectiveness of informal enforcement methods. All modes of reciprocal cooperation depend on transparency, so that each party can correctly interpret the actions of a contracting partner and send an appropriate signal in response. When the relationship calls for the parties to undertake highly interdependent actions, the import of each individual action as cooperative or opportunistic becomes opaque. Under these conditions, reciprocity may break down. Sorting through these complex interactions may require an authoritative adjudicator or referee to impose appropriate sanctions according to a predetermined set of rules as a substitute for individual acts of generosity or retaliation.

The dilemma, however, is that these two systems of enforcement do not appear to work in harmony. Rather, the available evidence indicates that, where formal enforcement extends over the entire domain of a relationship, it suppresses the instinct to reciprocate and thus "crowds out" informal mechanisms that depend on reciprocity. The lesson gained from a comparative analysis of formal and informal enforcement, therefore, is that formal enforcement is best confined to the particular domain in which it alone is effective to ensure compliance with cooperative goals.

In Chapter 5, we apply our model of optimal enforcement to international law. Formal enforcement is significant and growing, even though most compliance with international obligations still depends on only informal enforcement. We describe in some detail the capacity of international bodies to make decisions that take direct effect in national law as well as the willingness of at least some national judiciaries to carry out the mandates of international law independently of other national lawmakers. At the same time, the persons who act on behalf of states in fashioning international law manifest a concern about reputation and retaliation and some preference for reciprocal fairness. In particular, we conduct an extensive review of current state practice to illustrate an interplay between formal enforcement and informal enforcement in international law. We focus largely on treaties, both bilateral and multilateral, but also touch on state practice regarding customary international law.

In Chapter 6, we compare the observed practice of international law enforcement to what our model predicts. Many different treaty regimes recognize a distinction between verifiable and observable conditions, that is, on the one hand, states of the world that can be recognized by participants in the treaty relationship and demonstrated convincingly to objective third parties at a reasonable cost, and, on the other hand, those that can be recognized but not demonstrated. Treaty obligations involving observable conditions are enforced informally, whereas formal enforcement turns on verifiable conditions. This pattern can be seen in such diverse areas as arms control, environmental protection, trade liberalization, human rights, and the protection of property interests.

We also present case studies involving trade treaties, human rights, and European integration. In each instance, threats of formal enforcement induced resistance to the international obligation in question. In two instances in which the threat ended, deeper commitments to the underlying obligation followed. These episodes suggest that formal enforcement can frustrate the achievement of otherwise attainable international cooperation.

In Chapter 7, the final chapter, we come back to the question of the limits of formal enforcement of international law. Our model of optimal enforcement provides useful criteria for evaluating various proposals to strengthen formal enforcement in international law. We examine in particular the ambitions for the new International Criminal Court, proposals to enhance the powers of WTO dispute resolution, efforts to obtain formal enforcement of decisions of the ICJ through actions in domestic courts, controversies over the domain of international treaties that expressly look to domestic courts for enforcement, and the existence of a general power in the judiciary to enforce customary international law. Our analysis suggests that adherents of these proposals have not adequately considered their likely consequences. Although motivated by the noblest of ideals, these projects may have the paradoxical effect of undermining international respect for law and discouraging cooperative efforts to promote broader standards of decency and respect for all people. International lawyers now have available the tools for exploring the relationship between obligations, enforcement mechanisms, and compliance. A failure to use them can doom the best intended reforms.

# 2 STATES, FIRMS, AND THE ENFORCEMENT OF INTERNATIONAL LAW

Almost all nations observe almost all principles of international law and almost all of their obligations almost all of the time.

LOUIS HENKIN, HOW NATIONS BEHAVE 47 (2nd ed. 1979)

WHY DO PEOPLE INVEST IN THE ENFORCEMENT OF INTERNATIONAL law? This question lies at the heart of this study. Our answer, in a nutshell, is that people will make investments that increase the likelihood that actors will cooperate in a collective project – the joint production of social welfare. Absent these investments, actors would not meet their obligations and social welfare would suffer. The greater likelihood of valuable cooperation provides the principal incentive for states to absorb the cost of enforcement.

This claim rests on several premises, which we discuss in the coming pages. We argue that decisions about enforcement are bound up with choices about the voluntary creation of international law obligations. It follows that the process by which international law is made is, for our purposes, akin to the process by which people make binding commitments by forming contracts. We anticipate many objections to each of these premises and attempt to meet them. Understanding the thread of our argument requires an appreciation both of how international law creation works and the state of the debate among political scientists, international lawyers, and other academics about what explains international relations.

We also elaborate on what we mean when we say that "people" make international law. The traditional conception of international law depicts states as the makers. But the state is an abstraction, as it can act only through people. Moreover, more recent conceptions of some kinds of international law challenge the idea that states have a monopoly on international law creation. We use "people" thus to signal two different ideas: Even when states act, the people who represent states may have preferences and incentives that do not align perfectly with state interest, and, in any event, collective bodies other than states may make international law, again acting through people as their agents.

## JOINT PRODUCTION OF COLLECTIVE WELFARE

First, our interest is in the *enforcement* of international law, rather than international law as such. As a result, we focus only on that portion of international law that in its purposes corresponds to contract, which is to say international law that results from voluntary undertakings that contemplate the joint production of collective welfare. As we discuss later in this chapter, legal regimes differ in the incentives that they create for people to comply. A rule that drivers must drive on the right costs little to enforce, because once the rule is announced, drivers will know that regardless of state actions to punish rule breakers, driving on the wrong side of the road brings no general advantage and does create great risks of harm. In contrast, a rule that you must pay the agreed price for customized goods you have ordered but not yet received requires some investment in enforcement, because if you determine that you have no use for the goods, you have some incentive not to give up anything for them.

Much of international law – both treaties and that body of unwritten rules and standards called customary international law – involves either memorializing practices that everyone already has an incentive to follow or organizing action in ways that benefit all at little or no cost. An example of the first kind of rule is the customary norm that restricts attacks by warships on unarmed enemy fishing boats: Navies, at least before the era of modern total war, had better things to do with their resources.[1] Allocation of the broadcast spectrum for purposes of international communications is an example of the second kind. There are a limited number of "places" on the spectrum and each can serve no more than one signal, yet (ignoring sunk costs) in general no broadcaster cares which particular place it gets. In neither case is enforcement an important question, because the rule by its nature creates incentives for compliance.

But, as we demonstrate later in this chapter, a growing body of international law, both treaty-based and customary, does entail commitments that require the joint production of collective welfare and thus presents the same fundamental enforcement dilemma that parties face when entering into contracts. When states form a common market, or engage in reciprocal disarmament, or attack global environmental problems, each has an incentive to shirk on its own

[1] JACK L. GOLDSMITH & ERIC A. POSNER, THE LIMITS OF INTERNATIONAL LAW 27–28, 66–78 (2005).

obligation while reaping the benefits of the actions of other states. Knowing that these incentives exist, everyone has a reason to take costly precautions against shirking or to pass up the project altogether. Enforcement decisions here, as in the law of contract, seek to change those incentives.

## ENFORCEMENT CHOICES

A critical assumption in our analysis is that people make choices about how to enforce international law. When rulemakers design a standard to govern future conduct, one part of the design is the enforcement mechanism. This seemingly simple extension of a straightforward story – that international lawmaking results from a deliberative process involving collective decision making and voluntary consent, rather than from random or magical events – requires some unpacking, however. Too often scholars and policy makers take the enforcement decision for granted. Lawyers, for whom thinking about enforcement as an analytically distinct issue should be second nature, to some extent have encouraged this inattention.

Let us consider first how private contracts are enforced. Typically the parties write obligations and assume that enforcement mechanisms will follow. They understand that if they have succeeded in making a legally enforceable agreement, one party can go to court to recover damages caused by breach, and under certain conditions can obtain a judicial injunction ordering or forbidding certain conduct. A money judgment in turn entitles its beneficiary to enlist the assistance of public authorities in attaching and selling the assets of the person against whom the judgment runs. A judge may enforce an injunction with monetary penalties, and under certain conditions with imprisonment of a contemptuous violator of the order.

But contract enforcement is not limited to these conventional remedies. First, parties can design their own enforcement mechanism, as with a provision for liquidated damages.[2] They can commit to use alternative dispute settlement procedures, as with an arbitration clause.[3] They can decide to rely on self-help rather than third-party sanctions.[4] And in every instance, courts can look at agreements in which these choices are not explicit and make decisions about enforcement for the contracting parties.[5]

---

[2] See Charles J. Goetz & Robert E. Scott, *Liquidated Damages, Penalties and the Just Compensation Principle: Some Notes on an Enforcement Model and a Theory of Efficient Breach*, 77 COLUM. L. REV. 554 (1977).

[3] *E.g.*, Vimar Seguros y Reaseguros, S.A. v. M/V Sky Reefer, 515 U.S. 528 (1995) (recognizing arbitrability of a dispute over a sea carrier's obligations to shipper).

[4] See Robert E. Scott, *A Theory of Self-Enforcing Indefinite Agreements*, 103 COLUM. L. REV. 1641 (2003).

[5] *See* Robert E. Scott, *The Case for Formalism in Relational Contract*, 94 Nw. U. L. REV. 847 (2000).

How does international law enforcement resemble contract enforcement? First and most obviously, two or more states, acting through their governments and with the requisite parliamentary approvals, can form an agreement that specifies an enforcement procedure. Typically these agreements nest the enforcement mechanism in preexisting institutions and understandings. For example, when Canada, Mexico, and the United States decided to include strong protection for foreign investors in Chapter 11 of NAFTA, they specified an international tribunal from which investors could seek monetary compensation for government action that infringed their rights under that agreement.[6] The agreement incorporated by reference another international instrument, the Convention on the Settlement of Investment Disputes Between States and Nationals of Other States (the ICSID Convention), to which all three countries already were parties.[7] For the framers of NAFTA, the ICSID Convention represented both a set of explicit procedures – for example, in the absence of a contrary agreement, the disputants form a tribunal by each unilaterally selecting one arbiter from a list of approved persons, and agreeing to a third – and, as of the time of signing NAFTA, twenty years' worth of practice that elaborated on and modified the express understandings of what the Convention meant.

Similarly, the framers of the 1957 Treaty of Rome, the agreement that established the European Economic Community (renamed the European Community by the 1992 Maastricht Treaty), created the European Court of Justice (the ECJ) to interpret and apply Community law and authorized the ECJ to impose monetary damages that would have direct effect in the legal systems of the states that belonged to the Community.[8] Initially, the framers had no direct experience with this institution, although they clearly used French administrative courts as a model. By the time of the later revisions of the Treaty as well as the accession of new members, however, the parties acted against a concrete historical background. When the ten latest members joined the Community in 2004, they had a pretty clear idea of what ECJ enforcement means in practice.[9]

---

[6] North American Free Trade Agreement, arts. 1101–39, Dec. 17, 1992, H.R. Doc. 103–159 (1993), 32 I.L.M. 605, 639 (1992).

[7] Convention on the Settlement of Investment Disputes Between States and Nationals of Other States, Mar. 18, 1965, 17 U.S.T. 1270, T.I.A.S. No. 6090, 575 U.N.T.S. 159. The United States not only signed this agreement and obtained Senate approval pursuant to Article II of the Constitution, but also enacted 22 U.S.C. §1650a to give U.S. federal courts jurisdiction to enforce pecuniary awards issued by tribunals pursuant to the Convention. Another provision, 28 U.S.C. §2414, in turn requires the Secretary of the Treasury to honor judgments issued by federal courts.

[8] For the current version of these obligations, see Consolidated Version of the Treaty Creating the European Community, Dec. 24, 2002, OJ (C 325) 33 (2002), arts. 220–45, 256.

[9] One should recall that the power of the U.S. courts to exercise judicial review, that is directly to enforce the Constitution against the federal and state governments, also arose gradually over the first several decades of the nation's history. SYLVIA SNOWIS, JUDICIAL REVIEW AND THE LAW OF THE CONSTITUTION (1990). In this sense the hardening process in EC law enforcement replicated U.S. constitutional law development.

But international law, much less international law enforcement, does not result only from explicit agreements. A murkier and more controversial area comprises *customary international law*. This body of rules and norms is derived and observed, rather than made. Authoritative commentators – putting aside for the moment who fits this description – proclaim that a custom exists when they detect state practice that, in their opinion, results from a sense of legal obligation. A range of institutions, both national and international, can, and in the view of some commentators must, apply this law to the disputes before them.[10]

Because customary international law is not formally constituted (using the terminology of H. L. A. Hart, customary international law lacks a rule of recognition, or at least one with wide acceptance), it eludes precise description.[11] It involves two sets of arguments, one over what rules fall into the category of customary international law and another over who gets to address the first question. We briefly consider both.

Under some accounts, an "invisible college" of international law specialists determines both who belongs to the rulemaking group and uses general normative principles such as human dignity, good faith, and fairness to decide what counts as a binding norm.[12] In particular, some authorities assert that there exists a body of customary international law, called *jus cogens*, that transcends the principle of state consent by applying even to states that expressly reject them.[13] But, according to other versions of customary international law, rules based on normative rather than descriptive claims do not count, and only persons exercising official power, such as judges and government officials, have

---

[10] For extensive accounts, see ANTHONY A. D'AMATO, THE CONCEPT OF CUSTOM IN INTERNATIONAL LAW (1971); MICHAEL BYERS, CUSTOM, POWER, AND THE POWER OF RULES: INTERNATIONAL RELATIONS AND CUSTOMARY INTERNATIONAL LAW (1999); KAROL WOLKE, CUSTOM IN PRESENT INTERNATIONAL LAW (2nd rev. ed. 1993).

[11] Hart observed:

It is indeed arguable, as we shall show, that international law not only lacks the secondary rules of change and adjudication which provide for legislature and courts, but also a unifying rule of recognition specifying "sources" of law and providing general criteria for the identification of its rules.

H. L. A. HART, THE CONCEPT OF LAW 209 (1961).

[12] *See, e.g.,* Oscar Schachter, *Human Dignity as a Normative Concept,* 77 AM. L. INT'L L. 848 (1983); Oscar Schachter, *The Invisible College of International Lawyers,* 72 NW. U. L. REV. 217 (1977).

[13] The Restatement (Third) of the Foreign Relations Law of the United States defines *jus cogens* or peremptory norms as follows:

Some rules of international law are recognized by the international community of states as peremptory, permitting no derogation. These rules prevail over and invalidate international agreements and other rules of international law in conflict with them. Such a peremptory norm is subject to modification only by a subsequent norm of international law having the same character. It is generally accepted that the principles of the United Nations Charter prohibiting the use of force ... have the character of jus cogens.

AMERICAN LAW INSTITUTE, RESTATEMENT (THIRD) OF THE FOREIGN RELATIONS LAW OF THE UNITED STATES §102, comment k (1987).

the capacity to recognize (as opposed to describe) what the set of customary international law rules contains.[14] There also exists a strand of scholarship that criticizes many conventional views about the content and function of customary international law.[15]

Whether state choices have much to do with customary international law depends on which of these accounts applies. A version that does not rest on state consent and that looks to normative principles rather than to overt expressions of state behavior as a source of rules is inconsistent with the premises of our analysis. We concede at the outset that we have little, if anything, to say about one widely held view of a significant part of international law, and hence of its enforcement.

This is not too much of a concession, however. The extremely normative and insular version of customary international law that we cannot fit within our framework resides largely in the academy and the staff of various international organizations, and has little official support from governments and judges, a few rhetorical sallies aside. The actual application of customary international law, as opposed to its invocation, looks rather different. Officials usually base a determination that a norm exists on manifestations of state support for it, an approach that assumes some element of choice.[16] They also find that customary international law works in a smaller sphere than that to which the academic supporters assign it.[17]

Nor is the normative version the only game in town, even in the academy. Some academic proponents of an expansive account of customary international law have found room for rational-choice explanations of how customary law is made. For example, Eyal Benevisti argues that at least some customary international law represents an efficiency-driven solution to a transactions-cost problem. He argues that states recognize in advance that straightforward negotiations may fail to produce desirable outcomes, either because differences in state interests may thwart recognition of a globally desirable result or because

---

[14] *See, e.g.,* Flores v. South Peru Copper Corp., 343 F.3$^{rd}$ 140, 156–58 & n. 26 (2nd Cir. 2003) (dismissing suit based on customary international law against polluter; rejecting view that scholarly opinion alone can create customary international law); United States v. Yousef, 327 F.3rd 56, 99–103 (2nd Cir. 2003) (rejecting argument based on scholarly opinion that customary international law limits national jurisdiction to prosecute extraterritorial acts as crimes).

[15] JACK L. GOLDSMITH & ERIC A. POSNER, note 1 *supra,* at 21–78.

[16] Thus the vocabulary of *opinio juris* has been explained as a shorthand for a kind of state consent that implies voluntary choice. Maurice H. Mendelson, *The Formation of Customary International Law,* 272 RECUEIL DES COURS 155, 268–93 (1998); George Norman & Joel P. Trachtman, *The Customary International Law Game,* 99 AM. J. INT'L L. 541, 544, 570–71 (2005).

[17] Curtis A. Bradley & Jack L. Goldsmith, *Customary International Law as Federal Common Law: A Critique of the Modern Position,* 119 HARV. L. REV. 815, 357–58 (1997); Jack L. Goldsmith & Eric A. Posner, *A Theory of Customary International Law,* 66 U. CHI. L. REV. 1113 (1999).

domestic interest groups may block one or more states from acceding to that outcome. He gives as an example the allocation of jurisdiction over waterways that affect multiple states. Faced with obstacles to beneficial agreements, Benevisti argues, these states delegate to a disinterested and expert third party, such as the ICJ, the authority to reach an appropriate outcome. The third-party decision maker in turn invokes customary international law, which does not depend on the inevitably incomplete set of express international agreements, to reach the optimal result.[18]

Benevisti's argument is one example of a trend. At least in the legal academy, a group of scholars, mostly younger than the celebrated proponents of normative customary international law, argue that all types of international law result from rational choices by authoritative officials acting on behalf of states.[19] Although this literature has not achieved any consensus on what kinds of behavioral regularities, coupled with what kinds of signals about a sense of legal obligation, count as evidence that a particular rule exists, it does take as a given that a custom cannot arise except as a reflection of state choices. For these scholars, at least, our approach may make a contribution to the understanding of customary international law and its enforcement.

When one turns from recognition of the existence of international law to its enforcement, the conceptual and methodological problems become complicated. Most scholars focus on the use of domestic institutions to enforce international law. Yet others maintain that international law says nothing about domestic implementation of international obligations. If left unqualified, this last claim clearly is false. Both NAFTA Chapter 11 and the European Court of Justice are examples of international commitments that deal expressly with domestic implementation. At most one can say that there exists some separation between the question of what obligations exist under international law and what national governments must do to meet their obligations.[20]

---

[18] Eyal Benevisti, *Customary International Law as a Judicial Tool for Promoting Efficiency*, in THE IMPACT OF INTERNATIONAL LAW ON INTERNATIONAL COOPERATION – THEORETICAL PERSPECTIVES 85 (Eyal Benevisti & Moshe Hirsch eds. 2004).

[19] *See, e.g.*, JACK L. GOLDSMITH & ERIC A. POSNER, note 1 *supra*, at 21–78; Francesco Parisi & Vincy Fon, *International Customary Law and Articulation Theories: An Economic Analysis*, 2 INT'L L. & MGT. REV. 1 (2006); Tom Ginsburg, *International Judicial Lawmaking*, 45 VA. J. INT'L L. 631 (2005); Andrew T. Guzman, *A Compliance-Based Theory of International Law*, 90 CAL. L. REV. 1823 (2002); George Norman & Joel P. Trachtman, note 16 *supra*; Edward T. Swaine, *Rational Custom*, 52 DUKE L. J. 559 (2002); Pierre-Hugues Verdier, *Cooperative States: International Relations, State Responsibility and the Problem of Custom*, 42 VA. J. INT'L. L. 839 (2002).

[20] For one statement of the separation claim – that international law does not control domestic enforcement – see ANTONIO CASSESE, INTERNATIONAL LAW 168 (2001):
Apart from the general rule barring States from adducing domestic legal problems for not complying with international law, and the treaty or customary rules just mentioned that impose the

This separation of right and remedy complicates analysis, because different national legal systems offer various arrays of enforcement tools. The United States, at one of the extremes of the spectrum, has a robust tradition of private civil litigation as a tool for the advancement of public goals. Other countries regard public policy as largely the province of public officials acting through institutions such as the criminal justice process. To what extent should this variation in national enforcement mechanism matter when one stipulates that an international law rule exists?

A traditional formulation is that the question of domestic enforcement is independent of the existence of a rule of international law. Thus, Beth Stephens has argued, certain human rights norms exist as customary international law, even though state practice about what the custom means in the domestic legal system varies enormously.[21] This move makes possible a second claim, namely that the norm for enforcing any law in the U.S. legal system is through adjudication, whether in an independent civil suit or as a component of preexisting domestic legal claims, even if other states approach enforcement differently. To state the proposition technically, in the United States international law provides a rule of decision that judges must apply to cases before them. Thus, some argue, an international norm barring the execution of a person for committing a crime when under the age of eighteen both obligates courts not to impose a capital sentence in cases submitted for their judgment and provides a basis for prospective relief against sentences already pronounced but not yet carried out.[22]

The legal argument that international law by its very nature empowers U.S. domestic judges as enforcers is simple, if also simplistic. The Supremacy Clause of the Constitution states that "all Treaties made, or which shall be made, under the Authority of the United States, shall be the supreme Law of the Land; and the Judges in every State shall be bound thereby, . . ."[23] Louis Henkin, perhaps the preeminent authority on U.S. foreign relations law, argues that this language generally commits the U.S. judiciary to give effect to rights created by treaties. More controversially, he also maintains that this language bars the president and the Senate from unilaterally altering the meaning of treaties for domestic purposes. Thus, in his view, the Senate's long-standing practice

     obligation to enact implementing legislation, international law does not contain any regulation of implementation. It thus leaves each country *complete freedom* with regard to how it fulfils, nationally, its international obligations.

[21] Beth Stephens, *Translating* Filártiga: *A Comparative and International Law Analysis of Domestic Remedies for International Human Rights Violations,* 27 YALE J. INT'L L. 1 (2002).

[22] *See* Roper v. Simmons, 543 U.S. 551 (2005).

[23] U.S. Constitution, Art. VI.

of attaching qualifications to treaties at the time of adoption to bar direct enforcement produces only a legal nullity.[24] In Henkin's world, the separation principle in international law does not translate into U.S. enforcement flexibility. To the contrary, the United States must write domestic nonenforcement into the body of a treaty to keep its courts from participating in the interpretation and application of the rules included in the text.[25]

If Henkin's position accurately captures the views of U.S. lawmakers, then little separation exists between the choice whether to recognize a norm as international law and decisions about its enforcement. Enforcement by independent judges operates as the norm, and the obstacles to avoiding this outcome are high. This structure does not make a theory of international law enforcement based on rational choice irrelevant, but it does limit the scope of the theory by constraining the domain over which it can apply. The United States, at least, would have to be understood as facing only all-or-nothing choices, with the decision to accept an international rule as binding automatically resulting in a particular formal enforcement mechanism.

Again, we must concede a weakness in our theory, but not an insurmountable one. The nonseparation hypothesis, as we shall call it, has two significant deficiencies. First, it does not describe actual U.S. practice. The courts have declined to enforce a wide array of obligations that the United States has assumed under international law.[26] Recent Supreme Court decisions point in different directions, but they seem to recognize a power in the president and the Congress,

---

[24] Louis Henkin, *U.S. Ratification of Human Rights Treaties: The Ghost of Senator Bricker*, 89 Am. J. Int'l L. 341, 346 (1995). For development of the argument, see Lori Fisler Damrosch, *The Role of the United States Senate Concerning "Self-Executing" and "Non-Self-Executing" Treaties*, 67 Chi.-Kent L. Rev. 515 (1991); Jordan Paust, *Self-Executing Treaties*, 82 Am. J. Int'l L. 760, 760 (1988); David Sloss, *Non-Self-Executing Treaties: Exposing A Constitutional Fallacy*, 36 U.C. Davis L. Rev. 1 (2002); Carlos Manuel Vázquez, *The Four Doctrines of Self-Executing Treaties*, 89 Am. J. Int'l L. 695, 716–17 (1995). For a critical response, see Curtis A. Bradley & Jack L. Goldsmith, *Treaties, Human Rights, and Conditional Consent*, 149 U. Pa. L. Rev. 399, 442–56 (2000).

[25] Henkin (and the others who take this position) presumably would allow the United States to make an international agreement without calling the instrument a "treaty." The United States then could adopt a statute specifying and limiting domestic judicial enforcement, as Congress did do when approving NAFTA in 1993 and the Uruguay Round Agreements in 1994. North American Free Trade Agreement Implementation Act, §102, *codified at* 29 U.S.C. §3312 (2001); Uruguay Round Agreements Act of 1994 §102, *codified at* 29 U.S.C. §3512(2001). At least one prominent public law scholar, however, argues that the Constitution does not permit this option. Laurence H. Tribe, *Taking Text and Structure Seriously: Reflections on Free-Form Method in Constitutional Interpretation*, 108 Harv. L. Rev. 1221 (1995). For support of this position by an international law scholar, see Joel R. Paul, *The Geopolitical Constitution: Executive Expediency and Executive Agreements*, 86 Calif. L. Rev. 671 (1998).

[26] For a review of this practice, see Tim Wu, *When Do American Judges Enforce Treaties?* 93 Va. L. Rev. (2007).

exercised together and perhaps separately, to preclude judicial enforcement of particular international obligations.[27] Second, the nonseparation hypothesis does not rest on an intelligible theory of constitutional interpretation. It is universally conceded that, in the domestic field, legislative power implies the authority to control enforcement, including the exclusion of judicial enforcement.[28] The proponents of the nonseparation hypothesis have not given a satisfactory explanation of why international law should receive different treatment.

The enforcement of customary international law in the United States presents a similar conundrum. Many authorities maintain that customary international law automatically constitutes federal law that, under the Supremacy Clause, all U.S. courts must apply in cases over which they have jurisdiction.[29] An argument also exists that any violation of customary international law that produces an injury can lead to a tort suit in federal court. The courts do not seem to have embraced the most expansive version of this position, but an ill-defined capacity to apply customary international law and to base tort compensation on at least some violations may exist.[30] Again, it suffices for our purposes to

---

[27] In *Sosa v. Alvarez-Machain*, 542 U.S. 692, 728, 735 (2004), the Supreme Court appeared to take for granted that where the president and Senate have expressed an intention that a treaty not have domestic effect, the judiciary should respect that decision. But in *Roper v. Simmons*, 543 U.S. 551, (2005), the Court cited the International Covenant on Civil and Political Rights, Dec. 19, 1966, 999 U.N.T.S. 171, as evidence of an international consensus about the impermissibility of executing persons for crimes committed as a juvenile that in turn informed its interpretation of the Eighth Amendment, even though the president and the Senate when acceding to that treaty had expressly rejected this limitation on capital punishment. *Roper*, however, is not directly on point, as it did not give the treaty direct effect, but rather used the treaty's existence as an element of constitutional interpretation.

[28] It is quite common, for example, for Congress to provide exclusively for criminal punishment of a particular rule. *E.g.*, Canada v. R.J. Reynolds Tobacco Holdings, Inc., 268 F.3rd 103 (2nd Cir. 2001) (private enforcement of RICO statute not coextensive with scope of RICO criminal offense); Lamb v. Phillip Morris, Inc., 915 F.2nd 1024 (6th Cir. 1990) (no application of Federal Corrupt Practices Act in private suit). It also is not uncommon for Congress to limit the sanction for the violation of a federal rule to a loss of some federal benefit, such as some kind of funding. *E.g.*, Alexander v. Sandoval, 532 U.S. 275 (2001) (no private rights under disparate impact regulations implemented by federal agency under Title VI of Civil Rights Act of 1964); Gonzaga University v. Doe, 536 U.S. 273 (2002) (Family Educational Rights and Privacy Act of 1974 does not create a private remedy for persons injured by unauthorized disclosures). *Cf.* Cannon v. University of Chicago, 441 U.S. 667, 730 (1979) (Powell, J., dissenting) (criticizing judicial implication of private rights of action).

[29] AMERICAN LAW INSTITUTE, RESTATEMENT (THIRD) OF THE FOREIGN RELATIONS LAW OF THE UNITED STATES §§111, 115 (1987); LOUIS HENKIN, FOREIGN AFFAIRS AND THE CONSTITUTION 219 (1972). For a critical response, see Curtis A. Bradley & Jack L. Goldsmith, note 17 *supra*. For defenses against this criticism, see Ryan Goodman & Derek P. Jinks, *Filartiga's Firm Footing: International Human Rights and Federal Common Law*, 66 FORDHAM L. REV. 463 (1997); Harold Hongju Koh, *Is International Law Really State Law?* 111 HARV. L. REV. 1824 (1998); Gerald Neuman, *Sense and Nonsense About Customary International Law: A Response to Professors Bradley and Goldsmith*, 66 FORDHAM L. REV. 371 (1997); Beth Stephens, *The Law of Our Land: Customary International Law as Federal Law After Erie*, 66 FORDHAM L. REV. 393 (1997).

note that U.S. courts regard themselves as possessing some authority to both detect and enforce customary international law, but the scope of this authority remains undetermined and the receptivity of the courts to guidance from the political branches on enforcement questions remains unclear.

Stepping back to generalize, it seems reasonably clear that the makers of international law have the capacity to address and control enforcement. They often let this issue be settled by default, but ascertaining which outcome serves as the default remains controversial. The array of enforcement decisions is not unlimited, and various capacity constraints exist. Some forms of enforcement – going to war, imposing an economic embargo – entail great costs and require cooperation with other states, thus adding obstacles to their implementation. But, as an analytic matter, choices about enforcement are no different than decisions about what obligations constitute international law.

## Enforcement versus Compliance

We ask why people invest in the enforcement of international law. Note what the question does not ask, and what our answer does not say. We do not ask why nations comply with international law, much less what norms or rules count as "international law." As Louis Henkin's famous epigram suggests, both of these issues have inspired a vast body of scholarship. But our interest is different. We want to isolate, as best we can, the causes and consequences of enforcement.

Enforcement may explain why people comply with international law, but other forces also may be at work. Consider, for example, a rule that may constitute an obligation imposed by international law, but which costs a state nothing to observe. Jack Goldsmith and Eric Posner offer as an example the norm we mentioned earlier that requires the navies of belligerent states not to harass fishing boats.[31] If interfering with fishermen brings few advantages and diverts naval vessels from more productive uses, we would expect a high level of compliance. But this compliance would have nothing to do with enforcement, because states have every reason to choose this behavior without any additional investment.[32]

---

[30]   *Sosa v. Alvarez-Machain*, 542 U.S 692 (2004), endorsed a limited version of the no-automatic-application position, in the sense that it accepted that not all customary international law constitutes federal law. Technically speaking, however, the issue was not one that the Court needed to decide, as the plaintiff in that case satisfied the requirements of diversity jurisdiction and thus did not have to establish the existence of a federal question.

[31]   Jack L. Goldsmith & Eric A. Posner, note 1 *supra*, at 27–28, 66–78.

[32]   In formal terms, we would expect there to exist no enforcement mechanism other than the actors' own willingness to comply with the norm. The compliance cost thus would be limited to the benefits that could be derived from the foregone behavior, which by hypothesis have a low value.

More generally, many behavioral regularities that, at least in the eyes of some authorities, constitute "international law" require little or no investment in enforcement because actors have little or no incentive to defect. In general, these norms represent either a genuine coincidence of interest or solutions to what political scientists call *coordination problems*, situations where actors can derive a benefit from cooperation but where compliance with the norm does not create incentives for others not to comply. Classic examples include the assignment of rights in the spectrum of wavelengths and of positions along the geometrical space on which satellites can attain a geosynchronous orbit around our planet. Each actor might have a preferred allocation, but once assignments have been made, there is little to be gained from disregarding them.[33] Similarly, Tom Ginsburg and Richard McAdams explore cases decided by the ICJ, an international law institution that arguably represents a low-cost investment in enforcement.[34] They observe that the Court, which has no capacity to induce compliance with its decisions, enjoys its greatest influence in cases that present only coordination issues.[35]

But none of these observations demonstrates that international law deals *only* with coordination problems. Even if some prominent international law institutions – in particular, the ICJ – do not have the capacity to deal effectively with problems that require enforcement mechanisms, this does not mean that international law as a whole lacks the resources to deal with such problems. We focus on the growing body of international law that does respond to costly cooperation and thus requires some attention to enforcement.

Enforcement becomes a central issue when, to attain the benefits of coopera-tion, actors must make themselves vulnerable to exploitation by their partners. Scholars often refer to these situations as *collective action problems*.[36] A classic

---

[33]  For an extended discussion, see Duncan Snidal, *Coordination versus Prisoners' Dilemma: Implications for International Cooperation and Regimes*, 79 AM. POL. SCI. REV. 923 (1985).

[34]  Whether the ICJ represents a low-cost investment turns in part on assessments of the reputational effects of decisions by states not to comply with that body's decisions. One finds many assertions in the literature to the effect that states regard defiance of the Court as costly, but typically these represent normative claims about the value of the institution rather than careful analysis of the effects of its decisions. *See, e.g.*, CONSTANZE SCHULTE, COMPLIANCE WITH DECISIONS OF THE INTERNATIONAL COURT OF JUSTICE 404 (2004). We discuss the ICJ in detail in Chapter 5.

[35]  *See* Tom Ginsburg & Richard H. McAdams, *Adjudicating in Anarchy: An Expressive Theory of Inter-national Dispute Resolution*, 45 WM. & MARY L. REV. 1229 (2004). As a formal matter, the UN Security Council has the authority to require compliance with the judgments of the ICJ. UN Charter arti-cle 94(2). But the Security Council cannot act without the support of the five permanent members, a limitation that makes enforcement against the United States, the European Union, Russia, or China highly unlikely.

[36]  Students of game theory and of the rational-choice perspective on international relations will recognize the general form of the problem as that of the prisoners' dilemma. This heuristic stipulates an interaction where the actors can improve their welfare by cooperating, but where cooperation

and much discussed example in international law involves foreign direct investment, where an investor sinks resources (often literally, in the case of mining and oil drilling) into an enterprise over which the host government retains power.[37] Once the investment has been made and a profitable enterprise established, the host country might do better by seizing the enterprise, either literally or through regulation and taxation, than by accepting its previously agreed share of the proceeds. Knowing of this risk, the investor may take precautions against seizure (perhaps sabotaging the project or bribing local officials) or choose to pass up a socially valuable undertaking. To avoid this outcome, the parties might invest in a mechanism that alters the host country's incentives so as to make expropriation unprofitable.

The investor example illustrates several aspects of a collective action problem. Most fundamentally, the socially valuable task requires parties with diverse interests to expose themselves to the risk of opportunistic behavior by their counterparties. Opportunism may come in many forms. The counterparty may simply shirk in carrying out its responsibilities if it can obtain some part of the benefits of the common enterprise regardless of its own level of effort, or it may behave more aggressively to appropriate the value created by the

requires each actor to make itself vulnerable to opportunism by the other. Using a two-by-two matrix to represent two actors, A and B, and two possible actions, cooperate and defect, we can assign ordinal rankings to the four possible outcomes (Player A's outcome listed first, rankings from first preference to last):

|  | Player B Cooperate | Player B Defect |
|---|---|---|
| Player A Cooperate | 2,2 | 4,1 |
| Player A Defect | 1,4 | 3,3 |

In single interactions, the game has a stable solution of mutual noncooperation (defect, defect). A vast literature explores the conditions under which increased iterations, party discount rates, and enforcement mechanisms can change this result to stable cooperation. *See generally* Paul G. Mahoney & Chris William Sanchirico, *Norms, Repeated Games, and the Role of Law*, 91 CAL. L. REV. 1281 (2003).

[37] *See* Paul B. Stephan, *Redistributive Litigation – Judicial Innovation, Private Expectations and the Shadow of International Law*, 88 VA. L. REV. 789 (2002).

first party, as in the example of host state expropriation of foreign investment. Mechanisms to address these risks present different kinds of costs. In categorical terms, we can speak of ex post precautions to safeguard against the possibility that a counterparty defects from its cooperative obligations once a project is under way, and ex ante decisions to forego objectively desirable projects because amelioration of the risks is too costly. Contract theory in turn looks at ways to design mechanisms that minimize these costs for given levels of benefits.

Other examples abound. We discuss in detail investor protection, an area of growing importance, in Chapter 5. Arms limitations agreements similarly present collective action problems, at least in cases where participants plausibly might use force in their dealings with each other. The Washington Naval Treaty of 1922, for example, exposed its signatories to opportunistic harm that became all too apparent when Japan attacked Pearl Harbor. Environmental projects, such as the Kyoto Protocol on the emission of greenhouse gases, present a risk that some countries might shirk in implementing costly antipollution measures in response to the success of other countries' investments. Reductions in trade barriers, by increasing specialization in production and greater economic interdependence, expose participants to the risk of exploitation. The struggle against terrorism presents collective action problems because of the diversity of nonstate groups inclined toward violence and the consequent variance of terrorist threats that different countries face. The benefits of eradicating al-Qaeda, for example, may disproportionately accrue to the United States, but considerable costs might fall on people in Western Europe if repressive measures antagonize their significant immigrant minorities.

The first part of our claim, then, is that collective action problems have growing significance in the contemporary world. Technological change, the transformation of communications and information processing, and greater economic interdependence both are the product of, and present increased incentives for, wider and deeper participation in the kind of international cooperation that presents a risk of defection. As the potential benefits from international cooperation increase, so does the significance of risks associated with defection. And as both benefits and costs grow, so does the value of enforcement mechanisms that can deter defection.

This argument about the role of enforcement in international law should seem familiar to students of private contracting behavior. The standard and widely accepted account of why both contracting parties and society expend resources to enforce contracts is to encourage the undertaking of socially desirable cooperative projects that entail a risk that contracting parties will behave opportunistically.[38] We maintain that, in essence, international law enforcement responds to the same concerns.

## INTERNATIONAL LAWMAKERS AND PRIVATE ACTORS

In arguing that the enforcement of both international law and private contracts reflect similar behavioral issues and instrumental objectives, we do not mean to suggest that private actors and the persons that produce international law (for the most part, but not exclusively, nation states) are fundamentally alike. To the contrary, firms and states are governed by decision makers bound by different constraints and facing different incentives, have different expectations of the future, and operate against vastly different historical and cultural backgrounds. We argue only that these differences are not so great as to render irrelevant contract theory models of optimal investment in international law enforcement.

Some specialists in international law and international relations seem to take a different view, however. In general, they emphasize the exceptional character of international law and its enforcement. We consider several arguments underlying this position and find them unpersuasive.

### States Are Different

That the application of legal rules to states works differently than the application of rules to individuals is a commonplace in the instrumental analysis of the law as well as in mainstream international relations theory.[39] States cannot be imprisoned, and the agents whose choices result in legal liability seldom bear the direct costs of any money judgment.[40] But the same is true of other complex organizations, such as private firms or nonprofit entities. And these limitations affect all kinds of legal rules, not just international ones. We need to look closely, then, at the question of whether such distinctions as exist between states and other complex entities might affect the instrumental consequences of international law.

---

[38] *See* Alan Schwartz & Robert E. Scott, *Contract Theory and the Limits of Contract Law*, 113 YALE L.J. 541, 559–62 (2003).

[39] The best recent analysis of this problem by a legal academic is Daryl Levinson, *Making Government Pay: Markets, Politics, and the Allocation of Constitutional Costs*, 67 U. CHI. L. REV. 645 (2000).

[40] For a persuasive explanation of the public benefits from the particular limits on the liability of governments and governmental agents in U.S. domestic law, see John C. Jeffries, Jr., *The Right-Remedy Gap in Constitutional Law*, 109 YALE L. J. 87 (1999); John C. Jeffries, Jr., *In Praise of the Eleventh Amendment and Section 1983*, 84 VA. L. REV. 47 (1998).

One difference between firms and states is the prospect of survival. In theory, both have an indefinite expected life, unlike people, whose end is inevitable. But firm death is common and predictable. Firms frequently liquidate, either voluntarily or in bankruptcy, or become absorbed into another entity. State death, by contrast, is rare and, to the extent it occurs, is determined more by exogenous factors, such as the nature of a state's neighbors, over which political leaders have no control.[41] This difference conceivably might affect both the sensitivity of states to externally imposed sanctions and the *discount rate* that states use to assess future costs and benefits.

But both states and firms act through agents, and the relevant issue is how law and its enforcement affect the agents' incentives when they commit their principals to particular courses of conduct. There is no reason to believe that differences in the principal's survival prospects systematically affect those of its agents. States, without disappearing, may experience a change in regime, as when a democratic leadership replaces authoritarian rulers or vice versa. Even when a regime (by which we mean the fundamental aspects of a political system that determine both political leadership and policy making) remains stable, different coalitions or parties may come to power, exiling (either figuratively or literally) the losers.[42]

The leaders of all organizations must account in some way to their constituencies, whether we are talking about firms and their stakeholders, non-profits and their donors, or states and those to whom they must account for their actions (sometimes, but not always, the electorate). Whatever the differences in the organizational form and accountability mechanism, there is no reason to believe that the characteristics of the groups to which the organizational leaders must answer, and in particular their respective discount rates, vary according to the form. As Albert O. Hirschman demonstrated in his groundbreaking study *Exit, Voice, and Loyalty: Responses to Decline in Firms, Organizations, and States*, common factors, in particular adjustment of incentives, provide at least a partial explanation for the way that states and other complex organizations respond to changes in their environment.[43]

One also might argue that firms deal with a limited range of human endeavors, namely profit-motivated transactions, whereas states necessarily must respond to, and participate in, the full scope of human activity. States organize

---

[41] *See* Tanisha Fazal, *State Death in the International System*, 58 INT'L ORG. 311 (2004).

[42] For more on this point, see Robert E. Scott & Paul B. Stephan, *Self-Enforcing International Agreements and the Limits of Coercion*, 2004 WIS. L. REV. 551, 583–85.

[43] ALBERT O. HIRSCHMAN, EXIT, VOICE, AND LOYALTY: RESPONSES TO DECLINE IN FIRMS, ORGANIZATIONS, AND STATES (1970). For an insightful application of Hirschman's work to one particular international regime, see J. H. H. Weiler, *The Transformation of Europe*, 100 YALE L.J. 2403 (1991).

violence, succor the needy, and seek to sustain and nourish the national culture. In this view, very little that states do seems to correspond to private transacting, so a body of law designed to facilitate the latter has little bearing on the lion's share of the tasks that confront states.

This objection overlooks the protean, innovative, and inclusive nature of private transactions. Contract law may seem a hoary legacy of the eighteenth and nineteenth centuries, as much Anglo as American, but the private transactional world is a challenging and constantly changing environment. New technological methods and organizational structures require new contracts, and those firms and people that fail to adapt struggle to continue. Moreover, transactions as often as not operate at the interface between different cultures, as members of groups with different backgrounds and assets interact. Law follows in the wake of transactional innovations: Contract law comprises a set of common themes and problems, not a rigid set of rules. It is the robustness of the concept of contract, not its doctrinal details, that has inspired so many social philosophers – Hobbes, Locke, Rousseau, and Rawls all come to mind – to use the contract metaphor to explain and justify states.[44]

One can derive a different objection to a comparison of states and other organizations by starting with the claims of realism, the still dominant theory of international relations among U.S. political scientists. Realists see the basic analytical unit as the nation state and material interest as the driving force motivating each state's interactions with the rest of the world. Many realists assume that national security constitutes the core material interest, which they regard as a function of relative rather than absolute capacity. Their world has a strongly Darwinian cast: Leaders and policy élites who fail to maximize state security find themselves superseded. But realists insist that security is always a relative issue. Leaders are indifferent to the state's power in absolute terms, but care deeply about how much (or less) stronger is their state than are state rivals.[45] With firms, by contrast, the prospects for cooperation seem greater, and the challenges from competition less grave, because of the greater ability of firms to specialize.

Concentrating on relative, rather than absolute, gains complicates cooperation. Much economic theory rests on an implicit assumption about the sequence of considerations: Actors first calculate the marginal value of

---

[44] For earlier scholarship that applies contract theory to problems in international relations, see, *e.g.*, Joel P. Trachtman, *The Theory of the Firm and the Theory of International Economic Organization: Toward Comparative Institutional Analysis*, 17 Nw. J. INT'L L. & BUS. 470 (1996–97); Jeffrey L. Dunoff & Joel P. Trachtman, *Economic Analysis of International Law*, 24 YALE J. INT'L L. 1 (1999).

[45] For an influential restatement of this position and a critique of other perspectives on international relations, see John J. Mearsheimer, *The False Promise of International Institutions*, 19 INT'L SECURITY 5 (1994–95).

cooperative endeavors, and only then determine how to divide the profit. An exclusive focus on relative gains rules out the possibility of most win-win scenarios: Actors will reject any cooperative activity that alters the relative distance between them (using whatever metric they consider relevant), even if that activity increases the welfare of all.[46]

Consider a hypothetical world occupied by states A through Z, each with an initial endowment of 10 units. Suppose that some cooperative action among these states would produce a net benefit of 105 (perhaps reduction of a terrorist threat), with 5 of the gain going to state A and gains of 4 each going to states B through Z. Using the analysis conventionally used by economists, the cooperative action is pareto-optimal, because all are better off and none is worse off. But if the only salient criterion is relative welfare, then states B through Z would be worse off as a result of cooperating, as they would move from a world of equality with A to one where A has 15 units to their 14. Accordingly, none would cooperate with A.

In a world in which states care only about changes in their well-being relative to that of other states, there will not exist many instances where collective action will seem desirable. The conditions for cooperation to succeed are too stringent: The action must not only produce gains, but the gains must be distributed in such a manner that the relative welfare of the cooperating states does not change. Where states do seem to act collectively, as in the case of the creation of international organizations, realism will surmise that the appearance may be deceiving. In particular, realists doubt that states would delegate real power to such an organization, especially the power to enforce commitments, because most delegations would alter the relative position among states.

Because realism discounts both the reasons for states to pursue collective action and the capacity of international institutions to induce compliance with rules, it has little use for international law and even less for international law enforcement. As Anne-Marie Slaughter observed more than a decade ago, the postwar dominance of realism among international relations theorists effectively divorced mainstream political science from international law.[47] But facts on the ground as well as new theoretical perspectives have challenged the core premises of international relations theory.

The critical step involves identifying international relations problems where the value of absolute gains dominates concern over relative gains. Several trends over the last thirty years make this easier. A greater awareness of the

---

[46] As Norman and Trachtman put it, "Realists reject the possibility of cooperation where it results in relative gains to a competitor." George Norman & Joel P. Trachtman, note 16 *supra*, at 547 n. 32.

[47] *See* Anne-Marie Slaughter Burley, *International Law and International Relations Theory: A Dual Agenda*, 87 Am. J. Int'l L. 205, 206 (1993).

international implications of particular aspects of human well-being, exemplified by the environmental and human rights movements, have drawn international relations into fields where relative gains simply do not matter. Changes in the world economy, partly technological (e.g., the information processing and communications revolutions) and partly structural (e.g., the growth of global capital markets), have required states collectively to adapt to new challenges, rather than simply to compete with one another. And a shift in international security issues from state-based threats, in particular the bipolar nuclear balance of terror, to transnational terrorism and similar nonstate threats has transformed the most fundamental problems of international order. In each of these areas, the gains from cooperation seem clear and the relative distribution of these gains among states is of secondary importance. A quarter-century ago, the principal security issue was the threat that the Soviet Union and the United States each posed to the other. Today, we might list AIDS, an influenza pandemic, climate change, economic disruption, and terrorism as comparable threats to long-term survival, but none of these problems involves the kind of symmetries that superpower competition entailed.[48]

As to both the incentives facing decision makers and the relative importance of cooperative projects, then, firms and states share salient attributes. Key decision makers fear demotion or dismissal, independent of the fate of the entity, and seek to avoid that outcome. The trade-offs these decision makers make between present and future benefits and costs (in short, their discount rate) will vary, but there is no reason to believe that this variation will depend fundamentally on whether the decision makers are acting on behalf of states or firms. Firms face collective action problems, but increasingly so do states. The mechanisms states employ to address collective action problems, then, should resemble those used by private actors, at least at the analytic level.

## States Do Not Make International Law

Yet another objection to the mining of contract theory for insights into international law and its enforcement is that similarities between firms and states do not matter, because states play a diminished (and diminishing) role in the development of international law. The classical view of international law, as the product of interstate bargains, always was incomplete, and in the modern world, some say, verges on the irrelevant. What is new and interesting about international law is the connections between, on the one hand, affinity

---

[48] For a recent restatement of this claim, see Laurence R. Helfer & Anne-Marie Slaughter, *Why States Create International Tribunals: A Response to Professors Posner and Yoo*, 93 CALIF. L. REV. 899, 931–36 (2005).

groups whose membership transcends national borders and, on the other hand, supranational organizations that in turn shape the choices national actors make.[49]

Among international lawyers, the most prominent proponent of a perspective that shifts focus away from states is Anne-Marie Slaughter. In *A New World Order*, she develops her central thesis:

Stop imagining the international system as a system of states – unitary entities like billiard balls or black boxes – subject to rules created by international institutions that are apart from, "above" these states. Start thinking about a world of governments, with all the different institutions that perform the basic functions of governments – legislation, adjudication, implementation – interacting both with each other domestically and also with their foreign and supranational counterparts. States still exist in this world; indeed, they are crucial actors. But they are "disaggregated." They relate to each other not only through the Foreign Office, but also through regulatory, judicial, and legislative channels.[50]

The new world order that Slaughter describes works through information exchange and deliberations rather than by coercion and incentives. Collaboration, not compulsion, is the order of the day. Rules and norms come out of this discourse, but enforcement results from discrete actions by national governments and their various components, not from the direct action of international organs.[51]

---

[49] For a recent review of the role of supranational, subnational, and extranational actors in international lawmaking, see Duncan B. Hollis, *Why State Consent Still Matters – Non-State Actors, Treaties, and the Changing Sources of International Law*, 24 BERKELEY J. INT'L L. 137 (2005).

[50] ANNE-MARIE SLAUGHTER, A NEW WORLD ORDER 5 (2004). This book synthesizes more than a decade of work that has had a significant impact on international lawyers as much as international relations experts. For examples of her influence on the work of younger scholars, see José E. Alvarez, *The WTO as Linkage Machine*, 96 AM. J. INT'L L. 146 (2002); Laurence R. Helfer, *Overlegalizing Human Rights: International Relations Theory and the Commonwealth Caribbean Backlash Against Human Rights Regimes*, 102 COLUM. L. REV. 1832 (2002); Jenny S. Martinez, *Toward an International Legal System*, 56 STAN. L. REV. 429 (2003); Diane F. Orentlicher, *Whose Justice? Reconciling Universal Jurisdiction with Democratic Principles*, 92 GEO. L.J. 1057 (2004); Kal Raustiala, *The Architecture of International Cooperation: Transgovernmental Networks and the Future of International Law*, 43 VA. J. INT'L L. 1 (2002).

[51] In all these examples, the key players are national government officials who exercise the same array of coercive and persuasive powers on behalf of transgovernmental decisions that they do domestically. They can coerce, cajole, fine, order, regulate, legislate, horse-trade, bully, or use whatever methods that produce results within their political system. They are not subject to coercion at the transgovernmental level; on the contrary, they are likely to perceive themselves as choosing a specific course of action freely and deliberately. Yet having decided, for whatever reasons, to adopt a particular code of best practices, to coordinate policy in a particular way, to accept the decision of a supranational tribunal, or even simply to join what seems to be an emerging international consensus on a particular issue, they can implement that decision with the limits of their own domestic power.
ANNE-MARIE SLAUGHTER, note 50 *supra*, at 185.

There is much to admire in Slaughter's work. Her highlighting of regulatory networks, especially those linking governments (as distinguished from legislatures or judiciaries) is important and useful. At the same time, we believe that she overstates the extent and power of these networks, especially regarding legislatures and judges, and at the same time understates the capacity of international judicial bodies to exercise coercive power. Some of these errors reflect a conflation of normative aspirations and positive analysis, and in particular a discomfort with the choices that working systems of democratic accountability seem to produce. To use Hirschman's terminology, increasingly complex networks and other relationships across national boundaries might expand the exit option for many actors, but voice, in the sense of participation in a collective decision-making process in ways that maximize participation, fairness, and legitimacy, remains the monopoly of states.[52]

Slaughter's core claim, that states play only a formal role in international relations and derivatively in the production of international law, has a lengthy and important history. Engels proposed that the state constituted an epiphenomenal structure, the nature and actions of which depended on the modes of material production and the nature of class relations.[53] Hobson and Lenin used this conceptual apparatus to explain international relations, in particular the rise of European great power imperialism at the end of the nineteenth century.[54] In spite of the general discrediting of classical Marxism that followed the collapse of the Soviet state and its ideological as well as economic aspirations, claims about the domination of corporate interests and the irrelevance of the state still crop up in radical critiques of contemporary globalization.[55] Indeed, a standard radical left account of the contemporary international economic and political system rests on a belief that multinational corporations and their ilk

---

[52] For a perceptive argument about the inherent tension between the development of international law and parliamentary accountability, see Jack L. Goldsmith & Stephen Krasner, *The Limits of Idealism*, 132 DAEDALUS 47 (2001). For criticism of Slaughter's claims along these lines, see Kenneth Anderson, *Squaring the Circle? Reconciling Sovereignty and Global Governance Through Global Government Networks*, 118 HARV. L. REV. 1255 (2005).

[53] FRIEDRICH ENGELS, THE ORIGIN OF FAMILY, PRIVATE PROPERTY AND THE STATE (1972) [1884].

[54] J. A. HOBSON, IMPERIALISM: A STUDY (1965) [1902]; VLADIMIR I. LENIN, IMPERIALISM THE HIGHEST STAGE OF CAPITALISM – A POPULAR OUTLINE (1939) [1917].

[55] For scholarly studies, see, *e.g.*, SASKIA SASSEN, LOSING CONTROL? SOVEREIGNTY IN AN AGE OF GLOBALIZATION (1999); SUSAN STRANGE, THE RETREAT OF THE STATE – THE DIFFUSION OF POWER IN THE WORLD ECONOMY (1996). For more popular and explicitly political treatments, see, *e.g.*, JOHN GRAY, FALSE DAWN: THE DELUSIONS OF GLOBAL CAPITALISM (1998); NOREENA HERTZ, THE SILENT TAKEOVER: GLOBAL CAPITALISM AND THE DEATH OF DEMOCRACY (2002); NAOMI KLEIN, NO LOGO: TAKING AIM AT THE BRAND BULLIES (1999). Similar critical analyses of transnational networks come from the right. Consider the argument implicit in the claim, repeatedly encountered by one of us in elegant Parisian circles, that "[Israeli Prime Minister Ariel] Sharon is the real leader of the United States."

have developed networks that effectively crowd out national and local decision making.[56]

What distinguishes Slaughter's perspective is its optimism about the disappearance of the state from international relations. Rather than manipulating state choices in ways that harm the general welfare, her transnational networks transfer best practice, reinforce progressive impulses, and improve the management of regulatory challenges that globalization presents. Some scholars with different normative impulses accordingly have attacked her work as formalistic, naive, and otherwise ill-founded. Her embrace of the international regulatory and cultural status quo disturbs those who see this world from a critical and radical perspective. For them, she comes across as not much more than apologist for an empire resting on global capital.[57]

We believe these critics overlook another difficulty with Slaughter's story. Its focus on the production of soft law means that it slights the formal enforcement of international law and thus leaves a distorted impression of how enforcement works. There is both greater international power, and less network-based collaboration, than her account admits.

First, as noted in Chapter 1, a number of international bodies have enforcement powers that are effectively indistinguishable from those possessed by national courts. They can hear cases brought by private parties, rather than only those selected by governments, and they can order money damages and, in the case of international criminal courts, impose prison terms. Those subject to their power, including states, might resist enforcement, but this does not distinguish the enforcement capacity of these tribunals from those of domestic courts, where reluctant judgment debtors sequester assets, flee the jurisdiction, and otherwise seek to frustrate the workings of the law.[58]

Other work by Slaughter, coauthored with Laurence Helfer, describes international tribunals as often effectively constrained by national decision makers, and thus not fully independent lawmakers.[59] They argue that domestic political actors limit the policy space in which these tribunals can act, and that

---

[56]  *E.g.*, Noam Chomsky, Hegemony or Survival: America's Quest for Global Dominance (2003); Michael Hardt & Antonio Negri, Empire (2000); Robert J. S. Ross & Kent C. Trachte, Global Capitalism: The New Leviathan (1990).

[57]  Martti Koskenniemi, The Gentle Civilizer of Nations – The Rise and Fall of International Law 1870–1960, at 488 (2002); Jean Louise Cohen, *Whose Sovereignty? Empire Versus International Law*, 18 Ethics & Int'l Affairs 1 (2004–05).

[58]  *See* In re Grand Jury Subpoenas Dated March 9, 2001, 179 F. Supp. 2nd 270 (S.D.N.Y. 2001) (discussing Marc Rich case).

[59]  Laurence R. Helfer & Anne-Marie Slaughter, note 48 *supra*; Laurence R. Helfer & Anne-Marie Slaughter, *Toward a Theory of Effective Supranational Adjudication*, 107 Yale L.J. 273 (1997).

group-based ethics of appropriateness further constrain the members of these bodies. But these considerations do not distinguish international judges from domestic ones. Moreover, the existence of constraints based on professional identity seems unrelated to the question of whether these tribunals exert effective power independent of national governments. By Helfer and Slaughter's account, the groups that generate these identities operate across national borders, and therefore cannot function as a *national* check on judicial policy making.

Slaughter's work also does not adequately consider how a domestic judiciary's independence affects the enforcement of international law. As we explore in detail later in this book, domestic courts have the potential to augment the enforcement of international law, and can choose to do so in ways that national lawmakers only partly can control. One straightforward way to avoid legislative accountability is for a national court to absorb an international rule into domestic constitutional law, thus insulating it entirely from the political branches. The Supreme Court has played with this approach, most recently in *Roper v. Simmons*.[60] Alternatively, courts can adopt international law as a method for interpreting domestic legislation and count on the many obstacles to domestic lawmaking to prevent a later repudiation. In the United States, the *Charming Betsy* canon of statutory construction, which admonishes courts to interpret the law so as to avoid putting the United States into violation of its international obligations, performs this task.[61]

Not only does Slaughter give a false impression of how the enforcement of international law can work contrary to the wishes of domestic governments, but she overstates the extent of transnational influences on legislators and judges. Interparliamentary cooperation, except as mediated by governments, is almost nonexistent in the contemporary world. The International Parliamentary Union in Geneva, the principal organ for such direct contacts as exist, has a low level of activity. Its status was diminished even further by the recent withdrawal of the U.S. Congress from membership.

The reasons why Slaughter specifically, and most international law scholarship generally, downplays legislatures are beyond the scope of this book. For present purposes, it suffices to note that transnational networks generally lack symmetry: They are strongest among private actors and the executive branches of states, and largely exclude national lawmakers. The kinds of cooperation that

---

[60] 543 U.S. 551 (2005).

[61] *E.g.*, F. Hoffman-Laroche Ltd. v. Empagran S.A., 542 U.S. 155 (2004) (interpreting jurisdiction of U.S. antitrust law as limited in accordance with customary international law). *See generally* Curtis A. Bradley, *The Charming Betsy Canon and Separation of Powers: Rethinking the Interpretive Role of International Law*, 86 GEO. L. J. 479 (1998).

networks promote effectively results in a transfer of power from legislatures to governments and from politicians to private actors.[62]

We conclude that nothing about the process of enforcing international law categorically distinguishes it from domestic law enforcement. In both instances, judges operate under conditions of constrained independence and have substantial, but not complete, authority to make enforcement choices that domestic political authorities might find unpalatable. Moreover, this observation is true of some, but not all, international as well as domestic tribunals. At the structural level, then, contract enforcement and international law enforcement seem more alike than different.

### Incentives Do Not Matter

By arguing that the enforcement of international law rests largely on an effort to encourage the joint production of social welfare, we implicitly assume that those who make and enforce international law seek to maximize social welfare, either self-consciously or as a result of selective pressure, and that this search dominates all other constraints. The attribution of rational instrumentalism to international law enforcement has its proponents, especially among U.S. professors of international law.[63] But many scholars reject this perspective and insist instead on the importance of cultural limitations on the producers, interpreters, and enforcers of international law.

It would be misleading to portray the culturalist and antirationalist work as monolithic. Rather, it is united only by a shared commitment to certain

---

[62] Paul B. Stephan, *Accountability and International Lawmaking: Rules, Rents and Legitimacy*, 17 Nw. J. INT'L L. & BUS. 681 (1996–97); Joel Paul, note 25 *supra*.

[63] For a representative sample of this work, see Kenneth W. Abbott, *Modern International Relations Theory: A Prospectus for Lawyers*, 14 YALE J. INT'L L. 335 (1989); Jeffrey L. Dunoff & Joel P. Trachtman, note 44 *supra*; Tom Ginsburg & Richard McAdams, note 35 *supra*; JACK L. GOLDSMITH & ERIC A. POSNER, note 1 *supra*; Andrew Guzman, note 19 *supra*; Oona Hathaway, *Do Human Rights Treaties Make a Difference?* 111 YALE L. J. 1935 (2002); John O. McGinnis, *The Decline of the Western Nation State and the Rise of the Regime of International Federalism*, 18 CARDOZO L. REV. 903 (1996); Jonathan R. Macey, *Regulatory Globalization as a Response to Regulatory Competition*, 52 EMORY L.J. 1353 (2003); Eric A. Posner & John C. Yoo, *A Theory of International Adjudication*, 93 CALIF. L. REV. 1 (2005); Warren F. Schwartz & Alan O. Sykes, *The Economic Structure of Renegotiation and Dispute Resolution in the World Trade Organization*, 31 J. LEGAL STUD. S179 (2002); John K. Setear, *Responses to Breach of a Treaty and Rationalist International Relations Theory: The Rules of Release and Remediation in the Law of Treaties and the Law of State Responsibility*, 83 VA. L. REV. 1 (1997); Edward T. Swaine, note 19 *supra*; Michael P. Van Alstine, *The Costs of Legal Change*, 49 U.C.L.A. L. REV. 789 (2002). We also have contributed to this literature. *See, e.g.*, Robert E. Scott & Paul B. Stephan, note 42 *supra*; Paul B. Stephan, *Courts, Tribunals and Legal Unification – The Agency Problem*, 3 CHI. J. INT'L L. 333 (2002); Paul B. Stephan, *The Futility of Unification and Harmonization in International Commercial Law*, 39 VA. J. INT'L L. 743 (1999); Paul B. Stephan, note 62 *supra*; Paul B. Stephan, *International Law in the Supreme Court*, 1990 SUP. CT. REV. 133.

methodological intuitions. Its perspectives run the gamut from continental critical theory (influenced in turn by certain of the last quarter-century's fashions in historiography, legal scholarship, and literary theory) to Kantian idealism and contemporary versions of natural law. What these various strands have in common is a conviction about the provisional and ideational nature of social life, international relations included. In this perspective, values and beliefs do not passively reflect social reality, but shape and condition it. To understand why states and their political élites behave as they do, we must examine their cognitive environment. These approaches ascribe primary significance to those factors that shape and filter perceptions of the material world, rather than to the supposedly objective conditions of that world.

For lawyers, one of the attractions of culturalist theories is the importance they attach to institutions of persuasion. If social reality is constructed rather than experienced passively, then surely law – the art of persuasion – plays a critical role in that process of construction. The connection is not necessary – one can assign primary importance to ideas and still dismiss law as mystification – but a natural affinity exists. Perhaps for this reason, many American international law professors adopt culturalist approaches.[64] A brief review of the most prominent scholarship over the last decade illustrates this tendency.

During the 1990s, senior American scholars offered two complementary and influential theories about international law that loosely fit into the constructivist category. Thomas Franck addressed the question of how a rule became international law. He argued that the operative principle was one of legitimacy, which he defined in terms of both process – the use of a process recognized as conveying validity – and content of the rule – its precision, expression of widely held values, and conformity with widespread practice. Legitimacy, according to Franck, strengthens the "compliance pull" of rules, which in turn converts the rule from an expression of aspiration into a behavioral regularity.[65]

Writing during the same period, Abram and Antonia Chayes described the managerial aspect of international law. In their conception, international law operates primarily as a form of bureaucratic rationality, a device through which technocratic élites in different countries structure their cooperative activity. This kind of rationality must be distinguished from the concept used by

---

[64] The legal academic literature on constructivism and international law is vast. An October 10, 2005, search of the Westlaw database of law journals turned up 196 references. The movement is distinct from, although related do, critical legal studies, which has exercised considerable influence in international law scholarship. *See, e.g.,* DAVID KENNEDY, INTERNATIONAL LEGAL STRUCTURES (1987); MARTTI KOSKENNIEMI, note 57 *supra.*

[65] Thomas M. Franck, *Legitimacy in the International System,* 82 AM. J. INT'L L. 705 (1988), *expanded and revised as* FAIRNESS IN INTERNATIONAL LAW AND INSTITUTIONS (1995).

economists: It entails the development of interchangeable and recognizable command structures, and hence is more cognitive than adaptive. For this perspective, international law represents the will of particular groups in domestic societies to rationalize and control international events.[66]

Younger scholars propounded other theories that also stressed the active role of international law in shaping state behavior. Harold Koh developed the concept of "transnational legal process." In his view, civil society groups cooperating across national borders promote norms of behavior, which national decision makers (whether legislatures, executives, or judges does not seem to matter) find persuasive and adopt. The prototypical case involves norms of decency and respect associated with the international human rights movement. A critical step in this process, although somewhat undertheorized in Koh's account, involves the domestic lawmaker's willingness, as a result of an internalization process, to attach coercive consequences to the norm in question. This willingness, Koh apparently believes, gives credibility and persuasive force to the norm.[67]

As we discussed earlier, Anne-Marie Slaughter has drawn on the work of political scientists Margaret Keck and Kathryn Sikkink studying advocacy networks in international politics to explain what international law does.[68] Normative claims imbued with the imprimatur of international law provide a focus for interest groups to organize both locally and across borders. These groups form "epistemological communities" that share experience and values and build expertise, on which they draw to persuade authoritative decision makers. International law thus involves horizontal avenues of  persuasion more than vertical impositions of authority. Slaughter apparently shares with Koh a belief that coercive enforcement of norms by local lawmakers enhances the credibility and persuasive pull of the contested claims.[69]

More recently, Ryan Goodman and Derek Jinks have brought an explicitly sociological perspective to the functional analysis of international law. They argue that international law constructs expectations, institutions, and behavior not just through its persuasive force, the fundamental process in the work of Franck, the Chayeses, Koh, and Slaughter, but also through acculturation. In their conception, it operates as a form of social pressure that induces conformity. Goodman and Jinks explicitly connect the functional effects of coercion

---

[66] ABRAM CHAYES & ANTONIA HANDLER CHAYES, THE NEW SOVEREIGNTY: COMPLIANCE WITH INTERNATIONAL REGULATORY AGREEMENTS (1995).

[67] Harold H. Koh, *Why Do Nations Obey International Law?* 106 YALE L.J. 2599 (1997); Harold H. Koh, *Transnational Legal Process*, 75 NEB. L. REV. 181 (1996).

[68] MARGARET F. KECK & KATHRYN SIKKINK, ACTIVISTS BEYOND BORDERS: ADVOCACY NETWORKS IN INTERNATIONAL POLITICS (1998).

[69] ANNE-MARIE SLAUGHTER, note 50 *supra*.

to this force. In opposition to Koh and Slaughter, they conclude that, "[u]nder certain conditions, binding third-party decision and material sanctions may weaken the effectiveness of acculturation."[70]

What do these various cultural theories add to our understanding of international law and its enforcement? First, they provide an alternative explanation as to how norms emerge in international practice. Second, and more relevant for our specific purposes, they indicate that enforcement turns not on concepts such as cost and investment, but rather on salience and intelligibility. What a rationalist (in the economic sense) might regard as an empty gesture – say, a judicial decision against a judgment-proof defendant – a culturalist might see as a significant enactment of a cultural norm.[71]

How effective are culturalist theories at providing a positive account of international legal rules? Consider, for example, the hypothesis that the nature of states as liberal or illiberal explains a wide range of international behaviors. This is a cultural theory, in the sense that the possession of liberal institutions serves as the relevant independent variable, rather than as the product of some social process. Liberal states, so the hypothesis goes, rarely go to war with each other and otherwise engage in more open and peaceable relations. An early article by Slaughter extended the point by demonstrating how legal doctrine distinguishes between liberal and illiberal states even in contexts where the rules purported to neutrality. In particular, she argued, the widely accepted but uncodified rules governing what constitutes an official act by a foreign state that domestic courts will not review take the liberal-illiberal distinction into account, even though the formal content of this doctrine does not expressly distinguish among types of states.[72]

As these examples illustrate, rational choice and cultural accounts of international law generate different, and on occasion contradictory, positive explanations and normative claims. They particularly differ on the implications of enforcement. For rational choice theorists, enforcement involves a cost-benefit analysis to determine what kinds of investments in the production of sanctions generates what kinds of compliance. For constructivists, enforcement is a kind of theater that teaches by example. The two approaches ask different questions and point to different answers.

---

[70] Ryan Goodman & Derek Jinks, *How to Influence States: Socialization and International Human Rights Law*, 54 DUKE L.J. 621, 698 (2004). For a case history to similar effect, see Laurence R. Helfer, note 50 *supra*.

[71] Recall that in the first wave of lawsuits under 28 U.S.C. §1350, the so-called Alien Tort Statute, the defendants almost always had no attachable assets within the jurisdiction of any U.S. court. Curtis A. Bradley, *Customary International Law and Private Rights of Action*, 1 CHI. J. INT'L L. 421 (2000).

[72] Anne-Marie [Slaughter] Burley, *Law Among Liberal States: Liberal Internationalism and the Act of State Doctrine*, 92 COLUM. L. REV 1978 (1992).

One of us has written about a similar tension regarding the general problem of legal construction of social norms.[73] Lawyers who work with economic models and methodologies seek testable hypotheses and reproducible results, but often must sacrifice realistic detail to model behavior. Those borrowing from anthropology and sociology use thick description to provide a full account of particular events, but sacrifice both the capacity to generalize results and to test hypotheses with quantitative analysis. "Without context no legal rule can be applied, but with nothing but context no legal rule can be found."[74] We repeat the conclusion reached there:

[E]fforts to enrich rational choice theory through the incorporation of endogenous preferences derived from social norms . . . have been frustrated thus far by the heroic but ultimately fatal step of trying to graft the complex and highly individualized process by which values and preferences are created and modified onto a formal analytical framework. A more profitable approach . . . is to deploy rational choice analysis on its own terms, but retain (as part of the analyst's frame of judgment) the situational sense of context-specific knowledge as an antidote to inapposite analogies and generalizations.[75]

## Political Élites Are Not Faithful Agents

There is a final and perhaps even more troubling objection to our argument that a contract theory model informs the enforcement of international law. Comparing the voluntary commitments made between states to contractual commitments made between firms may seem inapt to the extent that state actors are less faithful agents than corporate managers. For example, a critic might well argue that the claim that governing élites create international law in order to maximize the welfare of their citizens is far more problematic than the parallel claim that managers of firms seek to maximize shareholder welfare. After all, there are many more conflicts of interest between a dictator and his subjects than there are between a manager and shareholders. To put the point squarely: If a ruthless leader is maximizing his own gain at the expense of the interests of his subjects and he is dealing with a representative democracy, why should we be confident that any agreement that emerges between such different states will be welfare-enhancing for the people of both those countries?

There are several responses to this concern. One answer is simply to remind the reader that we have assumed that states design the content of international

[73] Robert E. Scott, *The Limits of Behavioral Theories of Law and Social Norms*, 86 VA. L. REV. 1603 (2000).

[74] *Id.* at 1646–47.

[75] *Id.* at 1647.

law to maximize welfare in order to isolate questions of enforcement, which present issues that scholars largely have ignored to date. A more substantive response is that evolutionary pressures to respond to the welfare of the people operate on governing élites, even undemocratic ones, just as they do on corporate managers. The differences are matters of degree and not differences in kind.

For example, assume that each state has a political élite that seeks to maximize its own welfare but faces uncertainty about the future. Assume further that the institutional constraints on the ability of any governing élite to pursue self-interested goals varies according to the characteristics of the domestic regime. States ruled by dictators or other authoritarian regimes only weakly constrain their leaders, in the sense that some choices might lead to an unacceptable high risk of domestic or foreign overthrow. By contrast, constitutional democracies exert much stronger constraints on self dealing both through mandated power sharing and checks and balances, as well as by posing a real risk of electoral defeat. Thus, it follows that the agency costs caused by the separation of interests between the élites and the people are potentially greater in some regimes than in others.

But the fact that some political élites may be faithless agents does not undermine the claim that the mechanisms of enforcement that apply to firms can usefully be applied to the international commitments undertaken by those states. First, it is not the case that agency costs are uniform across firms either. Celebrated examples such as Enron, Adelphia, and WorldCom show that the capacity of shareholders to monitor the actions of managers may vary dramatically. Yet these examples do not lead corporate law scholars to abandon the foundational assumption that firms seek to maximize shareholder wealth. Moreover, the fact that some governing élites are faithless agents does not directly undermine the claim that the international commitments undertaken by those élites are intended to promote the collective production of social welfare. After all, élites will seek rents primarily by diverting wealth to themselves or to the interest groups they represent. Thus, they generally will have little interest in degrading the quality of their international commitments. After all, these commitments create the welfare surplus that the élites may then attempt to divert. In sum, although we admit the analogy between firms and states is imperfect in its detail, we argue it is sufficiently plausible to sustain interest in the question: What are the optimal means of enforcing international commitments?

We are left, then, with both a strong and a weak claim. Our weak position is that rational instrumentalism provides a valuable, but also incomplete, perspective for understanding the enforcement of international law. The relative importance of welfare maximization and selective pressure, in contrast to cultural conditions, as an explanation for actual practice will vary with particular contexts. We maintain only that rational instrumentalism cannot be ignored. Our strong claim is that rational instrumentalism is as good at explaining the enforcement of international law as it is at explaining private contractual enforcement.

With these preliminary issues disposed of, we now consider what contract theory has to say about joint production of social welfare.

# 3 LESSONS FROM CONTRACT THEORY

A treaty is in its nature a contract between two nations, not a legislative act.

Foster v. Neilson, 27 U.S. (2 Pet.) 253, 314 (1829) (Marshall, C.J.)

INTERNATIONAL LAW COMPRISES A SYSTEM OF NORMS, CUSTOMS, RULES, treaties, and agreements that purports to govern the behavior of nation states toward their citizens, other states, and other states' citizens. The very breadth of international law frustrates categorization. At some level of abstraction, any generalizations about the purposes and functions of international law cannot avoid gross oversimplification. But some themes run through the field, even if they do not explain every aspect of the system.

Although nations may conform their behavior to international rules and norms for many reasons, the animating purpose of much international law is to foster mutually beneficial cooperation among states. Although the subject matter of any particular cooperative enterprise may vary greatly – from treaties and customs regarding a private investment agreement to a convention on global warming to the "laws" of war – the fundamental behavior remains the same. International law functions in many instances to encourage nations to cooperate where it is in their mutual self-interest to secure the cooperation of other states, but where deviations from the cooperative goal will secure even greater private advantage to any single defecting state. To solve this conundrum, a primary concern of any system of international law is insuring compliance with the cooperative goal. In this book, we take as a given the value of these various cooperative purposes and focus our attention on the single question of how best to induce the behavior necessary to achieve that objective.

In the previous chapter, we noted the claims of many contemporary experts that the domain of international law has moved well beyond the world of voluntary commitments by state actors, and now encompasses projects to which the concept of contracting is irrelevant. In response we observed that, although the aspirations of some advocates have expanded greatly in the years since World War II, there is scant evidence that there exists much international law that effectively binds actors without the voluntary participation of states. Rather, state consent has become more complicated.

First, states increasingly delegate lawmaking authority to organizations, such as the organs of the European Community, that to some extent can exercise their powers without going back to the member states for further approval. Second, states sometimes manifest consent to a rule or norm of international law not through the normal channel of an executive decision and legislative approval, but rather by a court embracing a rule on its own initiative. Even in this circumstance, however, the court usually purports to rely on its sense of what the political branches would want and leaves open the possibility that those branches can reverse its decision. Accordingly, as we set out in Chapter 2, it remains possible to conceive of international law as for the most part ultimately traceable back to voluntary agreements, even if not all scholars would agree entirely with this account.

This point is critical to our argument. The institution of voluntary commitment is the time-honored mechanism for achieving compliance with cooperative goals that benefit the collective interest of parties whose particular interests diverge. Contract is the means for attaching legal consequences to such commitments. This link between the mechanisms of private contracting and the purposes of international law has long been recognized. But policy makers and scholars often invoke this similarity only rhetorically. Reasonable people can debate, for example, whether Chief Justice Marshall's invocation of the contract concept to explain a treaty, quoted at the beginning of this chapter, represents a forensic flourish or instead has real analytical purchase. We propose to do something quite novel. We introduce systematically the tools of contract as a focal point for evaluating the question of how best to ensure optimal compliance with international law, however defined.

## THE ELEMENTS OF CONTRACT THEORY

First, we will review contemporary understanding of contracting. Although contract law has a long and distinguished pedigree, it is only in recent years that the underlying theory of contract has been systematically explored. Here we describe the current thinking about contract enforcement, and in particular theories predicting what types of contracts parties will elect to write under conditions of imperfect information and incentives to behave opportunistically.

Throughout, we assume that parties act rationally, within the constraints of their environment, in the sense that they wish to contract if they believe the arrangement will make them better off and not otherwise. Thus we must consider how contractors might deal rationally with known and anticipated information deficiencies and incentives to exploit the arrangement at the expense of joint benefits.

Parties who enter into contracts typically face a conundrum. They want to write a contract that is optimal ex ante, that is, one that at the time of contracting encourages each party to invest in the contractual relationship so as to maximize the anticipated joint benefits. But they also want to write a contract that is optimal ex post, that is, one that is still value maximizing after all future uncertainties have been resolved as of the time of performance. There is, of course, an inherent and irreducible tension between these two objectives. In order to motivate (and protect) investments in the cooperative enterprise, each investing party would like to ensure the commitment of the others. But subsequent events may render inflexible commitments inconsistent with the contractual objective of maximizing the joint surplus.

For example, suppose that unforeseen circumstances cause the cost to one of the parties to complete a promised investment to exceed the value that the counterparty expected to generate from the contract. Anticipating this, the parties would want the flexibility to adjust the investment whenever future circumstances make the contract no longer profitable. But if the contract is written to accommodate this desire to change its terms, the credibility of the investing party's commitment to the enterprise is undermined. This, in turn, may lead the other party to decline to undertake its reciprocal obligations under the contract. Thus, each party not only wants to insure the commitment of the other but also wants to preserve the flexibility to adjust to future uncertainties. This tension between the need for both commitment and flexibility influences the parties' decisions whether or not to contract and, if so, what kind of contract to write.

This conundrum exists in international bargaining as much as in private contracts. Imagine, for example, a trade agreement pursuant to which rich countries agree gradually to reduce barriers to agricultural imports coming from poor countries, in return for which poor countries agree to invest in intellectual property protection to the benefit of rich country exporters. Rich countries would make this deal if they anticipated that their own agricultural producers could shift production to crops that would not face import competition or otherwise could deploy their assets profitably. Suppose that the costs of restructuring domestic agricultural production turns out to exceed any joint benefits that might be derived from the agreement, perhaps as a result of unanticipated technological change in production, storage, or shipping methods. The rich countries would want the flexibility to adjust their obligations so as to reduce these costs, but their retained flexibility would reduce the incentive of poor countries to enter into and invest in this deal.

Contract theory has developed a set of analytic tools for understanding how this contracting conundrum might best be resolved. These tools rely on advances in the economics of information, a field that is less than thirty years old but has already produced three Nobel laureates.[1] The task for lawyers and legal academics, in turn, is to test the predictions of this theory by searching for real-world applications. In this chapter, we present a brief overview of the tools of contract theory and sketch their application to ordinary contracts and international agreements. This analysis provides the foundation for our effort to use this lens to understand the effects of, and relationship between, formal and informal mechanisms for stimulating cooperative behavior in international law.

Traditionally, the legal analysis of contracts took an ex post perspective. That approach analyzed the rights and obligations of the parties *after* the contracted-for performance had come due and one party or the other had failed to comply with its commitments. From this perspective, contract law appears to be a system of rules that imposes obligations on the promisor and specifies remedies available to the promisee for breach of those obligations.

This ex post perspective is not surprising, because the analysis of private law in general has tended to focus on litigated disputes and judicial decisions resolving those disputes as the key elements in the state's decision to interfere in private relationships. Thus, courts and commentators have tended to view contract from the lens of the litigants. Once a contract is breached (the commitment is broken), the "injured party" seeks to recover for losses incurred in reliance on the broken promise. A court judgment for the injured party is logically seen as compensation for the wrong that the breaching promisor did to the promisee. This analogy to tort law – that breach is compensation for harm inflicted by the broken promise – reflects the history of the common law action in assumpsit for breach of contract, which judges initially borrowed from tort law and which provided legal redress for a wrongful failure to perform a promised undertaking.[2]

---

[1]  Nobel prizes for work in the field of contract theory have been awarded to George Akerloff, Michael Spence, and Joseph Stiglitz. Their research is concisely summarized in Karl-Gustaf Lofgren *et al.*, *Markets and Asymmetric Information: The Contributions of George Akerloff, Michael Spence and Jospeh Stiglitz*, 104 SCANDINAVIAN J. ECON. 195 (2002).

[2]  JAMES BARR AMES, LECTURES ON LEGAL HISTORY 130–137 (1913); A. W. B. SIMPSON, A HISTORY OF THE COMMON LAW OF CONTRACT 210–15 (1986).

The first major conceptual advance in the law and economics of contracts was to shift the focus of analysis from the ex post judicial decision enforcing the contract to the ex ante decision to enter into the contract in the first place. The ex ante perspective has enormous payoffs for advancing our understanding of how and why people enter into contracts. It forces the analyst to recognize that contract regulates a consensual activity, and thus the parties have choices over whether or not to contract and, if they do, whether to accept the legal obligations that a court will impose on the parties should the deal break down. Similarly, as we have argued earlier, international lawmaking for the most part is a consensual activity, as states retain the capacity not to create obligations and to choose which consequences to attach to those obligations that they do create.

For the most part, the obligations of contract law are only *default rules* – terms that will be implied in the contract in the absence of a contrary agreement. Thus, the parties must determine whether to accept these default terms or to contract out of the legal defaults and negotiate their own alternative terms. Instead of asking the ex post question (What do courts do?), the ex ante perspective asks: Why do parties write the contracts that they do in light of what courts (and other legal entities) do?

From this ex ante perspective, then, one can isolate the key analytical questions: Why do parties enter into legally binding contracts? What factors determine whether they choose to write a complex contract (one that seeks to specify outcomes in many possible states of the world) or a simple contract (one that leaves many contingencies unaddressed and looks to renegotiation once the unknown future states are realized)? How do the parties deal with the central problem that each party has private information that the other does not have, and that some information known to both of the parties (i.e., the information is observable) may not be provable to a court (i.e., the information is not verifiable)? In the balance of this chapter, we offer a primer on the answers that contract theory provides to these basic questions.

## Why Do Parties Contract?

Why do parties enter into legally binding contracts? After all, much cooperative behavior goes on without contracting. Many people can and do enter into relationships that are enduring and effective but do not contemplate legal coercion if either party defects from the cooperative understanding. Indeed, as we will see, parties frequently make agreements that they specifically intend not to be legally binding. These agreements rely on informal (or nonlegal) mechanisms to motivate the cooperation necessary for parties to achieve a welfare-enhancing objective.[3] But as the discussion that follows makes plain, sometimes these informal mechanisms fail to work effectively. When that happens parties may consider the alternative of a legally binding contract.

A contract contemplates a commitment regarding future cooperative behavior. This commitment has an intertemporal aspect: Parties promise today to do something tomorrow. When parties choose to form a binding contract, therefore, they invoke the power of the state to coerce performance (or require a monetary substitute) from a promisor who later comes to regret having made the promise. Moreover, the fact that regret was caused by circumstances not expressly contemplated by the parties generally will not excuse the disappointed promisor. In this sense, then, contractual liability is a form of strict liability.

The intertemporal aspect of transactions makes contract law's strict liability highly salient. Contracting involves an unconditional promise to do something in the future and the future is unknown. Inevitably, therefore, such a commitment entails risks. The promise may be more costly to perform than the promisor anticipated, or the promise may not have the value to the promisee that was anticipated at the time of contracting. Thus, an initial question arises: Why do parties not simply wait until the future unfolds and then act on current knowledge to acquire the goods and services that they need? After all, a legal regime that respects and protects property rights is sufficient to support current, "spot market" exchange transactions.

The answer to this question illuminates what joint production of welfare entails. If promises were cost-free, then obviously a party who will rely on the actions of another would prefer to receive a promise in advance of a contemplated future activity. A promisee can always better plan for the future having received a credible promise from a promisor. The problem, of course, is that in a reciprocal relationship each party is *both* a promisee and a promisor. In order to obtain a promise from you, I must make a reciprocal commitment. So, why would anyone exchange a risky promise – where he is legally obligated to perform despite unanticipated hardships – in order to receive a return promise from someone else?

The most plausible answer is that this exchange of promises produces a welfare surplus. In simple terms, a rational actor model predicts that an exchange of promises will be, in expectation, a win-win situation for both parties. If the welfare gains that both parties anticipate are greater than the expected costs, including the predicted costs of regret, then both parties will be better off, in terms of expectations, if they mutually bind themselves. This is simply another

---

[3] For a discussion of "self-enforcing" agreements and other informal means of enforcement, see Robert E. Scott, *A Theory of Self-Enforcing Indefinite Agreements*, 103 COLUM. L. REV. 1641 (2003).

way of expressing the idea we introduced earlier – that cooperative behavior can be mutually beneficial to all the participants in the cooperative enterprise, even where each participant is required to produce, at its own expense, an investment the returns from which it then shares with others.

## Protecting Relation-Specific Investments

One obvious instance in which parties might contract, despite the risks, is where the desired objective requires some investment by either (or both) of the parties in a joint activity.[4] The initial motivation for each party to cooperate derives from a determination that, following the planned investment, the resulting joint venture is potentially more profitable (however one defines profit) than any alternative use of her time and resources. If this determination is well-founded, then each promisor's investment will be either wholly or partially relation-specific, that is, the resources constituting each party's investment will generate more valuable products if they are deployed in the relationship than if used for other purposes.

But there is an inherent dilemma for parties who contemplate such joint activity. Each party bears the full burden of her own investment in the cooperative enterprise but must share the future returns from that investment with her partner(s). This means that once a party undertakes a relation-specific investment, she is vulnerable to exploitation if her contracting partner fails to reciprocate fully.

These specialized investments can be of any sort. They might require the production of customized goods, or perhaps an investment in human capital to perform a particular service, or even investments by the parties in information, say about future price fluctuations. As an example, assume that a Seller of software systems produces off-the-shelf software that is suitable for many business needs. The Seller also takes on special orders for individual customers, creating software systems that are designed for a single buyer's needs. Buyer is interested in purchasing one of these systems. Assume that Seller can produce either system (but not both) in time to meet Buyer's requirements. The specialized software system configured to fit Buyer's particular business needs would cost $70,000 to produce and would be worth $100,000 to Buyer. Seller could also provide Buyer its off-the-shelf system at a cost of $40,000. Because the market for off-the-shelf business software is competitive, Seller also sells that system for $40,000. The off-the-shelf system is worth $50,000 to Buyer. If the parties did contract for the specialized system and Buyer subsequently breached, Seller

---

[4] The discussion of relation-specific investment is drawn from Alan Schwartz & Robert E. Scott, *Contract Theory and the Limits of Contract law*, 113 Yale L. J. 541 (2003).

could only resell that system on the market for $20,000 (the specialized system is tailored to the needs of Buyer and, thus, is not as valuable to another buyer). There are two key questions: What agreement would it be socially desirable for these parties to make? Second, what agreement would they make were contracts not enforceable?

The answer to the first question is easy. Recall that social welfare is the sum of the parties' gains from contracting. Thus, the total surplus is the difference between Buyer's valuation and Seller's cost. The off-the-shelf contract would produce a surplus of $10,000 ($50,000 Buyer's valuation less $40,000 Seller's cost). A contract for the specialized software would create a surplus of $30,000 ($100,000 Buyer's valuation less $70,000 Seller's cost). Therefore, joint welfare would be maximized if the parties contract to produce the specialized software system.

But in the absence of legal enforcement (and assuming the absence of any informal means of enforcement), Seller would never agree to produce the specialized software system. To see why, suppose that Seller did agree to produce the specialized system for a price of $85,000. Now consider the parties' positions *after* Seller has already incurred the $70,000 production cost. Buyer now knows that if he refuses to pay the agreed-on price, he can still purchase an off-the-shelf system on the market for $40,000 and receive a gain of $10,000. Seller knows that, if Buyer breaches, her only recourse is to sell the specialized software on the market for $20,000 and incur a $50,000 loss. On these facts, unless Buyer is concerned about his reputation or being subjected to other informal sanctions, he will propose to renegotiate the price (perhaps offering some pretext such as unanticipated hardship). The potential surplus from a renegotiation is $80,000 (the difference between the value of the system to Buyer ($100,000) and its value to Seller ($20,000)). One plausible result of a renegotiation is for the parties to agree to split the surplus equally. A renegotiation price of $60,000 achieves this division.

This example illustrates why, absent legal enforcement, the parties would not contract for the specialized system in the first place. A Seller who is not myopic would realize that, because the Buyer will renegotiate the price after the Seller invests, her true payoff under this contract will be a loss of $10,000, rather than the anticipated gain of $15,000 that the contract initially promises. Therefore, Seller will only produce and sell the off-the-shelf system. Seller's decision not to make specialized software follows directly from the fact that Buyer's initial promise to pay $85,000 is not credible. Both parties would realize at the time of contracting that Buyer will have an incentive to renege later. Because Seller cannot resell the specialized software system for a price above cost – this is the definition of a relation-specific investment – the specialized contract would yield an expected negative payoff for Seller.

This vulnerability points to one of the key insights of the ex ante perspective. Legal enforcement of contracts is traditionally understood to protect the injured promisee by awarding compensation for her reliance on the promise. Of course this is true, but the traditional understanding misses the main purpose of legal enforcement. If contracts were not enforceable – that is, if promises were not credible because there was no effective means of ensuring compliance – then parties would decline to put themselves in situations where they could be exploited by the other party's failure to perform. Instead, parties such as the Seller in our example would elect to redirect their energies and resources to interactions that would not lead to such vulnerability. By invoking a mechanism that commits her to perform in the future, the Buyer can enhance the credibility of her promise to pay and thus can secure a return investment from the Seller. Otherwise, the Seller might choose not to enter into the proposed commitment and instead walk away from the deal.

This insight can be extended to international relations. Consider the classical argument for free trade as developed by Hume, Smith, and Ricardo. Specialization of production yields benefits to all parties as long as countries that produce specialized goods can count on other countries supplying the products that they need, but do not make, at an acceptable price. Persuaded by this claim, Great Britain abandoned agricultural self sufficiency in 1846. But, unless a country has confidence that it can obtain what it needs from other countries, it will resist specialization in favor of autarchy. The necessary reassurance does not have to take the form of a legally enforceable promise – Great Britain in the nineteenth century relied principally on its naval hegemony – but it can. The WTO system, for example, reflects an effort to ground the international division of labor on a legal institution.[5]

What are the implications of this vulnerability in private contracting? In the jargon of contract theory, our hypothetical Seller, the investing party, risks being "held up" by Buyer, who can force a renegotiation of the contract as a condition of its reciprocal performance. This threat will be credible if Seller's investment cannot be used for other purposes outside the relationship. In that case, Seller's sunk cost investment will increase the risk that Buyer will threaten to walk away from the deal unless Seller agrees to renegotiate the initial contract terms.

---

[5] For an extended discussion of the vulnerability and trust implied in the international division of labor, see PAUL SEABRIGHT, THE COMPANY OF STRANGERS: A NATURAL HISTORY OF ECONOMIC LIFE 14–15 (2004).

But surely, a skeptic might respond, many parties would never behave strategically even where they are legally free to do so. Instead, they will be constrained by social norms, a desire to maintain their reputation in the relevant community, or the hope that they might deal with the promisee again in the future. Of course this is true. In many instances, therefore, the agreement between Seller and Buyer will be *self-enforcing* in the sense that the desire to protect his reputation or for possible future business dealings with Seller will motivate Buyer to perform even in the absence of third-party coercion compelling performance.[6]

The important point, however, is that reputation and future business prospects, though important ingredients to successful contracting, have their limits. Consider reputational incentives first. Social esteem and a reputation for keeping one's word are powerful motivations whenever other potential trading partners are able conveniently to learn why the parties' deal broke down. Reputations work well in small trading communities, especially those with ethnically homogenous members or other cooperation-inducing structures, where everything that happens soon becomes common knowledge and boycotts of bad actors are readily enforced.[7] Reputational sanctions also can be effective in industries that establish trade associations, because the associations can create a collective memory of the contracting behavior of their members.[8] Reputations are difficult to establish, however, in large, heterogeneous economies in which particular contracting parties often are anonymous.

As we will discuss in greater detail in Chapter 5, reputation also plays an important role in inducing compliance with the obligations of international law. Given the limited number of states in the world, the impossibility of anonymity, and the durability of state identities, one might believe that little else is needed. But reputations attach to regimes, not states, and regimes change with some frequency. As we noted in Chapter 2, some regimes might heavily discount their future prospects, and thus the significance of the reputational consequences of their actions. Thus, as in contract, reputation plays an important but constrained role as a means of enforcing international law.

---

[6] *See* Benjamin Klein, *Why Hold-Ups Occur: The Self-Enforcing Range of Contractual Relationships*, 34 ECON. INQUIRY 444 (1996); Robert E. Scott, *Conflict and Cooperation in Long-Term Contracts*, 75 CAL. L. REV. 2005, 2039–2050 (1987).

[7] *See* Janet Landa, *A Theory of the Ethnically Homogenous Middleman Group: An Institutional Alternative to Contract Law*, 10 J. LEGAL STUD. 349 (1981). An excellent survey of early informal enforcement mechanisms is Avner Grief, *Informal Contract Enforcement: Lessons from Medieval Trade* in 2 THE NEW PALGRAVE DICTIONARY OF ECONOMICS AND LAW 287 (Peter Newman, ed. 1998).

[8] For discussion, see Lisa Bernstein, *Private Commercial Law in the Cotton Industry: Creating Cooperation through Rules, Norms and Institutions*, 99 MICH. L. REV. 1724 (2001); Lisa Bernstein, *Merchant Law in a Merchant Court: Rethinking the Code's Search for Immanent Business Norms*, 144 U. PA. L. REV. 1765 (1996).

Contract theory also recognizes that agreements will be self-enforcing to the extent that the parties anticipate the prospect of future dealings. Specifically, when parties contemplate making a series of contracts, neither party will breach an early contract if the gains from one breach are lower than the expected profits from future contracts that a breach would eliminate. But this incentive has natural limits. Ongoing relationships inevitably come to an end. When parties come to realize that the relationship is soon to terminate (say when the promisor contemplates retirement or otherwise withdrawing from the trading community), the threat that the other party will no longer deal with the promisor is insufficient in and of itself to induce performance. Thus, all repeated interactions are subject to a familiar end-game problem. Indeed, in the limiting case, the anticipation of the last transaction may cause the entire cooperative pattern to unravel as each party anticipates that the next interaction will be the last interaction and that the promisor might defect.[9]

Similar dynamics apply to international law enforcement. Systems such as the WTO system rely exclusively on future interactions to induce compliance with its obligations. A state that has suffered an injury from another state's violation may take proportionate measures against the violator, but cannot take excessive measures or induce other states also to retaliate. States that have an ongoing, mutually beneficial trade relationship with each other thus have a strong reason to behave.

But for the same reason that regimes, as distinguished from states, bear the reputational consequences of both cooperation and violation, the shadow of the end-game problem hangs over the use of future dealings as an inducement to good state behavior. A regime can fail, and its successor may not have the same incentive to enforce its predecessor's interests. And a regime that senses that its end is near will not worry about future retaliation. Thus, as the likelihood of regime change increases the salience of threatened future interactions diminishes. Consider, for example, a nonaggression pact between neighboring powers. If one state believes that by violating the pact it can install new leaders in its neighbor, it may run the risk of retaliation.

The existence of limitations on these traditional means of self-enforcement do not, by themselves, justify formal legal enforcement of promises. As we discuss in detail in Chapter 4, there are strong reasons to believe that powerful norms of reciprocity enhance and extend the reach of the traditional means of self-enforcement, both for individuals and for states. In combination, therefore, these informal mechanisms can motivate cooperation even in arms-length interactions between complete strangers. The important point is

---

[9]  Robert E. Scott, note 6 *supra*.

that formal legal mechanisms matter where informal enforcement does not constrain the incentive to breach. In such an environment, legal enforcement is necessary to make a promise to perform credible and thus to induce valuable cooperation.[10]

## PROBLEMS OF ADVERSE SELECTION, MORAL HAZARD, AND VERIFICATION

One of the challenges parties seek to overcome when contracting is that, quite simply, prospective contracting partners do not know everything about each other. Rather, each party has private information about himself that the other does not know. We can illustrate this point with a simple example. Assume Buyer wishes to purchase a product – say, a new machine – from Seller, but Buyer is unsure about the quality of the goods or services that Seller can offer. In our example, Seller knows the quality of the machine that it has contracted to sell but Buyer does not. In the international context, regimes usually have a better sense of the limits of their domestic power, and thus their capacity to marshal resources or face risks in the course of international relations, than do other states.

To illustrate the problems that result from this asymmetry of information, assume that the sellers in this market fall into two groups – high-quality sellers and low-quality sellers. If quality varies among sellers, then buyers face a problem. Our Buyer does not know whether Seller's machine is of a high quality or a low quality. Unless the problem can be solved, Buyer has an incentive to offer only a blended price for the machine (a price less than the value of a high-quality machine but more than the value of one of low quality) reflecting the probability that Seller's goods are either high or low quality. Over time, this reluctance to pay full value will drive the high-quality sellers out of the market, because the blended price would not permit them to recover their higher costs. As a result, only low-quality sellers will remain in the market. This example illustrates the famous "lemons problem" caused by the *adverse selection* of low-quality sellers.[11]

---

[10]  Contract theory recognizes more functions for contract than inducing cooperation. A contract can have a risk management function by shifting a risk to someone who can bear it at a lower cost. For fuller discussion, see Alan Schwartz & Robert E. Scott, note 4 *supra*, at 562–65; Robert E. Scott & George G. Triantis, *Embedded Options and the Case Against Compensation in Contract Damages*, 104 COLUM. L. REV. 1428 (2004). Because we do not see as many analogs to this function in international law and relations, we do not discuss it further in this book.

[11]  *See generally* George Akerloff, *The Market for "Lemons:" Quality Uncertainty and the Market Mechanism*, 84 Q. J. ECON. 355, 366 (1970).

Parties can respond to this problem of *hidden information* in several ways. One familiar method is for the high-quality sellers to offer warranties to their buyers. Because high-quality goods perform better and last longer, a warranty of replacement or repair would cost the high-quality sellers less to provide, compared to their low-quality competitors. Warranties thus serve as valuable *signals* of quality to the extent that low-quality sellers cannot readily copy them. An effective signal creates a *separating equilibrium* in which both high- and low-quality sellers can exist in the same market.

But warranties are not a perfect signal because they are not self-executing. Rather, a buyer must be able to prove to a court that the seller has breached its warranty of quality. This merely moves the problem of hidden information one step further up the chain of the legal process. Recall that information may remain completely private, in the sense that no other person is able to observe the condition or quality at issue. Alternatively, someone interacting with the holder of the hidden information may be able to perceive the condition or quality, making the information observable. But for the legal process to be effective, information must not only be observable, but verifiable, in the sense that the person interacting with the holder of the information can, at a reasonable cost, convince a third party that its observation is valid. In this typology, not all observable information is verifiable, and only verifiable conditions or qualities can be used to specify an obligation that a third party can enforce.

To return to our example, if Seller gives a warranty of quality, and Buyer claims that the machine fails to meet the warranty standard, Buyer then bears the burden of proving to a court that the machine does not conform to the agreed standard. Even if Buyer can *observe* for himself that the goods fail to meet the warranty that they "are fit for the ordinary purposes for which such goods are used,"[12] it still must bear the additional burden of proving or *verifying* that fact to a court or other third party.

In addition to the problem of adverse selection caused by hidden information regarding the attributes or characteristics of a contract performance, the parties must also cope with the problem of moral hazard caused by the *hidden actions* or behavior of a contracting partner. Assume in our example that Seller warrants to use its best efforts to modify the contracted-for machine should Buyer encounter any problems in adapting it to Buyer's particular requirements. If Buyer is unable to monitor Seller's efforts to adapt the machine, then Seller's hidden actions create a problem of *moral hazard*. As the name implies, Buyer faces a risk that Seller will not fully exert its best efforts as promised, but rather

---

[12] *See* UNIFORM COMMERCIAL CODE §2–314(2)(c).

will (immorally) chisel on or shirk a portion of its responsibility. And even if Buyer can observe Seller's actions, once again it faces the difficulty of verifying to a court that the efforts actually undertaken by Seller fall short of the standard of "best efforts."

Information asymmetries caused by hidden information and hidden action thus operate at two distinct levels. Between the parties, hidden information or action may prevent the uninformed party from observing a key fact or condition (in our example, the level of quality or efforts produced by Seller). But even if the information known to one party is observable in the sense that a contracting partner can perceive it as well, it may not be *verifiable*, in the sense that the observing party is unable at reasonable cost to establish the fact sufficiently to convince a neutral third party such as a court.

Note, however, that verifiability is not a dichotomous concept (i.e., a fact is not either completely verifiable or not verifiable at all). Rather, proof to a court is a matter of degree. The ability to verify a condition of the contract will be determined by the interactive evidentiary strategies of the parties and the rules allocating burdens and standards of proof. At the conclusion of any litigation, a court makes a factual determination by comparing its confidence in the truth of a given fact against a standard of proof (such as the typical civil standard of "more likely than not"). The costs of verification are thus variable because the parties bear their own costs of evidence production as they fight over a fixed amount at stake.[13]

## Using Rules and Standards to Ameliorate the Verification Problem

One way that parties can reduce the burden of verification is by specifying substitutes or *proxies* for the underlying fact or condition in question. For example, qualitative performance obligations, such as duties of care or commitments to undertake best efforts, may seem at first blush to be nonverifiable . Even though contracting parties can observe each other's effort or level of care, the costs of proving a contracting partner's failure to exert a promised level of effort may seem greater than the gains from tying the contract performance directly to the level of those efforts. But courts typically do not search for direct measures of effort. Instead, they employ evidentiary proxies for the desired performance. For example, rather than assessing Seller's efforts directly, a court may rely on evidence of Buyer's profits as a signal of Seller's effort.

---

[13]  For discussion, see Robert E. Scott & George G. Triantis, *Anticipating Litigation by Contract Design*, 115 Yale L. J. 814 (2006).

Proxies such as these serve to reduce evidentiary cost, even at some sacrifice in accuracy.[14]

The utility of evidentiary proxies turns largely on the ability of the parties to translate contract-specific standards into objective equivalents. Damages for contract breach provide a familiar illustration. Suppose that contracting parties wish to set damages so that the breacher internalizes the expectation loss inflicted on the promisee. The parties have a choice between a liquidated damages provision and the legal standard of expectation damages. A liquidated damages clause typically will specify a fixed sum, readily verifiable to a court. But if the contract is enforced instead by expectation damages, a court will reject nonverifiable evidence based on the promisor's costs or the promisee's valuation. Instead, the court will invite the parties to select verifiable market-based proxies for the value of the promisee's lost expectation. Courts regularly require litigants to present market evidence of costs and values that they then use to measure damages.[15]

Assume, for example, that a buyer breaches a contract to purchase goods from a seller. Contract law holds that the seller's damages must equal the difference between the contract price and the market price of a resale of the goods to another buyer. This damage award assures the seller that it will receive its contractual expectation without ever having to offer any evidence of its nonverifiable production costs. Rather, a court determines the expectation-damages standard by proof of the prevailing market price of the contract goods, a readily verifiable fact. The parties' choice, therefore, is not whether to condition the contract on a verifiable liquidated damages clause or nonverifiable expectation damages. Rather, the choice is between two more or less efficient proxies for the promisee's expected losses from breach.[16]

As the preceding example illustrates, a core feature of contract design is the decision of how best to allocate resources between the drafting and the enforcement stages of contracting. Because there inevitably is a trade-off between the front-end and the back-end costs of the contracting process, this decision requires the allocation of resources between the two stages. Anticipating future litigation, the parties might elect to invest resources in negotiation and drafting by, for instance, contracting directly on key evidence – such as a liquidated

---

[14] *Id.* at 840–41.
[15] *See, e.g.,* UNIFORM COMMERCIAL CODE §2–708(1) (seller's market damages); §2–713(1) (buyer's market damages); §2–723(2) (proof of market damages: "If evidence of a [market] price prevailing at the times or places described in this Article is not readily available the price prevailing within any reasonable time before or after the time described or at any other place which in commercial judgment or under usage of trade would serve as a reasonable substitute for the one described may be used . . . ").
[16] *See* Robert E. Scott & George G. Triantis, note 13 *supra* at 817–18

damages clause – that establishes the existence or nonexistence of a particular condition (the expected losses from breach). For instance, such a contract might instruct a court to compel the defendant to pay $10,000 when the parties present evidence of a specific instance of nonperformance.

But the number of possible future states of the world and the corresponding contractual performances means that the up-front cost of a *complete contingent contract* is likely to be prohibitive. In the alternative, the parties might instead express their obligations in more general terms, and rely on a court to assign outcomes based on the evidence presented at trial. A vague term (such as an obligation to make a good faith effort to deliver goods on a certain date) gives the court much more discretion than a specific provision. Accordingly, one can divide contract terms into two categories – precise terms and vague terms (or, to follow the convention in characterizing legal regulation, *rules* and *standards*).

Evidence at trial proves directly whether a contractual *rule* is satisfied. In contrast, contractual *standards* are one step further removed from the evidence. Proof at trial establishes whether a proxy is satisfied, and then the court must determine what weight to give to the proxy in the enforcement of the relevant standard.

The choice between rules and standards in contracts thus concerns *who* chooses the evidentiary proxies for the desirable behavior and *when* the choice is made. Rules permit the parties to choose the proxy at the time of contracting, while standards delegate the choice of proxies to the court at the time of trial. Deciding between rules and standards in contracting thus turns on the trade-off between two different kinds of informational advantage. The parties know better than any court what objectives they desire from the contract and what actions are required to achieve those objectives. But the parties do not know what the future holds, while the court has the benefit of hindsight.

On the one hand, parties have a greater incentive to specify in advance proxies for a desired performance or contractual contingency when the proxy's accuracy is less likely to be affected by the future state of the world. On the other hand, parties have an incentive to use contractual standards to delegate to the court the later choice of proxies that are more likely to be contingent on unknown future events. Finally, the parties can create *combinations* of rules and standards that better define the space within which a court may later choose the relevant proxies.

The process of specifying contract terms thus proceeds along a continuum that extends from narrow rules to very broad standards. The ultimate objective is to lower contracting costs (or to improve the incentive gains from contracting) by shifting investments in contracting costs between the front and back end of the process. In short, the goal is to maximize the incentive bang for the contracting cost buck.[17]

In international law, we find the same combination of rules and standards that private contracts manifest, arguably for the same reasons. The WTO system, for example, contains both very precise numeric commitments to tariff levels and categories and broad standards such as a prohibition of "arbitrary or unjustifiable discrimination."[18] As we discuss in detail in Chapter 6, many international law obligations are conditioned on private information, such as a state's capacity to meet certain standards or a regime's assessment of the state's security. Some are irreducibly unverifiable, whereas others are susceptible to approximation through a verifiable proxy.

But international law presents an additional layer of complexity, because delegating the authority to enforcement organs to create proxies is less straightforward than in private contracting. As we discuss in Chapter 6, the international tribunals to which this authority may be delegated tend to be less institutionally developed, and have less of a track record, than the domestic courts that interpret and apply the standards found in private contracts. If the delegation is not to a tribunal, but rather to national courts as a class (which may be the case in customary international law), then the heterogeneity of national courts makes it highly unlikely that a single proxy will emerge. In either case, a state may have less confidence in the enforcer's ability to come up with satisfactory proxies. As a result, formal enforcement of international law standards, as opposed to rules, presents greater challenges than does the use of standards in private contracts.

In sum, our analysis suggests some caution when analyzing the optimal enforcement of contractual commitments according to whether or not the relevant conditions are verifiable. The question, at bottom, turns on whether appropriate proxies for the desired condition can be specified ex ante or whether a disinterested third party can be trusted to make such a selection ex post. The fundamental point is that verification necessarily requires the use of evidentiary substitutes for the underlying behavior or contingency. The availability of good substitutes, in turn, depends largely on whether the contractual condition at issue can be translated (without significant losses in accuracy) into relatively accessible objective equivalents. Therefore, in assessing whether or not a particular contractual commitment can be verified (and thus formally enforced), parties must consider both the cost of formal adjudication as well as the loss in accuracy occasioned by resort to the particular proxies in question.

---

[17] For a more complete discussion of the relationship between anticipated litigation costs and the choice between contractual rules and standards, see *id. passim*.

[18] For the quoted language, see General Agreement on Tariffs and Trade, art XX

## SIMPLE CONTRACTS AND THE PROBLEMS
## OF INCOMPLETE CONTRACTING

The preceding discussion illustrates how parties cope with the problems involved in verifying contractual commitments. It highlights the key fact that, *at the time of contracting*, parties will balance current investments in negotiating and drafting against prospective investments in enforcement. In theory, of course, parties can elect to invest entirely in the drafting process by identifying every possible state of the world that might materialize and specifying an appropriate contractual solution to each state. But, in reality, contracting parties confront a vexing problem: The future is unknown and unknowable. As a result, when the level of uncertainty is high, it simply costs too much for contracting parties to foresee and then describe appropriately the contractual outcomes for all (or even most) of the possible states of the world that might materialize. Under these circumstances, the ideal of the efficiently complete contingent contract – one that specifies the efficient payoffs for every relevant action and the corresponding sanctions for nonperformance – cannot be realized. Contracts will be incomplete in the sense that they will fail to discriminate between states of the world that optimally call for different obligations.

It is important to emphasize what we mean by efficient completeness. Parties can easily write an *inefficient* complete contract simply by specifying, for example, that no matter what circumstance may arise in the future, the buyer must always pay the seller the contract price. In such a contract the parties know at the time of contracting that in many of the realized states of the world, the contract will generate less surplus than their joint venture could have achieved. The challenge is to write an *efficient* complete contract, one that specifies the best outcome for both parties under all possible circumstances. This they cannot do.

Facing high uncertainty and high contracting costs, how should parties formulate the terms of their contracts? One option is to specify a simple contract with precise rules, that is, determinate outcomes that would apply across the board regardless of the state of the world that actually obtains. Returning to our earlier example, the parties could provide that Seller, who agrees to manufacture a specialized machine for Buyer, will deliver the machine to Buyer at a fixed price regardless of any subsequent events that might increase Seller's costs or reduce the value of the machine to Buyer. The advantage of a contract with such "hard" terms is that it binds each party to their respective commitments, thus ensuring the credibility of their promises. And, as we have seen, the promises' credibility will motivate the parties to undertake relation-specific investments as well as to take precautionary steps to reduce anticipated risk-bearing costs.

But unless the parties can fully and accurately anticipate the conditions that will exist at the time of performance, a contract containing only "hard" terms will always turn out to be suboptimal once the future arrives. Under conditions of uncertainty, any outcome that is based on expected values (i.e., one that is optimal "on average") will always tend to be wrong in the particular situation that ultimately materializes.[19] In short, once conditions change, a contract with hard terms will lead to outcomes that are less desirable than those the parties would have agreed to had they known the uncertainties in advance. Moreover, the prospect of incurring a loss ex post means that the parties will enjoy a smaller ex ante surplus. Each party will have an incentive to undertake costly precautions (purchasing insurance and the like) to guard against the risk of unfavorable future states. One solution to this problem is for the parties to renegotiate the contract ex post. But renegotiation of hard terms is costly; there is always the risk of a hold-up to the extent that one of the parties has made sunk costs investments in the contract.

In the alternative, if contracting costs are high, the parties might consider another option. They could draft a simple contract with broad standards, that is, "soft" terms that invite subsequent adjustment to take account of new facts on the ground. Thus, for example, the parties might agree to adjust the price term in the contract in good faith if subsequent events imposed significant hardship on one party or the other. By agreeing to "good faith adjustment," the parties seek to ensure that their contract is efficient ex post and that the resulting surplus is shared in some manner between both of them.

Assume, for example, that an unanticipated event causes the costs to Seller of manufacturing the contract machine to rise above the contract price. However, at the original cost the Seller can produce a substitute machine that is only slightly less valuable to Buyer. If Buyer insists on performance, the contract would still yield a surplus for Buyer but Seller would suffer a loss. Anticipating the prospect of a loss in certain states of the world will lead Seller to take costly precautions, including in the extreme case (when Seller is risk averse) deciding not to proceed with the contract. One solution, therefore, is for the contract to contain a standard of good faith adjustment by which Seller can provide the lower-cost substitute, perhaps with a price reduction for Buyer. Such a good faith renegotiation would reduce, if not eliminate, the need for precautions against unfavorable conditions that do not materialize.

International law contains many such soft terms. In trade law, for example, a state can back out of its hard commitment to tariff reductions if a resulting

---

[19] For discussion, see Charles J. Goetz & Robert E. Scott, *Principles of Relational Contracts*, 67 VA. L. REV. 1089, 1099 (1981).

surge of imports disrupts its economy. An entire body of *safeguards* law recognizes and regulates this action, using general standards rather than hard rules to determine when backing out is appropriate. More generally, the doctrine of *rebus sic stantibus* suspends international law obligations when a "fundamental change of circumstances" has occurred.[20]

But a contract or a treaty that uses such soft terms may raise the moral hazard problem that we identified earlier. Moral hazard results because a promisor who has the flexibility to adjust his performance in the future as conditions change will always choose the best alternative for him, even though it may not be best for the promisee or best for both parties in terms of joint welfare. Assume, in our earlier example, that Seller, claiming changed circumstances, offers to substitute an alternative machine at the original contract price because, as things turned out, its costs of producing the substitute machine are 10 percent less than the costs of producing the contract machine. Buyer values the substitute goods 20 percent less than the contract goods, yet still values those goods above Seller's cost and needs Seller's performance to fulfill its own obligations to third parties. Buyer, therefore, agrees to the adjustment.

The performance as adjusted leads to an efficient ex post trade because the contract as performed still produces a surplus that the parties can share. But this comes at a cost. The effect of the "good faith" adjustment is that Seller can capture a larger share of a smaller surplus. Viewed ex ante, Seller's actions reduce joint welfare, because the reduction in the Buyer's share of the surplus under the renegotiated deal is greater than Seller's gain.

Note that this particular moral hazard problem exists even where Buyer can monitor and observe Seller's actions under the contract to determine whether Seller's representations regarding its costs are true. The particular problem with soft terms such as "good faith adjustment" is one of verification. If a third party verifying the contract performance under a broad standard of good faith adjustment would permit the promisor to select a lower-cost proxy for the contract performance (say, by tendering the substitute machine), the promisor will do so even where this action results in an overall reduction in joint welfare.

The moral hazard problem is exacerbated whenever the seller's actions are effectively hidden from the buyer. In cases where the buyer cannot observe the seller's costs (or use any reliable proxy as a check on claims of increased cost), the seller has an incentive to claim hardship even where none has occurred in order to capture a larger share of the contractual surplus. In short, if a third party

---

[20] Vienna Convention on the Law of Treaties, art. 62, May 23, 1969, U.N.T.S. Regis. No. 18,232, UN Doc. A/CONF.39/27 (1969); David J. Bederman, *The 1871 London Declaration, Rebus Sic Stantibus and a Primitivist View of the Law of Nations*, 82 Am. J. Int'l L. 1 (1988).

cannot determine when a claim of good faith adjustment is genuine and when it is pretextual, the promisee is vulnerable to false claims of adjustment. Such a contract is inefficient because the buyer, anticipating the risk of the seller's subsequent claim of good faith adjustment, will take costly precautions (such as entering into contingent contracts with other suppliers) that will reduce the value of the Buyer's investment in the contract.[21]

Flexible (or soft) contract terms thus invite a party who is obligated to perform under an incomplete contract to attempt either to reduce its investment in the contract or, as in our example, to capture a larger share of the surplus from that investment. Recall that this happens because each party bears the full cost of its own investments but must share the resulting contractual surplus with its contracting partner. These moral hazard risks are often minimized by norms of trust, reciprocity, and desire for esteem – all of which bind people to perform obligations even where they share benefits. But, as we have indicated, in many arms-length transactions these self-enforcing mechanisms may fail adequately to reduce the moral hazard risk.

## Can the Hold-Up and Moral Hazard Problems Be Solved?

Economic theorists have devised ways of surmounting the hold-up and moral hazard problems that result, respectively, from ex post renegotiation or good faith adjustment. For example, they have imagined contractual mechanisms that induce revelation of private information with formally enforceable rules. These mechanisms, properly specified, can eliminate the incentive to exploit party vulnerability while retaining the flexibility to adjust for new information arising during the course of contract performance.[22] Other strategies include assigning the bargaining power in a renegotiation to the vulnerable party, either explicitly, by the assignment of property rights, or by using external factors to determine renegotiating capacities.[23] All these devices assume the existence of strong powers on the part of enforcement organs to compel truthful testimony and police renegotiation. In reality, domestic courts do not have such power even as to private contractors, and nothing in the international realm

---

[21] For discussion of these points, see Alan Schwartz & Robert E. Scott, note 4 *supra*, at 601–05.

[22] *See, e.g.*, Jean Tirole, *Incomplete Contracts: Where Do We Stand?*, 67 Econometrica 741 (1999); Benjamin Hermalin & Michael Katz, *Judicial Modification of Contracts Between Sophisticated Parties: A More Complete View of Incomplete Contracts and Their Breach*, 9 J. L. Econ. & Org. 98 (1993); Alan Schwartz & Robert E. Scott, The Law and Economics of Preliminary Agreements (2006).

[23] Sanford J. Grossman & Oliver D. Hart, *The Costs and Benefits of Ownership: A Theory of Vertical and Lateral Integration*, 94 J. Pol. Econ. 691 (1986); Oliver D. Hart & John Moore, *Property Rights and the Nature of the Firm*, 98 J. Pol. Econ. 1119 (1990); Aaron S. Edlin & Stefan Reichelstein, *Holdups, Standard Breach Remedies, and Optimal Investment*, 86 Am. Econ. Rev. 478 (1996).

contemplates the capacity of an independent body to control the ways in which states transact with each other.

We do not mean to dismiss these thought experiments. They are important contributions to our understanding of optimal contracting strategies because they show that, under carefully prescribed conditions, parties can write complex contracts that insure both efficient ex ante investment and efficient ex post trade and are invulnerable to exploitative renegotiation. Alternatively, the models show that parties can write simple contracts that anticipate renegotiation and yet constrain the renegotiation so as to limit the risk of hold-up. For our present purposes, however, the important point is that these models only work in a hypothetical legal system unlike any that exists today. Nothing in the world of international law enforcement, much less in the enforcement of private contracts, provides the kind of constraints on renegotiation that these solutions require.

The lessons from this work can be simplified as follows: If the parties can sustain the costs of writing complex, complete contracts, they would wish to invoke an enforcement mechanism that precluded renegotiation, because the ex ante contract, by definition, would have provided for the optimal outcome in all possible states of the world. But if the costs of contracting are high (because, for example, uncertainty is high), the parties would choose to write simple, incomplete contracts either with precise terms that solidify commitments or with broad standards that delegate flexibility to enforcing bodies ex post. In the former case, the parties would anticipate renegotiation and would wish to constrain that process so as to limit the hold-up risk. In the latter case, the parties would anticipate adjustment and would prefer that the adjustment process be constrained so as to limit the moral hazard risk.

As for theoretical models of complex contracts that preclude renegotiation, there exist applications both in domestic and international contexts. It is true that individuals generally have the freedom to renegotiate their commitments as long as they enjoy contractual capacity. But private firms to some extent can limit their power to renegotiate through internal governance rules, such as by requiring many layers of consent as a prerequisite to the assumption of a legal obligation. In addition, the law imposes some external limits on a firm's renegotiation autonomy, for example, by regulating conflicts of interests on the part of firm officials and in some cases allowing firm stakeholders to challenge transactions infected by such conflicts. In the United States, for example, shareholders can challenge the decision of a board of directors to renegotiate a contract by bringing a derivative action on behalf of the firm.

In international law, the issue of constraints on renegotiation is even more complex. States face substantial barriers to renegotiation whenever two conditions are satisfied. If a state's domestic legal order requires multiple approval layers (such as agreement by the executive and the legislature, perhaps with a supermajority rule for the latter) for international lawmaking and remaking, and if the capacity to seek enforcement is dispersed rather than monopolized by the government, modification of the international obligation entails great costs. Imagine, for example, a state that cannot denounce a treaty or otherwise alter its international commitments without legislative approval (unlike the situation in the United States, where the executive apparently can repudiate treaties without the participation of Congress).[24] Further assume that the international obligation in question is subject to formal enforcement, which means that some group of interest-holders can seek to vindicate their rights before a body with authority to impose sanctions (not necessarily a domestic court) without government approval. Under these conditions, altering the international rule would require either cooperation on the part of the executive and legislature or the provision of effective inducements to all the interest-holders not to act.

Imagine, for example, that the next round of multilateral trade negotiations produced an agreement to require formal enforcement of at least some trade rules, such as the "national treatment" obligation not to discriminate against imports other than by imposing duties. Further imagine that the United States were to fulfil its obligations under this deal the way it typically implements trade agreements, namely by enacting a statute. Perhaps a tribunal of the WTO would have the power to assess monetary sanctions for violation of the rule, and the legislation would give U.S. courts the power to enforce the awards of such tribunals.[25] Were the government of the United States to later regret this decision, perhaps because of dissatisfaction with the choice of proxies that the tribunal used to determine what constitutes impermissible discrimination, it could not simply renounce the commitment. Rather, it either would have to procure a new law from Congress or induce all potential claimants not to bring any proceedings before the WTO.

The difficulty of modifying formally enforced international law obligations may increase their ex ante efficiency by increasing the credibility of the commitment to honor the obligation. In our trade law example, the value of the commitment not to discriminate would be greater and might induce more

---

[24] Some scholars dispute whether the executive enjoys a unilateral power to repudiate international obligations, but the courts have not interfered when this happens. Goldwater v. Carter, 444 U.S. 996 (1979) (rejecting challenge to President Carter's denunciation of the Panama Canal Treaty).

[25] *Cf.* 28 U.S.C. §2414, which gives the Attorney General discretion to effect compliance with the monetary award of an international tribunal, but which requires the Secretary of the Treasury to pay a monetary judgment ordered by a federal court.

investment around the world in the production of goods for export. But, for the same reason, ex post efficiency will be reduced whenever the option of a complex contract is not feasible, because of the higher barriers to implementing a modified obligation. Were formal enforcement the only means of inducing compliance with international law, then, international lawmaking could reliably increase welfare only in areas presenting a low risk of changed circumstances. In our contemporary world, buffeted by technological innovation and rapid economic and social transformation, these conditions are likely to be satisfied only rarely. As a result, the domain of international law would be small indeed if all its obligations necessarily invoked formal enforcement.

In reality, parties to simple contracts and the makers of international law instead can turn to informal mechanisms of self-enforcement. Under some circumstances, they provide the best available means of regulating the inevitable renegotiation and adjustment problems so as to insure against exploitation of the vulnerable party. If the parties can rely on reputation, the prospect of future interaction, or social norms of reciprocity, they can approximate in practice the theoretical goal of writing a simple contract that looks to renegotiation or adjustment, and yet still achieves efficient trade without compromising investment efficiency.

## CONCLUSION

The lesson from contract theory is that actors can solve contracting problems by employing the full range of enforcement methods (both self-enforcement and formal legal enforcement) depending on the simplicity or complexity of the contract that they have written. Where transactions costs are low, the parties can write a complex, complete contract. Such contracts will frequently require the parties to make sequential, interactive investments in the joint venture. As we will explain in Chapter 4, the individual components of these more complex contracting strategies tend to be opaque, thus making it hard for either party to characterize accurately their partner's actions as cooperative or not. Complex contracts, therefore, often require third party arbiters, such as courts, to unpack the parties' respective obligations in the particular circumstances that unfold. Such contracts anticipate that the arbiter can verify the responses appropriate to the particular contingencies and states of the world specified in the contract.

Where transactions costs are high relative to the gains from contracting, parties will choose to write simple, incomplete contracts that lump together many future states of the world so that their respective obligations are transparent and iterative. But simple contracts create moral hazard and hold-up risks. Parties will either write simple contracts with "soft" contract terms (using standards such as "good faith adjustment") and anticipate opportunistic claims for adjustment, or they will write simple contracts with precise or "hard" terms and anticipate the risk of hold-up. In either case, exclusive reliance on formal enforcement of such agreements creates an enforcement risk that arbiters cannot police easily. In the case of simple contracts with soft terms, the risk is that the investing party will substitute alternative performances that reduce joint welfare or otherwise will seek to shirk or chisel on the obligation to perform. In the case of simple contracts with hard terms, the risk is that the investing party will be exploited strategically in a subsequent renegotiation. This exploitation is hard for third parties to police because a claimed incapacity to adjust to new circumstances often will reflect a party's alternatives to a renegotiated deal, which typically rest on private information.

In the face of the evident shortcoming of formal legal mechanisms, parties to simple contracts often have an incentive to use informal means of enforcement to ensure efficient adjustment in the case of contracts with soft terms, or to ensure that the renegotiation process does not exploit vulnerable parties in the case of contracts with hard terms. This is even more true with respect to international agreements, because of the difficulty of modifying obligations for which multiple persons have the capacity to seek enforcement. In the next chapter, we turn to the question of how informal enforcement works, and how it affects resort to formal enforcement.

# 4 A MODEL OF OPTIMAL ENFORCEMENT

It must not be forgotten that although a high standard of morality gives no advantage to each individual man over other men of the tribe, yet that an advancement in the standard of morality will certainly give an immense advantage to one tribe over another. A tribe including many members who were always ready to aid one another and to sacrifice themselves for the common good would be victorious over most other tribes; and this would be natural selection.

Charles Darwin, THE DESCENT OF MAN 178–79 (1874)

Partners in trade call one another brothers; and frequently feel toward one another as if they were really so. Their good agreement is an advantage to all.

Adam Smith, THE THEORY OF MORAL SENTIMENTS, Part VI, section II (1790)

THE MODEL OF OPTIMAL ENFORCEMENT OF INTERNATIONAL LAW THAT we develop in this book rests on two methodological building blocks. The first uses the tools of contract theory and the economics of information that we explored in the previous chapter. These allowed us to think more rigorously about the difficulties facing individuals, firms, and states who rely on formal mechanisms to promote cooperation and constrain incentives to defect from jointly beneficial objectives. In this chapter, we introduce the second methodological building block, exploring the allied disciplines of experimental economics, anthropology, and evolutionary theory. Here we analyze the strengths and the limits of informal mechanisms for enforcing commitments and address the central question of the relationship between informal and formal enforcement.

## THE LIMITATIONS OF FORMAL ENFORCEMENT

As a prelude to our discussion of the role of informal enforcement, we summarize the lessons gained from our examination of the formal enforcement of contractual commitments. Recall that in the previous chapter we introduced the concept of *verification* – the actions necessary to prove to a neutral party disputed facts or conditions known to each of the disputants. In formal enforcement proceedings, the information available to the court or arbiter comes from the parties themselves. Based on that information, the arbiter must make an evidentiary finding on disputed facts, determine the relevance of that finding for the particular contractual obligation (whether precise rule or broad standard) and impose an appropriate sanction. The arbiter's task in verifying the occurrence of the contingency is harder with respect to the application of a broad standard than in the case of a precise rule. All things being equal, the evidentiary proxies selected under a standard will be a noisier signal for the occurrence of the contractual contingency.

To illustrate this point, assume the parties wish to pair particular future contingencies to corresponding performance obligations, that is, when X occurs, the promisor must pay $Y. The parties can define X in several different ways. X may be a precise rule, that is, a relatively specific fact, such as the delivery of a widget with a specified weight. Here the parties only delegate to the court the determination of what evidence is sufficient to satisfy X and trigger the promisor's payment obligation. Alternatively, X can be a vague standard, such as the delivery of a widget in excellent condition. Here the court must determine not only what evidence is sufficient to establish the weight of the widget, but also the degree to which weight is relevant to the determination of whether the widget satisfies the standard.[1]

In general, therefore, standards are more costly to verify than rules. But standards do permit the parties to harness the advantage of hindsight, because a court gets a case only after the relevant future events have come to pass. As a result, standards reduce the ex ante costs of writing the contract – the costs incurred in foreseeing the future states of the world, calculating the efficient outcome in each state, and providing specifically for low-probability states. By trading off the informational advantage of standards for the accuracy benefits of rules, contracting parties can sometimes write more complete contracts and thus can enhance their incentives to make jointly beneficial investments. This makes possible a greater range of socially beneficial joint production.

Given these trade-offs, what are the basic options for parties who rely on formal enforcement? If conditions are unlikely to change much in the future (the level of uncertainty is low), and thus the cost of contracting is low relative to the anticipated gains, parties can best reduce verification costs by

---

[1]   Robert E. Scott & George G. Triantis, *Anticipating Litigation in Contract Design*, 115 YALE L. J. 814, 831 (2006).

writing a complex, complete contract. Such a contract will contain many precise terms – or rules – that pair particular contingencies with an appropriate contractual performance. Assuming that the parties to such a contract can forestall renegotiation, they will have an incentive to make jointly beneficial investments (in the jargon of economics, the contingencies and their respective performance obligations are "contractible"). These complex contracts are well suited to formal enforcement.

But formal enforcement does not work as well where the future is uncertain (the optimal actions for each party are highly dependent on the future state that materializes) and the costs of contracting are high. Under these conditions, parties are likely to write simple contracts that lump together many future states of the world and provide for the same obligations across the different states. Here the choice is between the Scylla of hard terms (precise rules) and the Charybdis of soft terms (vague standards). Where the level of uncertainty is high, a simple contract containing only hard terms will always be suboptimal ex post. This is necessarily so because the contract specifies the same obligation for many different possible contingencies that ideally would require different obligations.

Alternatively, parties may respond to a high level of uncertainty by writing a simple contract that contains many vague standards that delegate to courts ex post the task of finding proxies for the relevant contingencies and their respective performances. These soft-term contracts take advantage of a court's ability to assess the respective contract performances after all uncertainties have been resolved. But as we have seen, soft-term contracts also can create severe problems of verification. Unless there are objective surrogates for the performances in question, simple contracts with soft terms raise the moral hazard risk discussed earlier (where the promisor will always choose the performance proxy that is the least costly for him even where an alternative proxy under the same broad standard would be jointly profitable). In short, simple, rule-based contracts require renegotiation and thus undermine incentives to invest, whereas the costs of verifying simple, standard-based contracts will often exceed the associated benefits. Parties writing more complex contracts can ameliorate this problem by using combinations of standards and rules, but high contracting costs can make this strategy infeasible.[2]

To illustrate the relevance of the verification problem, consider the following example.[3] Assume that a buyer in New York wishes to get a single shipment of

---

[2]  For discussion of rules-standards combinations, see *id.* at 851–56.
[3]  The following example draws on Robert E. Scott, *A Theory of Self-Enforcing Indefinite Agreements*, 103 COLUM. L. REV. 1641, 1667 (2003).

the highest quality carved rosewood furniture – coffee tables, trunks, chests, etc. – from India. She anticipates using this shipment in a promotion of luxury home furnishings that she plans to market for the holiday season. The cost to the seller of fabricating high-quality furniture is $50,000. The buyer values the high-quality furniture at $70,000. The seller can also deliver furniture of average quality at a cost of $40,000. The lower-quality furniture, however, is worth only $50,000 to the buyer.

Assume that seller offers to fabricate the high-quality furniture for $55,000 and the average-quality goods for $45,000. Assume finally that both seller and buyer can observe high quality but cannot verify this condition to a court (at a reasonable cost). Further assume that a court can verify that goods do not meet merchantable quality. In other words, a court can apply only a legal standard of fair, average quality.[4] Both parties would prefer to contract for the high-quality goods because that contract promises the largest joint surplus. But the buyer will never agree to a contract that specifies (nonverifiable) high-quality furniture because she faces the downside risk that the seller will instead deliver only average-quality goods and demand the $55,000 contract price for high-quality goods. Because high quality is not verifiable, the first best option is not contractible.

Thus, if the only contracting option is formal enforcement, the buyer will propose a simple contract in which the parties condition performance on precise, verifiable contingencies. This contract will pay the seller $45,000 to fabricate furniture of ordinary merchantable quality. Because this contract is legally enforceable, should the seller deliver goods of less than merchantable quality, the buyer can recover compensatory damages.[5] But, as this illustration shows, formal enforcement does not enable the parties to take up the contracting opportunity that they both would prefer. The key question, which we discuss later, is whether the parties can expect to do any better if, instead of using formal, legal enforcement, they rely on informal means to enforce their respective promises.

Functionally equivalent problems arise in international agreements. Consider the example we used in Chapter 3, where rich countries propose to

---

[4] The standard of merchantable quality is verifiable because there are objective proxies readily available; specifically, the evidence of the level of quality the market regards as acceptable. *See, e.g.,* UNIFORM COMMERCIAL CODE §2–314 (2)(a), which provides that goods must be "at least such as would pass without objection in the trade under the contract description." Thus, under this standard a court can determine if the attributes of the goods are consistent with the contract description and also are "fit for their ordinary purposes for which such goods are used" by considering evidence from experts as to the general standard of merchantable quality. UNIFORM COMMERCIAL CODE §2–314(2)(c).

[5] *Id.* §§2–/14(2), 2–/15, ROBERT E. SCOTT & JODY S. KRAUS, CONTRACT LAW AND THEORY 1109–1122 (Rev. 3rd ed. 2003).

accept more imports of agricultural products from poor countries in return for greater protection of the intellectual property rights that their exports carry. Assume further that whatever agreement is reached will be subject to formal enforcement. The level of liberalization (expressed as a combination of higher quotas and lower tariffs) should be a function of the difficulty that domestic producers will encounter in shifting to other activities. If rich countries could reserve a right to reduce their commitment in the face of unexpected obstacles to successful adjustment by their domestic producers, they might commit to a high level of liberalization. But if a third party cannot verify the significance of the obstacles, and if the liberalization commitment will be backed up by formal enforcement, the parties will commit to less liberalization than they optimally would prefer. Conversely, difficulties in specifying and monitoring the level of enforcement against intellectual property theft that poor countries undertake may discourage rich countries from making a commitment to liberalize imports.

## Expanding Informal Self-Enforcement through Reciprocity

The power of informal enforcement has been well understood since the classic work of Stuart Macaulay, who advanced the empirical claim that most agreements between business persons were self-enforcing, and that powerful informal norms, rather than legal rules, govern most contracting behavior.[6] Indeed, even parties who lack the commercial sophistication to band together in trade groups can choose to rely on self-enforcement of their promises rather than on costly, legal enforcement. It follows that if the parties themselves can employ efficient extralegal mechanisms that make their promises credible, then they would be (and should be) indifferent to the high verification costs of legal enforcement of those promises.[7]

But any argument for informal enforcement as the preferred alternative to an expansive regime of legal enforcement must overcome a major difficulty. Scholars have long understood that reputational sanctions and the discipline of repeated interactions are effective means of enforcing commitments under certain conditions. But, as we suggested in Chapter 3, these conditions for self-enforcement are quite stringent. Ongoing relationships inevitably come to an

---

[6]  Stuart Macaulay, *Non-Contractual Relations in Business*, 28 Am. Soc. Rev. 555 (1963). Anticipating by forty years the experimental evidence, summarized later, that formal enforcement may "crowd out" informal enforcement, Macaulay's subjects reported that legal sanctions were not only unnecessary but might well have undesirable effects, as the invocation of legal enforcement might be seen as a betrayal of trust or an instinct to engage in sharp practice. *Id.* at 558.

[7]  *See generally* Robert E. Scott, *Conflict and Cooperation in Long-Term Contracts*, 75 Calif. L. Rev. 2005, 2051–53 (1987).

end and, consequently, repeated interactions are subject to the end-game problem. Reputation, in turn, will work to make promissory commitments credible only if other contracting parties can conveniently learn about the reasons why any particular transaction broke down. A reputation for trustworthiness is difficult to establish, therefore, especially in heterogeneous environments where most participants are unfamiliar with the past behavior of any particular contracting party.[8] As we observed in Chapter 3, this problem extends to international relations, because the regimes that act on behalf of states can come and go.

Recent work in experimental economics suggests, however, that the domain of informal enforcement of contracts may be considerably larger than has been conventionally understood. A robust result of these experiments is that a significant fraction of individuals behave as if *reciprocity* were an important motivation (even in isolated interactions with strangers).[9] Ernst Fehr and Klaus Schmidt have developed a theory of *inequity aversion* that captures the key results of the experiments by combining the features of both altruism and envy.[10]

Under the inequity aversion theory, a person is altruistic to others if her payoffs are above an equitable benchmark and is envious of the others if their payoffs exceed that benchmark. In other words, people compare themselves with others in their group (and with the other party in a two-person relationship) by using a benchmark of equality of distribution. Thus, inequity aversion (which also can be termed a *preference for reciprocal fairness*) holds that many

[8] Alan Schwartz & Robert E. Scott, *Contract Theory and the Limits of Contract law*, 113 Yale L. J. 541, 557 (2003). As we suggest in the text, small, homogeneous communities are best suited to use reputation as a means of self-enforcement. In these settings, contracting behavior soon becomes common knowledge, and sanctions against untrustworthy parties can effectively be imposed. See Janet Landa, *A Theory of the Ethnically Homogenous Middleman Group: An Institutional Alternative to Contract Law*, 10 J. LEGAL STUD. 349 (1981); Avner Grief, *Informal Contract Enforcement: Lessons from Medieval Trade* in 2 THE NEW PALGRAVE DICTIONARY OF ECONOMICS AND LAW 287 (Peter Newman, ed. 1998). Reputation is also effective where industries establish trade associations that can identify bad behavior and impose appropriate sanctions, such as boycotts. The contracting behavior of the members of the association thus becomes part of the group's collective memory. See Lisa Bernstein, *Private Commercial Law in the Cotton Industry: Creating Cooperation through Rules, Norms and Institutions*, 99 MICH. L. REV. 1724 (2001); Lisa Bernstein, *Merchant Law in a Merchant Court: Rethinking the Code's Search for Immanent Business Norms*, 144 U. PA. L. REV. 1765 (1996).

[9] See, e.g., Matthew Rabin, *Incorporating Fairness into Game Theory and Economics*, 83 AM. ECON. REV. 1281 (1993); David K. Levine, *Modeling Altruism and Spitefulness in Experiments*, 1 REV. ECON. DYNAM. 593 (1998); Ernst Fehr & Klaus Schmidt, *A Theory of Fairness, Competition and Cooperation*, 114 Q. J. ECON. 817 (1999); Ernst Fehr, Simon Gächter, & Georg Kirchsteiger, *Reciprocity as a Contract Enforcement Device: Experimental Evidence*, 65 ECONOMETRICA 833 (1997). For a review of the literature, see Ernst Fehr & Klaus Schmidt, *Theories of Fairness and Reciprocity – Evidence and Economic Applications*, in ADVANCES IN ECONOMICS AND ECONOMETRICS: THEORY AND APPLICATIONS, EIGHTH WORLD CONGRESS, VOLUME I, at 208 (Mathias Dewatripont, Lars Peter Hansen, & Stephen J. Turnovsky, eds. 2003).

[10] Ernst Fehr & Klaus M. Schmidt, *A Theory of Fairness, Competition and Cooperation*, note 9 supra.

individuals will respond to an inequity in a contractual relationship either by rewarding a generous action or by punishing a selfish action. This theory predicts that informal enforcement of many types of agreements, even those among perfect strangers, can be more efficient than the alternative of legal enforcement.

Fehr and Schmidt's work complements a claim by evolutionary theorists that an evolutionary basis exists for what they label "moralistic reciprocity," as distinguished from simple reciprocity.[11] Moralistic reciprocity embodies a willingness to punish defectors in ways that include social ostracism, reduced status, and withdrawal from relationships. In the simple form of reciprocity, punishment for defection takes the form of withdrawal of future cooperation (e.g., if you cheat, I will not deal with you anymore). Moralistic reciprocity refers to more elaborate forms of punishment, including social ostracism, reduced status, fewer friends, and fewer mating opportunities. Evolutionary theorists argue that simple reciprocity cannot support large-scale human cooperation. Withholding cooperation is too crude a mechanism to maintain cooperation in large groups. But moralistic reciprocity offers a more plausible basis for establishing large-scale patterns of cooperation because it provides many more ways that cooperators can punish defectors.

The key challenge is to explain why people would incur costs to impose such punishments. Theorists solve this problem by assuming that reciprocators punish both defectors and cooperators who fail to punish. But that then raises the further question of why moralistic cooperators will punish those activities only in a manner that is mutually beneficial to the group. The evolutionary theorists' response is to model behavioral change as a "process of cultural evolution." By this they mean that people will differ as to what behaviors produce joint benefits and thus deserve protection through moralistic punishment. Groups that protect through punishment only those activities that support mutual benefit will secure higher payoffs. Others in turn will imitate those behaviors, which through imitation will spread to others.

To clarify what underlies the inequity aversion theory, let us summarize the three key findings of a substantial body of experimental evidence. First, many people behave in a reciprocal manner that deviates from purely self-interested behavior.[12] Reciprocity means that individuals respond cooperatively to generous acts, and, conversely, punish noncooperative behavior.[13] Second,

---

[11]   Robert Boyd & Peter J. Richerson, SOLVING THE PUZZLE OF HUMAN COOPERATION (2005).

[12]   Experimental economists have gathered overwhelming evidence that systematically refutes the self-interest hypothesis. The recent experimental evidence suggests that people differ with regard to how selfishly or fair-mindedly they behave. This difference has important economic and legal consequences. For discussion, see Robert E. Scott, note 3 *supra.*

[13]   Ernst Fehr & Klaus Schmidt, *Theories of Fairness and Reciprocity,* note 9 *supra,* at 209–10.

individuals will repay generosity and punish selfishness in interactions with complete strangers even if doing so is costly for them and yields neither present nor future material rewards.[14] And third, the observed preference for reciprocity is heterogeneous. Some people exhibit reciprocal behavior and others are selfish. Taking all the experimental data together – gathered from diverse countries and cultures – the fraction of reciprocally fair subjects ranges from 40 to 60 percent, as does the fraction of subjects who are selfish. In short, the evidence indicates that roughly half of us are fair and the other half are self-interested.[15]

The last finding of heterogeneity provides a convincing explanation for the apparent anomaly of the robust evidence of reciprocal fairness in bilateral interactions and the equally robust evidence from experiments in competitive markets where almost all subjects behave as if they were self-interested. The explanation rests on the insight that the observed behavior is a function of the economic environment. In bilateral experiments, the presence of a fraction of reciprocally fair individuals can create incentives for selfish types to make fair offers. Alternatively, in a competitive market a few selfish players can drive the price to the competitive level and no single fair person can affect that price.[16] But in general and in many environments, heterogeneity means that even selfish parties will behave reciprocally as long as the population of fair types in the general population corresponds to what the experimental evidence indicates. If this condition is satisfied, there exists a positive probability that a contracting partner, even though a stranger, is predisposed to behave fairly. Thus, in a heterogeneous world, reciprocity pays, even for those who are selfish.

The reciprocal fairness experiments indicate, for example, that it pays to write trust contracts – that is, agreements based on observable but not verifiable conduct – even where the promisee is uncertain whether the promisor is a fair or selfish type. So long as the population is heterogeneous (i.e., there is a significant fraction of fair types in the population), reciprocity yields better enforcement outcomes in experimental settings *on average* than does the alternative of third-party (or legal) enforcement. This result indicates that even selfish parties will respond reciprocally to an offer to enter into a trust contract as a result of the positive probability that the promisor will behave fairly.

Even more interesting, for our purposes, are the experiments that ask anonymous subjects to enter into agreements that have the potential of enhancing the joint surplus if both act cooperatively and decline opportunities to shirk. The parties can choose self-enforcement or third-party enforcement with formal

---

[14] Ernst Fehr & Simon Gächter, *Fairness and Retaliation: The Economics of Reciprocity*, 14 J. ECON. PERSP. 159 (2000).

[15] *Id.*

[16] Ernst Fehr & Klaus Schmidt, *Theories of Fairness and Reciprocity*, note 9 *supra*, at 246–48.

sanctions. These experiments show that people who rely on moralistic reciprocity – that is, they reward generosity and punish unfairness – produce greater
joint returns *on average* than those who choose formal means of enforcement.

The inequity aversion theory has important implications for the choices
of means to enforce obligations. It suggests that in many contexts informal
enforcement, on average, provides the better strategy. If one can count on
self-enforcement to deliver the same gross benefits as formal enforcement,
self-enforcement will be superior simply because it is less costly. In addition,
parties to self-enforcing agreements can condition performance on observable
factors that might not be verifiable to a third party. This extension of the domain
of contracting leads to more joint production of social welfare.[17]

At the same time, we invoke the theory with caution. Scholars have not
yet seriously tested the experimentally observed preference for reciprocity in
real-world contexts. Thus, any use of the reciprocal fairness concept raises the
question of whether real parties will behave as did the experimental subjects.
Moreover, the experimental evidence does not establish whether the observed
preference for reciprocity is an intrinsic motivation or instead an adaptive
behavior.

Consider an argument for adaptation. It would not be surprising if people
learn over time that cooperative strategies generally work, because most interactions present a possibility of repeat play and reputational effect. Once the
lesson is learned, it is costly for any cooperator to adjust a strategy that is broadly
successful just to maximize a private advantage in a single interaction with a
stranger. After all, sometimes one might mistake an interaction that promises
future dealings for an opportunity to exploit a stranger and get punished or pay
an unexpected reputational price.[18] Thus, a preference for reciprocal fairness
may evolve as an adaptive heuristic that enhances individual welfare over a
large range of circumstances.

Alternatively, some theorists have suggested that strangers may signal to each
other their "standing" in a community by actions that are either cooperative
or not. This notion of "indirect reciprocity" relies on the assumption that
the cooperative behavior between two individuals will be contingent on their
previous behavior toward others. Under some models, the evolution of indirect
reciprocity leads to trusting behavior in relations between strangers.[19]

Theorists of cultural evolution also have adduced persuasive reasons why
cultures generate norms of moralistic reciprocity. These norms are part of a

[17] For discussion, see Robert E. Scott, *A Theory of Self-Enforcing Indefinite Agreements*, note 9 *supra*, at
1682–85.
[18] *Id.* at 1674–75.
[19] Karthik Panchanathan & Robert Boyd, *A Tale of Two Defectors: The Importance of Standing for
Evolution of Indirect Reciprocity*, 224 J. Theoretical Biology 115 (2003).

process that selects for cooperative behaviors that favor particular groups or tribes over others.[20] There is substantial evidence of a great diversity in social norms among human groups. At the same time, norms create conformity within those groups. The existence of persistent differences among groups and conformity within groups thus supports the hypothesis that groups with more cooperative norms are more likely to prevail in group conflict, and thus that evolutionary pressures will lead to the selection of their norms.[21]

But a theory of cultural evolution must also account for individual selection and the extensive evidence of selfish behaviors within groups. Robert Boyd and Peter Richerson, the most prominent scholars in this discipline, suggest that a dual "gene-culture" evolutionary theory is needed to account for the evolution of both cooperative and self-interested behaviors.[22] Their models support a claim that cultural evolution of cooperative behaviors is coextensive with genetic evolution of selfish behaviors. Rudimentary cooperation favored genetic selection of individuals who could avoid punishment and could acquire norms that promoted the group's survival. Over time, genetic changes led to emotions such as shame and the capacity to learn and internalize local practices. Moral emotions, in turn, enhanced the scale of cooperation. Further rounds of coevolutionary change continued until eventually individuals were able to cooperate with distantly related individuals and to punish others who violated the group's rules. In this way "a growing reliance on cultural evolution led to larger more cooperative societies among humans over the past 250,000 years or so."[23]

In modern society, however, these tribal instincts favor smaller groups (coalitions, cabals, etc.) in ways that lead to selfish behaviors. Evolutionary theories suggest that selfish instincts are suppressed by "work-arounds" in which cultural evolution harnesses tribal instincts for larger purposes. For example, large national and religious groups create ideologies with symbols of inclusion (e.g., the flag) that stimulate tribal cooperative instincts on a larger scale.[24]

That these work-arounds are only awkward compromises may explain the heterogeneity of preferences that are uniformly observed in the experiments on

[20] For a discussion of this literature and its implications, see Peter J. Richerson, Robert T. Boyd, & Joseph Henrich, *Cultural Evolution of Human Cooperation* in GENETIC AND CULTURAL EVOLUTION OF COOPERATION 357 (2003).

[21] Ernst Fehr & Urs Fischbacher, *Social Norms and Human Cooperation*, 8 TRENDS IN COGNITIVE SCIENCE 185, 189 (2004).

[22] See ROBERT T. BOYD & PETER J. RICHERSON, CULTURE AND THE EVOLUTIONARY PROCESS (1985).

[23] Peter J. Richerson, Robert T. Boyd & Joseph Henrich, note 20 *supra*, at 368. For the incorporation of this work into economic theory, see PAUL SEABRIGHT, THE COMPANY OF STRANGERS: A NATURAL HISTORY OF ECONOMIC LIFE (2004).

[24] Peter J. Richerson, Robert T. Boyd, & Joseph Henrich, note 20 *supra*, at 372–73.

reciprocal fairness. The cooperative adaptive behaviors that worked well in the small tribal groups of the Paleolithic era fit larger, impersonal social institutions only imperfectly. This might explain an equilibrium in which some people use a strategy of reciprocal fairness in dealing with strangers while others behave selfishly.

The cultural evolutionary hypotheses provide a context for appreciating the significance of the experimental evidence of reciprocal fairness. The preference for reciprocity does not undermine a conception of human behavior premised on rational self-interest, but rather extends its reach. To the extent that informal enforcement is linked to reciprocity, it depends significantly on the clarity and predictability of the responses to uncooperative behavior. Selecting an appropriate response to, say, an instance of shirking becomes more complicated when the defecting party's behavior cannot be readily characterized. Parties rarely shirk by directly announcing their unwillingness to perform as promised. They typically affirm solidarity, protest helplessness in the face of intractable problems, or act in subtle ways that are difficult to evaluate. In other words, nonperformance can be a "noisy" signal and systematic misperception of the other's actions may cause inappropriate responses.[25]

All this underscores the fact that, to work effectively, informal enforcement requires the imposition of a punitive sanction on a party who breaches a promise or otherwise reneges on a commitment. Even if the breaching party understands and "accepts" the punishment, retaliation will threaten the durability of any contractual relationship. This explains why all parties have an interest in cementing their contractual relationship within an embedded framework based on reciprocity. Reciprocal fairness offers a particularly stable foundation for a general strategy of conditional cooperation even between parties with no past and no prospect of a future. The strategy ameliorates the problems caused by the difficulty of detecting a defection and of selecting a proportional punishment.

## INEQUITY AVERSION IN INTERNATIONAL RELATIONS

To sustain our model of optimal international law enforcement, we must do more than defend the claim that the observed phenomena in laboratory experiments extends to real-world interactions among individuals. We also must explain why we also might observe a preference for reciprocal fairness when states interact with each other. Even if individuals manifest inequity aversion,

---

[25] Robert E. Scott & Paul B. Stephan, *Self-Enforcing International Agreements and The Limits of Coercion*, 2004 WIS. L. REV. 551, 568.

does it follow that complex organizations of people, either a firm or a state, will do so as well?

In an earlier era, international law governed the relationships of royal sovereigns, and then only those who ruled "civilized nations." This was largely true until the late eighteenth century, and had continuing salience until the collapse of the Austro-Hungarian, German, and Russian empires at the end of World War I. Among such a small and homogenous group as European royalty, the conditions for developing a preference for reciprocal fairness clearly were present. But the world of modern states, whether democratic or not, is radically different. Individuals still function as agents of the state, but, a few despots aside, there no longer exist situations where a single individual effectively exercises state power. In this environment, should we expect states, like firms, to exhibit the same opportunistic behavior that we see in individuals operating in competitive markets?

Our response to these questions consists of arguments bolstered by anecdotes, rather than extensive empirical research subjected to careful quantitative analysis. We cannot prove that a preference for reciprocal fairness necessarily motivates firms or states, but we can offer plausible explanations why it may. These explanations at a minimum justify further research to explore the hypothesis, and support taking our model of optimal international law enforcement seriously.

First, just as firms tend to interact and contract through specialists, the conception and negotiation of international agreements typically involves years of work in which technical experts have an important, and sometimes dominant, role. These experts often interact in multiple contexts, not just in the particular venue of a negotiation. It is not far fetched to imagine that often they form distinct, relatively homogenous groups of the sort that, consistent with the claims of evolutionary theorists, develop norms of inequity aversion.

Some international relations specialists, as we noted in Chapter 2, model international lawmaking as the product of transnational networks comprising epistemic communities.[26] As we indicated, we do not find that work entirely convincing, and in particular we regard the claim that national judges now populate such a network as overstated. But the observation that technical experts who contribute importantly to international lawmaking function as a distinct community is apt. This finding in turn provides a basis for our

---

[26] ANNE-MARIE SLAUGHTER, A NEW WORLD ORDER (2004); MARGARET F. KECK & KATHRYN SIKKINK, ACTIVISTS BEYOND BORDERS: ADVOCACY NETWORKS IN INTERNATIONAL POLITICS (1998); José E. Alvarez, The WTO as Linkage Machine, 96 AM. J. INT'L L. 146 (2002); Kal Raustiala, The Architecture of International Cooperation: Transgovernmental Networks and the Future of International Law, 43 VA. J. INT'L L. 1 (2002).

claim that a preference for reciprocal fairness may affect the actions of these experts. Groups of relatively small, relatively homogenous people can more easily identify and sanction both opportunists and those who fail to sanction opportunists.

More generally, states typically carry out international relations through bureaucracies.[27] Ministries of foreign affairs, trade, and the armed forces shape policy in the overwhelming majority of states. It seems plausible that these bureaucracies might display the tendency generally observed in such structures, namely, *ceteris paribus*, maximization of discretionary authority.[28] And exhibiting inequity aversion seems a good strategy for optimizing interactions with counterpart bureaucracies, which in turn should maximize each bureaucracy's power *vis-à-vis* its political masters.

A possible response to this conjecture might be that tension rather than cooperation may optimize bureaucratic power. Military bureaucracies in particular might increase their authority by minimizing interactions with their counterparts as part of a broader strategy of stoking tensions and feeding insecurity. One strand of late-twentieth-century thought, for example, maintains that a U.S. national security complex fattened its budgets and expanded its influence by contriving a permanent sense of crisis.[29]

On balance, however, this rejoinder seems far fetched. By and large, uncooperative behavior that fuels international tension creates disproportionately great risks for foreign policy élites. A crisis brings their performance under more scrutiny than usual, may set in motion dangerous events with consequences beyond the élite's control, and otherwise unsettles the stable rationality that bureaucracies generally seek. We suspect that the link between conventional bureaucratic incentives and inequity aversion is strong, although by no means absolute.

Studies indicate that even military bureaucracies exhibit some preference for reciprocal fairness. In the arms control field, for example, states have committed to confidence-building measures as a means of reducing the risk of conflict with their adversaries. The Treaty on Conventional Armed Forces in Europe exemplifies such arrangements.[30] One might think that professional military

---

[27] The following discussion is drawn from Robert E. Scott & Paul B. Stephan, note 23 *supra*, at 593–96.

[28] MAX WEBER, THE THEORY OF SOCIAL AND ECONOMIC ORGANIZATION (A. M. Henderson & Talcott Parsons, trans. 1947); WILLIAM A. NISKANEN, JR., BUREAUCRACY AND PUBLIC ECONOMICS (1994); William A. Niskanen, *Bureaucrats and Politicians*, 18 J.L. & ECON. 617 (1985).

[29] NOAM CHOMSKY, HEGEMONY OR SURVIVAL: AMERICA'S QUEST FOR GLOBAL DOMINANCE (THE GLOBAL EMPIRE PROJECT) (2003); GAR ALPERWITZ, ATOMIC DIPLOMACY: HIROSHIMA AND POTSDAM: THE USE OF THE ATOMIC BOMB AND THE AMERICAN CONFRONTATION WITH SOVIET POWER (1985).

[30] Treaty on Conventional Armed Forces in Europe, Nov. 19, 1990, S. Treaty Doc. No. 102–8 (1991). *See generally* S. V. Kortunov, *Basic Principles of Reduction and Limitation of Conventional Forces* in

organizations would oppose an agreement that constrains weapons deploy-ments and the size of deployed forces. But the Treaty has substantial reporting and inspection requirements that enlist the support of military experts and rests on measures such as embedded observers, as also did earlier agreements.[31] These techniques engage military personnel in a range of cooperative behaviors with their counterparts, interactions that those involved seem to find desirable.

Additional evidence of the existence of a preference for reciprocal fairness within many states can be inferred from the growth in number, scale, and scope of international organizations devoted to facilitating cooperative behav-ior. Growth may reflect many factors, of course, but it seems reasonable to associate an organization's reputation, which accumulates over time, with increased attraction for regimes already disposed to reciprocal fairness. To cite some important but by no means exclusive examples of growth, the Inter-national Monetary Fund and the World Bank had 29 members in 1946, 173 in 1992, and 184 in 2005; the GATT had 23 founding members in 1947, 102 in 1979, and its successor, the WTO, had 148 in 2004; the European Communities had 6 founding members in 1957, grew to 15 in 1994 and 25 in 2004. Each of these institutions also evolved from a specific-purpose entity (postwar recon-struction, currency stability, tariff reduction) to a much broader governance institution. We are prepared to believe that these organizations may stand for less than they seem.[32] But even discounting for the gap between their ambitions and accomplishments, the proliferation of these bodies suggests that a growing number of regimes prefer the kind of reciprocal and cooperative relations that membership in the organizations promotes.

Further research, we believe, would document convincingly that a substan-tial and significant portion of the interactions among people that leads to the establishment of international rules and norms takes place with the participa-tion of groups that share a common professional, technical, or bureaucratic identity that, in turn, is conducive to the development of a preference for recip-rocal fairness. As a result, the domain of informal enforcement of international law should be relatively broad. Even though the fragility of regimes might limit the value of sanctions based on future dealings and reputation, the conduct of international lawmaking through specialist groups will increase the likelihood of compliance with costly obligations in the absence of formal enforcement.

INTERNATIONAL LAW AND INTERNATIONAL SECURITY – MILITARY AND POLITICAL DIMENSIONS 186 (Paul B. Stephan & Boris M. Klimenko, eds. 1991) (analysis of Treaty and its implications by leading Soviet expert).

[31] ABRAM CHAYES & ANTONIA HANDLER CHAYES, THE NEW SOVEREIGNTY – COMPLIANCE WITH INTER-NATIONAL REGULATORY AGREEMENTS 147 (1995).

[32] For expression of this skepticism, see Paul B. Stephan, *Accountability and International Lawmaking: Rules, Rents and Legitimacy*, 17 NW. J. INT'L L. & BUS. 681 (1996–97).

## The Role of Formal Enforcement in a World of Informal Enforcement

We turn now to the central question: What role does (and should) the law play in a world where informal enforcement is pervasive and robust? To answer that question, let us review the unique benefits of informal enforcement. Recall that the experimental evidence tells us that informal enforcement, when it is effective, is both *cheaper* and *better* than formal enforcement. Informal enforcement is *cheaper* because a party needs to expend costs only to observe the other's behavior, while formal enforcement requires the parties to expend *additional* resources (attorneys fees, court costs, etc.) in verifying that behavior to a court. Second, less obvious perhaps but even more significant, is the fact that informal enforcement is also *better*. It permits parties to make credible promises regarding observable but nonverifiable measures of performance, thus increasing joint surplus.[33]

Recall, for example, the buyer who wished to acquire high-quality furniture fabricated by an Indian seller. The problem was that the parties were unable to write a formal contract describing precisely the quality of the contract goods (and the associated price) that would be jointly optimal. This was because the attributes of high-quality furniture were not verifiable and thus "high quality" was not contractible. Consequently, the legally enforceable contract for merchantable goods that the parties wrote instead failed to maximize joint welfare.

But imagine that the parties entered into a different agreement. The buyer might instead propose a legally unenforceable bonus agreement as a supplement to their formal contract. This agreement might propose a lower base price (say, $40,000) for goods that are sold "As Is," subject only to a minimum contract description.[34] In addition, the buyer would promise to pay a bonus of *as much as* $20,000 if the seller delivers high-quality goods satisfactory to the buyer. Here, in other words, the buyer is offering to share a portion of the greater contractual surplus with the seller in return for the enhanced effort necessary to produce the specialized high-quality goods that maximize the buyer's value. But this proposal has a twist. Under the common law indefiniteness doctrine,

---

[33] Robert E. Scott, *The Death of Contract Law*, 54 U. TORONTO L. REV. 369, 385–86 (2004).

[34] Under an "As Is" contract, the seller makes no warranties of quality (see UNIFORM COMMERCIAL CODE §2–316(3)(a)), but the seller is responsible for delivering goods meeting the basic contract description (*e.g.*, "six rosewood tables, four carved trunks," etc.). *See* UNIFORM COMMERCIAL CODE §2–313(1)(b) (express warranties are created by any description of the goods which is made part of the basis of the bargain). Comment 4 to §2–313 explains that a clause generally disclaiming all warranties of quality under §2–316 (such as an "As Is" disclaimer) cannot reduce the seller's obligation to supply goods sufficient to meet the contract description.

an agreement will not be enforced as a contract if it is uncertain and indefinite in its material terms.[35] Thus, the buyer's promise to give a bonus if satisfied with the additional effort of the seller is not legally enforceable.

A rational choice theorist might predict that this unenforceable bonus agreement would motivate the Indian seller to choose a low effort level, thus delivering lower-quality goods for which the buyer must pay only $40,000. Expending the extra effort to produce higher-quality goods is costly and the extra effort will not earn a compensating bonus payment. After all, the bonus promise is discretionary, and thus a self-interested buyer will always decline to pay a bonus regardless of the efforts expended by the seller.

But do these predictions hold if one takes into account preferences for reciprocal fairness? A preference for reciprocity that causes a party to reward a generous action and retaliate against unfair behavior would enhance the performance of the bonus agreement. A fair buyer in this situation will respond to a high effort level from the seller by paying a generous bonus. Moreover, assuming that the fraction of fair types in the general population is consistent with the experimental evidence, the probability of a fair bonus being paid is sufficiently great to motivate the seller (regardless of his type) to expend the extra effort. Thus, if a substantial fraction of the population responds to opportunities to reciprocate, we would predict that the legally unenforceable bonus agreement would actually produce a better result for both parties than would a legally enforceable contract that contained no bonus.

But the hypothetical case also shows that informal enforcement has some significant limitations. After all, the reciprocal outcome is not guaranteed – the experiments show only that informal enforcement between strangers works better *on average*. Moreover, common observation tells us that ongoing relationships that rely on informal enforcement can break down, and when they do the parties often resort to costly litigation.

What can go wrong? The answer is that informal enforcement requires what we might call "*moral clarity*." Each party must be able to observe and properly characterize the other's behavior. Moral clarity dissipates when transactions are complex and the sequence of performances are interrelated. In complex interactions, a failure to cooperate may not be observable immediately, or a cooperative response may be mistakenly interpreted as a defection from the cooperative norm. Lacking clarity, either party may mischaracterize the other's actions. Under these circumstances, without the necessary linkage between

---

[35] *See, e.g.*, Varney v. Ditmars, 217 N.Y. 223, 111 N.E. 822 (1916); Joseph Martin, Jr., Delicatessen, Inc. v. Schumacher, 52 N.Y. 2d 105, 417 N.E. 2d 541 (1981); RESTATEMENT OF CONTRACTS §32 (1932); RESTATEMENT (SECOND) OF CONTRACTS §33 (1981); SAMUEL WILLISTON, A TREATISE ON THE LAW OF CONTRACTS, VOL. I, §§37 *et seq.* (1990).

action and response, reciprocity will be an ineffective mechanism for enforcement.

Where reciprocity breaks down in complex transactions as a result of low moral clarity, third-party arbiters such as courts can serve a valuable function by "calling fouls." A disinterested referee may be in a better position to sort out complex behavior and, by "blowing the whistle,"can both detect a breach and forestall attempts by the aggrieved party to respond disproportionately. For this reason, complex sporting games, such as basketball, football and baseball universally employ referees for formal competitions rather than relying on reciprocity to detect and punish violations of the rules of the game.

But if the only function of a third-party referee is to provide the parties with information concerning the nature of a complex interaction, it does not provide formal enforcement as we have defined that term. Recall that formal enforcement requires not only the promulgation of a set of behavioral rules, but also the imposition of predetermined sanctions for breach of those rules. Why do rule enforcers have to have the power to impose sanctions? Is the provision of key information to the parties all that is necessary to maintain a robust regime of informal enforcement? In the world of international tribunals, for example, is the ICJ or the WTO DSB fully adequate to resolve disputes even though it lacks the authority directly to impose sanctions?

If sanctioning power were unnecessary, then the many formal regimes for enforcing contracts that we observe around the world would seem to be seriously flawed. But if it is implausible that all systems of formal legal enforcement of contracts are unnecessary (and perhaps counterproductive), should we then question whether informal enforcement mechanisms really have widespread utility? Or are there contextual arguments that explain why we see formal enforcement, including the threat of sanctions, in some situations and not others?

Consider the difference between a sporting contest and a legal proceeding. A basketball game or a tennis match may require only a neutral arbiter acceptable to both parties. The information that the parties lack (who committed the foul, was the shot taken beyond the three-point arc?) is directly observable by third-party arbiters. Sanctions are not essential as long as the neutrality and the powers of observation of the referee are credible.

In a legal proceeding, by contrast, the key information *is provided by the parties themselves.* Once the parties offer evidence, the fact finder can then *verify* information that each may lack individually. But without a sanction for nonproduction, no disputant in a conflict situation would have an incentive to provide truthful information to the arbiter that might harm his position. Absent a sanction, a contracting party would be motivated to conceal evidence of any defection that was known only to it. To be sure, even with the threat of sanction, parties in litigation often will withhold information. Nevertheless, the ability of a court to sanction non-disclosure (for example, by allocating burdens and standards of proof) provides a powerful incentive for parties to reveal private information that is relevant to determining liability under the legal rule.

The capacity to induce disclosure of private information, then, is the key distinction between formal enforcement and other forms of third-party intervention. A formal arbiter obtains private information from both parties under threat of imposing a sanction, and only then does the arbiter verify the "facts" and their relevance in reaching a resolution of the dispute. Thus, any system of legal enforcement that relies on the parties to disclose private information must, of necessity, carry with it the power to sanction. Simply put, the power to impose sanctions is integral to the refereeing function of formal enforcement. Unhappily, as we will see, the sanctioning component of formal enforcement is also the key factor that may lead to suppression of the preferences for reciprocity that underlie informal enforcement mechanisms.

## RIVALROUS ENFORCEMENT SYSTEMS AND THE "CROWDING OUT" PHENOMENON

A central question remains: Because informal enforcement can break down, should the regime of formal legal enforcement be expansive and seek to replicate the reach of informal enforcement, or should it be restrained, and enforce only verifiable contract terms, including those in complex agreements that do not lend themselves to informal enforcement? The answer to this question depends on another: What are the possible effects of the alternative means of enforcement on each other?

There are three possibilities. First, informal enforcement and formal legal enforcement may function independently, if adding more expansive formal enforcement will have no effect on the benefits derived from self-enforcement. Second, informal enforcement and formal enforcement may be complementary, if increasing legal enforcement will increase the benefits from self-enforcement at no additional cost. Finally, informal enforcement and formal enforcement may be rivalrous, if increasing legal enforcement will suppress the preference for reciprocity and thus reduce the unique benefits of informal enforcement.[36]

Note first that the experimental evidence suggests that the various avenues of informal enforcement – retaliatory threats, reputational sanctions, and moralistic reciprocity – complement each other. For example, experiments have compared the effort levels of subjects given a single, anonymous opportunity

---

[36] Robert E. Scott & Paul B. Stephan, note 25 *supra*, at 579–80.

to respond to a generous offer with the effort levels in a similar game in which repeated interactions created an additional opportunity to retaliate against selfish behavior. The results show, first, that a significant fraction of individuals are motivated by reciprocity in a one-shot, anonymous transaction, and, second, that repeated interactions cause a significant *increase* in the effort levels of the subjects.[37]

This result makes sense. Informal sanctions are imposed implicitly and ex post. Thus, for example, a cooperator can punish a shirker's defection after the fact without risking offense to another potential cooperator by having to announce in advance that there will be a sanction for defection. Reciprocation also may lead to a virtuous cycle, in which engaging in cooperative behavior increases one's preference for more cooperative behavior. Successful cooperation that generates a reputation for trustworthiness or produces returns in ongoing transactions both furthers a person's self-interest and, one can argue, also causes the parties to learn to care more about each other's welfare. This feedback effect, in turn, may strengthen the willingness to reciprocate voluntarily even where the prospect of retaliation (or reward) is quite low.[38]

How, then, do formal legal obligations to abide by the terms of a contract interact with motivations of fairness and reciprocity? At first blush, the robust evidence that many people exhibit reciprocal behavior may seem to argue for the law explicitly to incorporate similar norms of fair treatment. To illustrate this point, consider a hypothetical problem, *The Case of the Falling Phosphate Prices*, that states the question more concretely.[39] Assume that a fertilizer manufacturer in the United States enters into a five-year contract with a Brazilian supplier of phosphate. The contract requires the buyer to purchase 250,000 tons of phosphate each year at a stated price. The contract contains a merger clause, stating that the written agreement represents the entire agreement of the parties and supersedes all prior understandings. Two years into the contract, the bottom falls out of the phosphate market and prices fall dramatically. Consequently, the buyer only orders 50,000 tons, one-fifth of the contract quantity.

---

[37]  Martin Brown, Armin Falk, & Ernst Fehr, Incomplete Contracts and the Nature of Market Interactions, Institute for Empirical Research in Economics, University of Zurich, Working Paper No. 38 (2002). *See also* Ernst Fehr & Klaus M. Schmidt, *Theories of Fairness and Reciprocity*, note 9 *supra*, at 214–15; Ernst Fehr, Simon Gächter, & Georg Kirchsteiger, *Gift Exchange and Reciprocity in Competitive Experimental Markets*, 42 EUR. ECON. REV. 1 (1998); Gary Charness, *Responsibility and Effort in an Experimental Labor Market*, 42 J. ECON. BEHAV. & ORG. 375 (2000); Ernst Fehr & Armin Falk, *Wage Rigidity in a Competitive Incomplete Contract Market*, 107 J. POL. ECON. 106 (1999); Simon Gächter & Armin Falk, *Reputation and Reciprocity: Consequences for the Labour Relation*, 104 SCAND. J. OF ECON. 1 (2002).

[38]  Robert E. Scott & Paul B. Stephan, note 25 *supra*, at 577–79.

[39]  The hypothetical is loosely based on the facts in *Columbia Nitrogen Corp. v. Royster Co.*, 451 F.2d 3 (4th Cir. 1971), and the discussion in Robert E. Scott, note 33 *supra*, at 372–74.

Negotiations break down and the seller seeks $1,000,000 for breach of contract based on the difference between the contract price of the remaining 200,000 tons and their market price at the time of delivery.

At trial, the buyer introduces evidence to show that the parties had dealt with each other numerous times in the past, and that both sides had adjusted the actual quantities ordered under their contract in light of fluctuations in the market. The buyer argues that the past practice of informal adjustment shows that the "hard" contract terms (specifying the quantity of phosphate that the buyer had to purchase) were subject to a broad standard of commercial reasonableness. The seller's obligation to make a good faith adjustment meant that the contract required the buyer only to order a "reasonable" quantity in light of the hardship caused by the falling phosphate prices.

An analyst might suggest that where an agreement such as this one creates an opportunity for beneficial reciprocity, a court should enforce such a duty when the parties themselves fail to behave fairly. But, surprisingly, the experimental evidence argues for a more cautious approach. As we have seen, the data indicate that, when offered a trust contract, a substantial number of individuals will both pay higher prices and extend higher levels of effort than narrow self-interest would dictate. But when offered the same choices *plus* the possibility of having a third party impose a monetary sanction if the promisor shirks, the average price offered by buyers and the average effort given by sellers declines significantly. First, shirking by sellers increases. This occurs even where the expected costs of shirking exceed the expected returns to the seller. Second, reciprocity either in the form of generous offers by buyers or reciprocating efforts by sellers vanishes almost completely. Where shirking was expected to benefit the sellers, they chose the minimum effort in the vast majority of cases. In addition, in those instances where buyers offered more generous prices above the minimum, sellers did not reciprocate with greater efforts.[40]

It seems that, absent a legally enforceable obligation, reciprocal fairness – operating alone – generates high levels of cooperative behavior. And the evidence indicates that, once the entire relationship, including its informal aspects,

---

[40]  Ernst Fehr & Simon Gächter, *Do Incentive Contracts Crowd Out Voluntary Cooperation?* IEER Working Paper No. 34 and USC CLEO Research Paper No. C01-3, 2001. There are other experiments that have reported similar effects from the introduction of formal enforcement. *See, e.g.,* Iris Bohnet, Bruno S. Frey, & Steffen Huck, *More Order with Less Law: On Contract Enforcement, Trust and Crowding,* 95 AM. POL. SCIENCE REV. 131 (2001); Uri Gneezy & Aldo Rustichini, *A Fine is a Price,* 29 J. LEGAL STUD. 1 (2000); Ernst Fehr & Bruno Rockenbach, Incentives and Intentions – The Hidden Rewards of Economic Incentives, University of Zurich (2000). An extensive literature in social psychology also considers the crowding out of intrinsic motivations. *See, e.g.,* Edward L. Deci, R. Koestner, & Richard M. Ryan, *A Meta-Analytic Review of Experiments Examining the Effects of Extrinsic Rewards on Intrinsic Motivation,* 125 PSYCH BULL 627 (1999).

is subject to formal enforcement, voluntary reciprocity declines along with the overall level of cooperation. These experimental results suggest that formal legal sanctions and informal sanctions based on reciprocity may well conflict with each other. In other words, formal enforcement may "crowd out" behavior based on moralistic reciprocity.[41]

A careful examination of the experimental evidence shows, however, that the crowding-out phenomenon is complex. A number of studies have confirmed the crowding-out hypothesis in single-shot interactions between strangers. In single-iteration experiments, where the parties must choose either informal or formal enforcement, the choice of formal enforcement uniformly suppresses the evidence of reciprocity that is found in the alternative scenario of no formal enforcement.[42] But recent experiments show that, where there is some probability that the same buyers and sellers will continue transacting in the next period, formal enforcement that is limited *only to the verifiable dimensions of the agreement* actually enhances cooperation in those dimensions of the agreement that are nonverifiable.[43]

As applied to the hypothetical *Case of the Falling Phosphate Prices*, these experimental results point consistently in the same direction. Formal legal enforcement can complement and support informal enforcement, but only when the contracting parties deploy it narrowly to supplement informal enforcement. Thus, when legal enforcement purports to enforce *only the verifiable terms of a contract*, and where the parties believe in the prospect of an ongoing relationship, the evidence suggests that the option of formal enforcement may stimulate trust, thereby enabling parties better to enforce the nonverifiable portions of the relationship.

But the experimental evidence of crowding out undermines the claims of many contemporary scholars that courts should go further and hold that relational contracts (such as the phosphate contract described earlier) create reciprocal "relational" duties.[44] In our hypothetical case, for example, the changed circumstances that materialized after the parties made the contract would impose severe losses on the buyer unless the court granted relief from the contract's specific quantity obligations. Scholars have argued that the severity

[41]  Robert E. Scott, *A Theory of Self-Enforcing Indefinite Agreements*, note 3 *supra*, at 1689–90.

[42]  *See, e.g.*, Bruno S. Frey & Reto Jegan, *Motivation Crowding Theory*, 15 J. Econ. Surveys 589 (2001); Bruno Frey & Matthias Benz, Motivation Transfer Effect, University of Zurich, Institute for Empirical Research in Economics (2001); Iris Bohnet, Bruno S. Frey, & Steffen Huck, note 40 *supra*; Ernst Fehr & Simon Gächter, note 40 *supra*.

[43]  Sergio Lazzarini, Gary J. Miller, & Todd R. Zenger, *Order with Some Law: Complementarity versus Substitution of Formal and Informal Arrangements*, 20 J. L. Econ. & Org. 261 (2004).

[44]  Robert Hillman, *Court Adjustment of Long-Term Contracts: An Analysis Under Modern Contract Law*, 1987 Duke L. J. 1.

of the consequences of applying available contractual remedies – whether specific performance or damages – implies that the disadvantaged party did not fully consent to the losses that enforcement would cause. In this situation, they maintain, courts should create broad contractual obligations – such as the obligation to adjust the contract terms so as to treat one's contracting partner "fairly." But this understandable instinct to relieve the burden on the disadvantaged party may well prove counterproductive in the long run. If the court grants the buyer's request for adjustment in the *Case of the Falling Phosphate Prices*, future parties negotiating similar contracts are likely to be disadvantaged. The evidence suggests that an attempt to extend formal enforcement to nonverifiable contract terms – such as the obligation to adjust terms in good faith – is likely to impair the efficacy of those informal means of enforcement that rely on reciprocity norms.

Significantly, the common law of contract has firmly resisted demands for expansion of its domain. The classical common law rules make contractual liability hard to assume and hard to escape once assumed. If a promise falls within the scope of legal enforcement, this body of law fills only a few gaps and uses simple, verifiable default rules when it does.[45] The common law's parsimonious approach to the domain of formal contract enforcement stands in sharp contrast, however, to the much more expansive approach of contemporary commercial statutes such as Article 2 (Sales) of the Uniform Commercial Code and the Convention on the International Sales of Goods (CISG). Each of these laws is replete with directions to judges to modify express agreements in light of postcontractual information subject to soft, generally unverifiable standards.

The evidence of powerful informal norms enforcing commitments that courts cannot readily verify suggests that the common law approach may prove to be the wiser one. Contracting parties may simply prefer to behave under two sets of rules – an explicit (and fairly hard) set of rules for those parts of their relationship that require legal enforcement and an implicit (and flexible) set of rules for those aspects that respond best to self-enforcement. The more general lesson for legal policy makers is that any effort to judicialize preferences for fairness and reciprocity may well destroy the very informality that makes them so effective in the first instance.

The experimental evidence suggests that the contemporary instinct of some policy makers to impose broad standards of reasonableness and fair treatment on contracting parties may actually undermine the very norms of reciprocity

---

[45] For discussion, see Robert E. Scott, note 33 *supra*; Robert E. Scott, *The Case for Formalism in Relational Contracts*, 94 Nw. U. L. Rev. 847 (2000); Robert E. Scott, *A Relational Theory of Default Rules for Commercial Contracts*, 19 J. Legal Stud. 597, 615 (1990).

that the legal system wishes to advance. If so, it is critical that we do not generalize about the potency of reciprocal fairness from litigated cases, as these disputes only arise when informal enforcement has broken down. The cases by themselves give no clue of the power of reciprocity in the enforcement of even agreements between perfect strangers. Understood in this broader context, the wisdom of the common law approach becomes clearer. And, as we will show, a strong case exists for extending this approach to international law enforcement.

## Explaining the Rivalry between Formal and Informal Enforcement

Why does the threat of losing profitable future dealings complement a prefer-ence for reciprocity while extension of formal legal sanctions to nonverifiable obligations undermine the very same preference? One possibility is that the explicit, ex ante nature of legal sanctions may signal an unwillingness to recip-rocate. Fair types may regard the threat of formal sanctions as simply unfair. Selfish types may interpret the willingness to expend resources to create a threat of legal sanction as a signal that the promisee is unlikely to be a reciprocator. The same formal threat does not exist where the sanction (say, terminating the relationship) is imposed ex post and only after defection has been observed. In that sense, ex post punishment may be perceived as "fairer" than the ex ante announcement of sanctions for breach of an obligation.[46]

There is another, and we believe even better, explanation for the crowding-out phenomenon. A careful analysis of the nature of reciprocal behavior and the constraints of formal sanctions shows that when formal rules and associated sanctions occupy the entire domain of a relationship, they interfere with the mechanisms that support reciprocity. An extended example best illustrates the point.

As any tennis player knows, in informal matches each player calls the oppo-nent's balls either inside or outside the lines on his side of the court. When the match is part of a formal competition, however, line judges and a chair umpire, who enforces the rules of the game under the threat of various sanctions rang-ing from loss of a point to forfeiture of the match, make the line calls. Most readers are familiar with the antics of Hall of Fame tennis player John McEnroe, who famously disputed many line calls during his very successful career as a professional tennis player. But what may not be as well known is that report-edly McEnroe was (and presumably still is) known for his generosity in giving

---

[46] Robert E. Scott & Paul B. Stephan, note 25 *supra*, at 580.

close calls to an opponent when playing tennis without a formal referee. What explains this apparent anomaly?

One explanation is that reciprocity simply does not work in formal settings where the parties agree in advance to abide by "the rules of the game" and arbiters impose sanctions for rule violations. Assume, for example, that John McEnroe plays a refereed match at Wimbledon and his opponent's serve strikes just inside the service line for an "ace," but the line judge calls the serve out. McEnroe, consistent with his preference for reciprocal fairness, points to where the serve has landed and generously concedes the point, *as he is permitted to do under the rules of the game.* Notice, however, that the opponent cannot easily and clearly reciprocate McEnroe's generosity so as to establish a "tit for tat" cooperative equilibrium. Assume, for instance, that in the ensuing game McEnroe's serve is almost an ace, but lands just outside the service line. Because the ball was close to the line, his opponent would like to concede the point to McEnroe as a reciprocating gesture. But the rules of the game – *which govern the entire interaction between the players* – prohibit this particular act of generosity. In a refereed match a player is not permitted to overrule the line call of a ball that is correctly called out. Of course, on an ensuing point the opponent can deliberately hit the ball into the net or otherwise sacrifice a point, but this action is ambiguous and any attempt to clarify the purpose of this action (say, by announcing that you are not going to try to win the next point) would risk a sanction from the chair umpire.

A skeptic might respond that the difference in behavior between refereed and self-called games only reflects incentives. Refereed games involve significant monetary compensation, whereas self-called tennis games typically involve only pride. But this response is unsatisfactory for two reasons. First, in the case of championship athletes, a lifetime of training typically results in the complete internalization of the desire to win, regardless of external incentives. Champions generally do not know how to shirk. Second, and more importantly, in games where moral clarity dominates, third-party referees are not used at all, even with very high monetary stakes. Professional golf, for example, dispenses prizes that if anything are greater than those used in tennis, yet it relies largely on self-enforced rules backed up by social norms and the possibility of boycotting opportunists.

One can construct similar examples to compare informal and formal (refereed) play of any game with predetermined rules that completely govern the game. The point is that formal enforcement of a comprehensive set of predetermined rules has the effect of substituting the enforcement of the rules for the underlying informal standards used by the participants themselves in the absence of a referee. The rules of the game as enforced by the third-party arbiter supplant the informal standards because informal standards depend on clear signals of reciprocity to function well. Formal enforcement of comprehensive rules reduces both the clarity of any opponent's response as well as opportunities to reciprocate in kind. Rules, by their nature inflexible, dispense with the flexibility needed to make a proportionate response.

But what of the formal enforcement of standards? To be sure, contract law permits the parties to set up the "contract game" according to broad standards whose content will be supplied subsequently by courts and not by ex ante rules established by the parties. But recall that courts do not apply contract standards directly to the underlying facts, as the parties themselves would in an informal reciprocal interaction. Rather, courts translate contractual standards into more or less accurate evidentiary proxies that they then use to verify compliance with the standards.

Over time, the proxies that courts use to verify contractual standards become "rule-like" in the sense that they are part of the legal "consequences" of contracting and are so understood by the parties ex ante. This process is most evident in the common law system of precedent in which specific applications of general standards become part of the ex ante set of rules that then influence the behavior of future parties. The only way to prevent evidentiary proxies for broad standards from becoming part of the structure of rules would be to return to the original conception of the English Star Chamber where the proceedings and their resolution would play out in a "black box." Yet the potential for unfairness and arbitrary decision making that characterizes the information-impoverished environment of such proceedings may explain why the Star Chamber evolved into a parallel system of equity "rules" that ultimately was absorbed by the courts of law.

## Summary

It may well be the case that only lawyers would see anything paradoxical in a world with increasingly complex relationships and only limited formal law. Their occupational hazard is to assume that without more law there is insufficient social order. As we observed in Chapter 1, international lawyers in particular seem to suffer from this problem, as they campaign for ever greater extensions of formal enforcement of international rules.

The theoretical basis for a claim that the choice of formal enforcement of a rule may make informal enforcement more costly is, we believe, reasonably well established. The claim, one must remember, does not mean that formal enforcement cannot be optimal. Rather, it asserts the necessity of considering the trade-off, in terms of losing the social welfare attributable to informal enforcement, that results when one establishes formal enforcement. Having established the plausibility of the theory, we now will test the theory in practice.

In the next two chapters, we will describe the formal enforcement of international law that currently exists, and then review the evidence that crowding out does operate. Documenting the phenomenon is challenging, because to some extent it requires us to prove a negative, that is, a drop in informal enforcement. We have chosen to focus on several case histories. In each there existed uncertainty about the availability of formal enforcement of a set of international rules. In two cases, a reduction in uncertainty resulting from a clear repudiation of the prospect of formal enforcement coincided with the expansion and deepening of the rules in question, although we cannot prove causation. In two other cases, the growing threat of more formal enforcement substantially undermined the regime in question. We regard this evidence, although only anecdotal, as sufficient to justify taking seriously the possibility that crowding out exists.

If we are right, there is a message for all legal policy makers: Beware of the myth of legal centrism. The consequences of an expansion of the domain of formal enforcement are likely to be a reduction in the potency of informal norms such as reciprocal fairness. Precisely because fairness matters, therefore, the law is wise to leave space for reciprocity to work. In short, the lesson may simply be that fairness imposed is fairness denied.[47]

---

[47] Robert E. Scott, *The Death of Contract Law*, note 33 *supra*, at 389–90.

# 5 PATTERNS OF INTERNATIONAL LAW ENFORCEMENT

[A] judge deciding in reliance on an international norm will find a substantial element of discretionary judgment in the decision.

Sosa v. Alvarez-Machain, 542 U.S.692, 726 (2004) (Souter, J.)

IN CHAPTER 1, WE INTRODUCED THE DISTINCTION BETWEEN FORMAL and informal enforcement of international law. Here we expand on the concept. Formal enforcement, as we have used the term, requires that the law enforcer enjoy independence from national political authorities and has powers that lend salience to its decisions. As either independence or powers wane, the enforcement function depends less on the authority of the enforcer and more on the cooperation of others. As enforcement becomes dispersed, it becomes informal.

A few examples illustrate the distinction. A tribunal (whether domestic or international) whose members serve for substantial terms, the docket of which is not subject to the control of national political authorities, and which has the authority to impose fines or otherwise punish offenders has greater independence than one formed on an ad hoc basis to resolve a dispute at the request of the affected governments.[1] The European Court of Justice (ECJ), the members of which serve for six years, which hears cases brought by individuals, national courts, and Community organs in addition to those brought by national governments, and which can impose money judgments with formal effect in national law, unambiguously carries out formal enforcement of

---

[1] For a fuller discussion of the factors that indicate the independence of a tribunal, see Eric A. Posner & John C. Yoo, *Judicial Independence in International Tribunals*, 93 CALIF. L. REV. 1, 26–27 (2005). We diverge from Posner and Yoo by including enforcement powers as a factor in tribunal independence.

Community law.[2] At the opposite extreme, the so-called Molotov-Ribbentrop Pact of 1939, the nonaggression treaty between the German Reich and the Soviet Union that cleared the way for the start of World War II, relied entirely on the two parties' resources to ensure compliance. Article V of the Treaty did state that the parties could refer disputes to arbitration, but it neither provided for any particular arbitral mechanism nor stipulated what authority the arbitration tribunal would have.[3] Community law, in other words, exemplifies hard law, and the Molotov-Ribbentrop Pact exemplifies the opposite.

## INFORMAL ENFORCEMENT

A first cut at explaining informal enforcement of international law involves showing what it is not. We understand formal enforcement as analogous to the strongest forms of domestic law enforcement, where interested parties can invoke the authority of a disinterested tribunal to obtain authoritative determinations backed up by credible sanctions under the tribunal's control. Take away one or more of these core elements of formal enforcement, and we have informal enforcement.

Informal enforcement is not nonenforcement. Consider again the Molotov-Ribbentrop Pact, which in hindsight seems the epitome of cynicism and contempt for law in the treaty process. Yet it would be wrong to say that the agreement did not work. To the contrary, it provided a temporary solution to problems that Germany and the Soviet Union faced in managing the imminent European crisis. The Pact identified a course of conduct that the signatories would undertake and then let their ensuing behavior bolster the prior commitments. Although the Pact died when Germany invaded the Soviet Union in June 1941, its consequences remain with us today. The Soviet Union relied on the Pact as a ground for its incorporation of the Baltic states, and today the Russian Federation cites the Pact as a basis for not compensating those states for the roughly fifty years of Soviet occupation.

During the life of the Pact, its division of Europe, shortly thereafter realized by force of arms, not only lowered the risk of post-invasion conflicts but gave each side the opportunity to signal trustworthiness and willingness to

---

[2] Note in particular Articles 244 and 256 of the Consolidated Version of the Treaty Establishing the European Community, which obligates the members of the Community automatically to enforce monetary awards by the Court through the conventional national civil procedure.

[3] Treaty of Non-Aggression, Aug. 23, 1939, F.R.G.-U.S.S.R., 1939 RGBl. II, No. 38, translated in 7 DOCUMENTS ON GERMAN FOREIGN POLICY, 1918–1945, at 245 (Series D) (U.S. Dept. of State 1956); Secret Additional Protocol, Aug. 23, 1939, in 7 DOCUMENTS ON GERMAN FOREIGN POLICY, *supra*, at 246.

cooperate. Compliance with the Pact was costly to the extent that either country passed up beneficial opportunities to seize different shares of Poland and the Baltic states and to safeguard against attacks in ways that could seem to pose a threat of aggression to each other. They absorbed these costs because the Pact produced at least modest benefits as well. During the period that Germany adhered to the Pact, both countries avoided confusion and uncertainty about the division of Europe and supplied each with information about the other's nature as a cooperating state. That the Soviet side spectacularly misinterpreted the significance of Germany's behavior, and thus found itself vulnerable to an opportunistic repudiation of the nonaggression obligation, should not obscure this last point.

Between the poles of the ECJ and the Molotov-Ribbentrop Pact lie many intermediate instances of informal international law enforcement. Consider the Dispute Settlement Body (DSB) of the World Trade Organization (WTO). The framers of the GATT, working in 1947, assumed that states would resolve trade disputes through diplomacy, with secrecy, pragmatism, payoffs, and freedom from precedential consequences dominating the process. By the 1950s, however, the parties found themselves referring their grievances not to diplomats but to trade law experts, who would respond with detailed and published legal opinions outlining the rights and duties of the parties in light of the GATT commitments. Panels of arbiters replaced trade negotiators as the preferred mechanism of dispute resolution. A 1979 agreement among GATT members codified this legalization of the dispute-resolution process.[4]

The 1994 Uruguay Round Agreements, which created the WTO to bolster the GATT, established the Appellate Body as a permanent institution for reviewing and rationalizing the extant panel process. The 1994 Agreements also contain a provision declaring that the decisions of the Appellate Body and the panels constitute binding determinations with regard to the rights and duties of the disputants, absent a consensus decision by the WTO members to alter the outcome. The DSB comprises the panel process, the Appellate Body, and the WTO membership acting in their dispute-resolution capacity.[5]

Other regional trade agreements contain similar dispute-resolution mechanisms. An incomplete list would include the European Free Trade Area (EFTA)

---

[4] Understanding Involving Notification, Consultation, Dispute Settlement and Surveillance, GATT Doc. L/4907 (Nov. 28, 1979).

[5] Understanding on the Rules and Procedures Governing the Settlement of Disputes, http://www.wto.org/english/docs_e/legal_e/28-dsu.pdf (last visited October 3, 2005). On GATT and WTO dispute settlement generally, see Andrew Guzman & Beth A. Simmons, *To Settle or Empanel? An Empirical Analysis of Litigation and Settlement at the World Trade Organization*, 31 J. LEG. STUD. S205 (2002); Paul B. Stephan, *Sheriff or Prisoner? The United States and the World Trade Organization*, 1 CHI. J. INT'L L. 49 (2000).

Court, Chapter 20 of NAFTA, Chapter 20 of the Central American Free Trade Agreement (CAFTA), and the Economic Court of the Commonwealth of Independent States (CIS). The EFTA Court and the CIS Economic Court, like the WTO Appellate Body, are standing institutions; the two Western Hemisphere free trade agreements use ad hoc panels of arbiters. All of these mechanisms limit participation to state parties and lack direct authority to impose sanctions. For our purposes, an analysis of their functions is subsumed in our discussion of the WTO DSB.

The WTO DSB has greater independence than the former GATT panel system had.[6] But, compared to the ECJ, it still operates under significant constraints. First, only states can initiate and terminate WTO dispute resolution. The real party in interest in trade disputes – exporting producers and consumers of imported goods faced with a trade barrier, or domestic producers seeking protection from foreign competition – cannot vindicate their rights directly, or even decide how much to invest in the dispute-resolution process. Although they may exhort their governments to take action, they cannot dictate to their governments what to do or what arguments to stress or ignore. Yet the incentives of governments and victims to prosecute a claim are likely to diverge greatly. Victims typically capture much of the benefit from resolution of a dispute, while the costs of success, such as retaliation by the losing side, usually are spread across diverse interests represented imperfectly by the government.[7]

Of even greater significance is the absence of any authority on the part of the WTO DSB to impose self-executing sanctions on wrongdoers. The body's finding that a member has suffered from another's failure to meet an obligation under one or more of the Uruguay Round Agreements results in a call for the offending state to bring itself into compliance with its responsibilities. If the offender does not remedy its lapse within a reasonable period of time, the victim can impose trade sanctions on the offender. The DSB must approve these measures, which cannot exceed what, in the view of the DSB, is necessary to compensate the victim for the ongoing effects of an unremedied violation.[8] In particular, the victim has no right to retrospective compensation, and even the "compensation" that applies prospectively operates only through increased

---

[6] For elaboration of the point, see Eric A. Posner & John C. Yoo, note 1 *supra*, at 44–46.

[7] *See* Alan O. Sykes, *Public versus Private Enforcement of International Economic Law: Standing and Remedy*, 34 J. Leg. Stud. 631 (2005); Mark L. Movsesian, *Enforcement of WTO Rulings: An Interest Group Analysis*, 32 Hofstra L. Rev. 1 (2003); Jide Nzelibe, *The Credibility Imperative: The Political Dynamics of Retaliation in the World Trade Organization's Dispute Resolution Mechanism*, 6 Theoretical Inquiries in Law 215 (2005).

[8] Understanding on the Rules and Procedures Governing the Settlement of Disputes, note 5 *supra*, art. 22.

duties that impose costs on the victim's consumers. As a result, the choice as to what costs the offender should bear rests ultimately with the victimized state, subject only to ceilings set by the DSB. As noted earlier, a state's government faces incentives that diverge from those of the exporters and consumers harmed by the illegal practice.

The International Court of Justice (ICJ) in the Hague is another international dispute settlement body that, like the WTO DSB, has the authority to determine the rights and obligations of states but not directly to enforce its decisions. Its Statute was promulgated in 1945, simultaneously with the UN Charter, and has not been amended. The ICJ has less independence than does the WTO DSB, inasmuch as much of its jurisdiction depends on special agreements by states to submit a dispute, rather than on ex ante commitments to recognize the ICJ as the authoritative interpreter of a particular treaty.[9] Like the WTO DSB, it can exhort the parties to a dispute to comply with its rulings but has no resources directly to induce compliance.

A naive reader of the UN Charter might observe that although the ICJ has no formal enforcement powers, the UN Security Council does. Article 94(1) of the Charter proclaims the duty of all UN members to comply with an ICJ judgment, and Article 94(2) gives the Security Council the right to "decide upon measures to be taken to give effect to the judgment." The passive voice used by this provision, however, betrays the limits of this authority. The Security Council has no coercive resources at its call; rather, it can only ask states to impose military or economic sanctions against wrongdoers. Perhaps because of this limitation, and perhaps because of the real possibility of any of the five permanent members (China, France, the Russian Federation, the United Kingdom, and the United States) exercising its veto right to forestall a Security Council decision, no state ever has invoked Article 94(2) as a basis for enforcing an ICJ judgment.

Finally, the International Tribunal on the Law of the Sea (ITLOS) adjudicates claims arising under the United Nations Convention on the Law of the Sea, a multilateral treaty that went into effect in 1994. For all practical purposes, only states have access to the ITLOS, just as in the case of the WTO DSB and the

[9] On the modern trend away from accepting ICJ jurisdiction in advance of a dispute arising, as well as the decline in the number of special agreement cases, see Eric A. Posner, The Decline of the International Court of Justice (John M. Olin Program in Law and Economics Working Paper No. 233, 2004); Eric A. Posner & John C. Yoo, *Reply to Helfer and Slaughter*, 93 CALIF. L. REV. 957, 971–73 (2005). Subsequent to the publication of these studies, the ICJ suffered yet another significant loss of jurisdiction when the United States withdrew from the Optional Protocol to the Vienna Convention on Consular Relations, a treaty that designated the ICJ as the authoritative interpreter of the Convention. The effectiveness of the U.S. withdrawal is controversial, and the ICJ in the past has asserted its own authority to disregard a state's withdrawal from its jurisdiction. *See* Case Concerning Military and Paramilitary Activities in and against Nicaragua (Nicaragua v. United States of America), [1986] I.C.J. 14, 23–25.

ICJ.[10] Moreover, a state can accede to the Convention without accepting ITLOS jurisdiction, except in the case of disputes over the detaining of a vessel or its crew.[11] Like the ICJ, the ITLOS expects parties to comply with its rulings but has no enforcement power. Article 296(1) of the Convention states that "Any decision rendered by a court or tribunal having jurisdiction under this section shall be final and shall be complied with by all the parties to the dispute." But nothing in the Convention says what happens if a party ignores this command.

To say that the WTO DSB, the ICJ, and the ITLOS embody informal enforcement of international obligations is not to argue that they are ineffectual. First, not all the work of these tribunals involves conflicts where enforcement matters. Some of the disputes they confront entail coordination problems where a definitive resolution has value regardless of its distributive consequences. In these cases, where no one loses (or at least no one loses much) as long as the tribunal provides a coherent decision grounded on familiar arguments plausibly derived from past authority, additional investment in enforcement is unnecessary. A study by Tom Ginsburg and Richard McAdams demonstrates that states regularly comply with ICJ determinations of boundary disputes, in spite of the absence of formal enforcement. Many of these conflicts involved rather small and peripheral territories, and clarity of the applicable rules seemed more important than the specifics of the boundary.[12]

But other disputes involve collective action problems where enforcement is salient. As the literature reviewed in the prior two chapters indicates, informal enforcement may provide robust, and in some circumstances, optimal, incentives for cooperation. We will postpone until Chapter 6 our analysis of whether informal enforcement, in the context of these tribunals, may be optimal. First, we want to look more closely at the specific forms of informal enforcement that the tribunals invoke.

## RETALIATION

In Chapter 3, we discussed how retaliation works to induce private cooperation. Given sufficiently low discount rates and indefinite prospects of ending the relationship, parties can optimize their cooperation by manifesting a

[10] The Convention on the Law of the Sea contains a Part XI that creates the International Seabed Authority, a regime for administering deep seabed mining operations, and envisions a time when disputes over that regime might be brought by interested persons to the ITLOS. But although the Authority has been created and occupies a resplendent headquarters in Jamaica, it has not entered into any contracts to exploit these resources and accordingly has engendered no disputes.

[11] Convention on the Law of the Sea, arts. 297, 298, Dec. 10, 1982, 1833 U.N.T.S. 397 (1994). Again, hypothetically the ITLOS has compulsory jurisdiction over seabed disputes, but at present these do not exist.

[12] Tom Ginsburg & Richard H. McAdams, *Adjudicating in Anarchy: An Expressive Theory of International Dispute Resolution*, 45 WM. & MARY L. REV. 1229 (2004).

willingness to retaliate against uncooperative conduct. Secure in the knowledge that these threats can work, the parties can invest in cooperation and divide the resulting surplus between themselves.

International law also uses retaliation as an enforcement mechanism. The WTO system in particular builds retaliation into its procedures. A study by Eric Reinhardt indicates that the decision to invoke the WTO DSB is strongly influenced by retaliatory motives. In investigating all GATT and WTO disputes between 1948 and 1998, he found that the single best predictor in determining whether a government would bring a claim against another state was the initiation of a claim against that government by the same state within the prior year.[13]

Retaliation in the WTO DSB goes beyond the decision to initiate a proceeding. When a party prevails, it acquires the right to impose otherwise impermissible trade sanctions against the transgressor. In several high profile disputes between the United States and the European Community, for example, the WTO DSB authorized targeted trade restrictions in the face of ongoing noncompliance. In three instances the offending state subsequently reached an accommodation with its critics; in two others the offender, as of this writing, has not yet responded.[14]

As we discuss later, retaliation is a less straightforward process than superficial analysis might suggest. A speculation by Richard Posner as to why states generally comply with international conventions on the treatment of prisoners of war hints at the shortfalls of this mechanism as an enforcement device. When engaged in war, Posner notes, states may wish to have a reputation for dangerous, even irrational ferocity but still adhere to minimum standards of decency regarding prisoners:

If both sides hold the same number of prisoners, each has a simple and effective means of retaliation if its opponent mistreats its prisoners. If one has very few

---

[13] Eric Reinhardt, Aggressive Multilateralism: The Determinants of GATT/WTO Dispute Initiation, 1948–1998 (Feb. 2000).

[14] See, e.g., European Communities – Measures Concerning Meat and Meat Products (Hormones), Original Complaint by the United States, Recourse to Arbitration by the European Communities under Article 22.6 of the DSU (WT/DS26/ARB, July 12, 1999); European Communities – Regime for the Importation, Sale and Distribution of Bananas, Recourse to Arbitration by the European Communities under Article 22.6 of the DSU (WT/DS27/ARB/ECU, March 24, 2000); United States – Tax Treatment for "Foreign Sales Corporations", Recourse to Arbitration by the United States under Article 22.6 of the DSU and Article 4.11 of the SCM Agreement (WT/DS108/ARB, August 30, 2002); United States – Anti-Dumping Act of 1916 (Original Complaint by the European Communities), Recourse to Arbitration by the United States under Article 22.6 of the DSU (WT/DS136/ARB, February 24, 2004); United States – Continued Dumping and Subsidy Offset Act of 2000 (Original Complaint by the European Communities), Recourse to Arbitration by the United States under Article 22.6 of the DSU (WT/DS217/ARB/EEC, August 31, 2004).

prisoners relative to the other, this means it is probably losing the war and so will fear punishment if it mistreats its few prisoners; also there will be few benefits, since the cost of maintaining only a few prisoners will be small. The winning side, which holds a disproportionate number of prisoners, can afford to maintain them, precisely because it is winning, and so has little to gain from mistreating them, especially since there is some, though perhaps only a small, risk that its opponent will retaliate against the prisoners that it holds.[15]

This example illustrates the dynamics of hostage taking, a well studied problem in the literature.[16] Absent hostages, however, retaliation becomes problematic where one side appears to have nothing left to lose. An abrogation of an agreement, such as the surprise end of the Molotov-Ribbentrop Pact, puts the denouncer in the position of expecting no further benefits from the arrangement and therefore makes it indifferent to any putative benefits that the counterparty might withhold. Under these circumstances, retaliation ceases to be a rational strategy: It costs the victim something to retaliate and the wrongdoer will lose nothing to which it otherwise believes itself entitled. After the German invasion, the Soviet Union no longer had any leverage under the Pact. Although it could resist the invasion and, ultimately, did invade and vanquish Germany, its capacity to punish Germany for its defection had nothing to do with the Pact itself.

The Molotov-Ribbentrop Pact example simply illustrates a point we made in Chapter 3: To work effectively as a means of informal enforcement of obligations, retaliation requires mutuality and anticipated future benefits from the reciprocal relationship. Once the parties envision the end game, mutuality and future gains disappear, and retaliation loses its sting. The dynamic functions in international law enforcement as much as it does in private contract. This observation, however, does not mean that other informal enforcement mechanisms also stop working.

[15] Richard A. Posner, *Some Economics of International Law: Comments on Conference Papers*, 31 J. LEG. STUD. S321, S325 (2002). The example exposes a puzzle, however: Why do states bother to codify the rules regarding prisoners of war if they know they will face retaliation if they lose? During World War II, for example, Japan was not a signatory to the 1929 Geneva Convention Relative to the Treatment of Prisoners of War, but after the war the United States still held war crime trials and executed many Japanese soldiers for mistreating U.S. prisoners. One possibility is to regard some instruments not as contracts, but rather as a form of coordination. From this perspective, a state adheres to the Geneva Conventions not only to bind itself, but to announce to potential future adversaries what standards it will apply to their conduct. Also, a state might join such an agreement to limit its obligations to those contained in the text, rather than facing the uncertain standards of victors' justice.

[16] The classic analysis remains Thomas Schelling, *An Essay on Bargaining*, 46 AM. ECON. REV. 281 (1956). *See also* Robert E. Scott, *A Relational Theory of Secured Financing*, 86 COLUM. L. REV. 901 (1986); Oliver E. Williamson, *Credible Commitments: Using Hostages to Support Exchange*, 73 AM. ECON. REV. 519 (1983).

REPUTATION

In Chapter 3, we discussed reputation as a complementary factor in inducing compliance with obligations. Reputations survive particular treaties and similar arrangements. A state that exploits an end game situation, as Germany did with respect to the Soviet Union, suffers a reputational loss in the eyes of all observers, not just those of its counterparty. To the extent a reputation for reliability induces valuable cooperation on collective action projects, a state will invest in behavior that augments this quality and will avoid otherwise beneficial behavior that incurs reputational costs.

What do tribunals add to this? The accessibility of WTO DSB, ICJ, and ITLOS decisions affects the reputational incentives of disputants. The dynamics of this process are complex, however, because the effect depends on the reputations of both the tribunal and the affected state, and both reputations are subject to updating and discontinuities. These factors require separate analysis, even though to some degree they are interdependent.

On the one hand, tribunal decisions lower the costs to third parties of determining whether a state honors its promises.[17] Rather than confronting an argument between interested parties about what took place and what it meant, other actors – states, international organizations, firms, news media, nonprofit organizations, and individuals – have a ready reference point for interpreting the dispute. Having a cheap and easy means of determining whether a state honors its obligations might induce a virtuous cycle. Lowering the cost of assessing a state's reputation should lead to more widespread reliance on reputation as a means of enforcement, which in turn might increase the returns to states that invest in acquiring a positive reputation.

On the other hand, endowing a tribunal with the power to make or break reputations is not a straightforward matter. Tribunals can make mistakes or pursue a separate agenda. An especially discreditable decision – one that appears poorly reasoned, unanticipated in light of prior legal authorities, or biased – may immediately undermine a tribunal's ability to affect the reputation of others. Moreover, where a tribunal has no direct powers of enforcement, persistent refusal by one or more significant states to comply with its decisions may diminish the tribunal's reputation for inducing compliance. Thus, tribunals can lose their capacity to affect reputations if they are seen as either wrong or ineffectual.

To complicate matters further, states can undergo internal changes that may offset reputational effects. Consider the so-called Rose, Orange, and Tulip

---

[17]   We take this to be the central point of Andrew T. Guzman, *A Compliance-Based Theory of International Law*, 90 CAL. L. REV. 1823 (2002). *See also* Andrew T. Guzman, *The Cost of Credibility: Explaining Resistance to Interstate Dispute Resolution Mechanisms*, 31 J. LEG. STUD. 303 (2002).

Revolutions in Georgia, the Ukraine, and Kyrgyzstan, each emulating to some degree Czechoslovakia's Velvet Revolution and the Aquino uprising that brought about the fall of the Marcos regime in the Philippines. Reaching further into the past, recall also the military coups of the 1960s and 1970s that ousted democratically elected governments in Argentina, Brazil, and Chile and the transition from authoritarian and militarist regimes to democratic rule in Spain, Portugal, and Greece. Common elements define these events: The formal state structure, as a matter of international law, continued, as did the fundamental domestic constitutional order; the transition to a greater or lesser extent employed extralegal mechanisms; and the new élite in each case presented itself internationally as representing a clear break with the past. We consider each of these events as a regime change, in the sense that the new government plausibly could face the outside world shorn of the reputation built up by its predecessor. For our purposes, it does not matter whether the effect is positive or negative: International reputations both good and bad can be shed as a result of internal events.

Conversely, normal political turnover does not constitute regime change. Consider the example of the United States. There are those who claim that new administrations can bring about profound changes in international relations, but the evidence suggests that replacing the party at the head of the Executive does remarkably little. Most of the instances, for example, in which the Bush administration has manifested an unwillingness to join multilateral regimes – the Kyoto Protocol, the International Criminal Court, the Comprehensive Test Ban Treaty, the International Land Mine Convention – reflect Senate opposition that antedated the 2000 election. Regime change in the United States requires a fundamental restructuring in the constitutional order and arguably last took place during the Roosevelt administration.

Both the WTO DSB and the ICJ illustrate the complexity of reputation development of an international organization.[18] Take the case of the ICJ first. One still can find scholars and policy makers who speak of the body's prestige and the existence of widespread support for it, but recent trends have not favored the ICJ.[19] China, France, and the United States have withdrawn from the compulsory jurisdiction of the court; no important state has accepted compulsory jurisdiction since those withdrawals; no major power (defined as the top ten

---

[18] Assessing the reputational value of the ITLOS is even more difficult, as so few disputants have sought to invoke its competence. In its first decade of existence, that tribunal has had jurisdiction over only twelve cases, only four of which involved anything other than vessel detention.

[19] For praise of the ICJ, see CONSTANZE SCHULTE, COMPLIANCE WITH DECISIONS OF THE INTERNATIONAL COURT OF JUSTICE 1 (2004): "Business is booming for the International Court of Justice (ICJ). Its prestige and activity have reached unprecedented heights."

national economies) has initiated a case in the ICJ since 1987, save one proceeding brought by Germany against the United States (producing a decision with which the United States refused to comply); and compliance with ICJ judgments generally has declined. A study by Eric Posner and Miguel Figueiredo has detected a pattern of bias in ICJ decisions.[20] Especially controversial have been a series of cases brought under the Vienna Convention on Consular Relations, where the court has rejected without reasoned analysis arguments about the appropriateness of applying procedural requirements to post-conviction challenges of criminal sentences. To date, the Supreme Court of the United States has acceded to the government's defiance of the ICJ.[21] And a Justice of the High Court of Israel, a jurisdiction where formal enforcement of international law is generally the norm, recently published a strikingly direct opinion attacking the integrity and competence of an ICJ judgment:

I read the majority opinion of the International Court of Justice at the Hague, and, unfortunately, I could not discover those distinguishing marks which turn a document into a legal opinion or a judgment of a court. . . . [T]he factual basis upon which the ICJ built its opinion is a ramshackle one. Some will say that the judgment has no worthy factual basis whatsoever. The ICJ reached findings of fact on the basis of general statements of opinion; its findings are general and unexplained; and it seems that it is not right to base a judgment, whether regarding an issue of little or great importance and value, upon findings such as those upon which the ICJ based its judgment. The generality and lack of explanation which characterize the factual aspect of the opinion are not among the distinguishing marks worthy of appearing in a legal opinion or a judgment. Moreover, generality and lack of explanation infuse the opinion with an emotional element, which is heaped on to an extent unworthy of a legal opinion. I might add that in this way, the opinion was colored by a political hue, which legal decision does best to distance itself from, to the extent possible. And if all that is not enough, there is the ICJ's almost complete ignoring of the horrible terrorism and security problems which have plagued Israel – a silence that the reader cannot help noticing – a foreign and strange silence.[22]

[20]  *See* Eric A. Posner & Miguel F. P. de Figueiredo, *Is the International Court of Justice Biased?* 34 J. LEG. STUD. 599 (2005).

[21]  Vienna Convention on Consular Relations (Paraguay v. United States), [1998] I.C.J. 426; LaGrand (Germany v. United States), [2001] I.C.J. 104; Avena and other Mexican Nationals (Mexico v. United States), [2004] I.C.J. 128. The corresponding Supreme Court decisions are Breard v. Greene, 523 U.S. 371 (1998); Federal Republic of Germany v. United States, 526 U.S. 111 (1999); Torres v. Mullin, 540 U.S. 1035 (2003); Medellin v. Dretke, 544 U.S. 660 (2005). The Court had yet another opportunity to address these issues in the joined cases Sanchez-Llamas v. Oregon, No. 04–10566 and Bustillo v. Johnson, No. 05–51, argued March 29, 2006.

[22]  HCJ 7957/04 Mara'abe and Others v. The Prime Minister of Israel and Others, 45 I.L.M. 202, 244–45 (2006) (Cheshin, V.P., concurring).

These trends underline a simple point: Even a tribunal that members of the international law community regard as central can find itself with an impaired capacity to affect reputations. As refusal to submit to ICJ jurisdiction and disregard of its decisions have become more common, the value of the information it generates about the law-abiding characteristics of states has depreciated. As the court becomes less useful, its irrelevance becomes manifest, and the cycle of reputational decline continues.

The WTO DSB presents a more complicated, but not necessarily different, story. The 1994 Uruguay Round Agreements both expanded the scope and scale of international economic law and created a permanent body to oversee the dispute-settlement process. Disentangling the consequences of these two fundamental changes is difficult, but cumulatively they have not enhanced the prestige of the WTO DSB and may have impaired it.

The Uruguay Round Agreements brought new areas under GATT discipline – primarily intellectual property, services such as banking and the professions, and investment requirements – and replaced general principles of nondiscrimination with more detailed and specific rules in several traditional areas of GATT regulation, particularly antidumping, export subsidies and food safety regulation. These new agreements comprised issues on which the negotiating states could not reach consensus and chose to delegate hard questions to the WTO DSB. A series of controversial decisions and some noncompliance followed.[23]

As noted earlier, the Uruguay Round Agreements also replaced a system of ad hoc arbitration of trade disputes with a permanent reviewing body that, as a formal matter, enjoys the final say on questions of WTO law. The WTO DSB acquired greater independence and discretion, independent of the expansion of scope and scale of the matters within its jurisdiction. Eric Posner and John Yoo have argued that with greater independence comes an inclination on the

[23] See Daniel K. Tarullo, Norms and Institutions in Global Competition Policy, 94 AM. J. INT'L L. 478, 494 (2000); Paul B. Stephan, note 5 supra. Appellate Body decisions that meet this description include European Communities – Regime for the Importation, Sale and Distribution of Bananas, AB-1997–3 (applying Agreement on Agriculture); European Communities – Measures Concerning Meat and Meat Products (Hormones), AB-1997–4 (applying Agreement on Sanitary and Phytosanitary Measures); United States – Tax Treatment for "Foreign Sales Corporations," AB-1999–9 (applying Agreement on Subsidies and Countervailing Measures); United States – Section 211 Omnibus Appropriations Act of 1998, AB-2001–7 (applying Agreement on Trade-Related Aspects of Intellectual Property Rights); United States – Continued Dumping and Subsidy Offset Act of 2000, AB-2002–7 (applying Agreement on Implementation of Article VI of the General Agreement on Tariffs and Trade 1994) . In only one of these cases has the offending state brought itself into full compliance with its obligations, although the United States twice has amended its legislation in response to the Foreign Sale Corporations dispute and the European Community has made certain adjustments in its bananas regime.

part of an international tribunal to exploit agency slack. Not having to justify its jurisdiction on a case-by-case basis, they contend, a tribunal might pursue an ideological or private agenda that none of the parties might wish. This in turn might lead states to seek other means of resolving their disputes and to resist those demands that the tribunal does make on their resources. They acknowledge that the data concerning the WTO DSB is inconclusive, although this is partly as a result of the relative newness of the system and the length of time it takes to determine whether a state will comply with a ruling or not. But they suggest that the increased independence of the WTO DSB may not have improved compliance under the Uruguay Round Agreements.[24]

Reputational benefits, in sum, are significant but remain subject to substantial contingencies. Tribunals do not come with reputations, but rather must build them over time on the basis of their observable work. Constructing a sufficiently great institutional reputation to justify regular compliance with a tribunal's decisions is costly. The interdependence between a state's reputation for complying with its obligations, on the one hand, and a tribunal's reputation for providing accurate and unbiased determinations of what those obligations are, on the other hand, may explain why we see relatively few permanent international tribunals of the type exemplified by the WTO DSB, the ICJ, and the ITLOS.[25]

## RATIONAL RECIPROCITY

The WTO DSB illustrates another aspect of informal enforcement that is related to, but distinct from, retaliation and reputational effects. As we discussed in Chapter 4, considerable evidence indicates that a substantial portion of individuals (roughly half) prefer reciprocity in their social interaction and will absorb some costs to satisfy that preference. This preference does not disappear when individuals act collectively, whether through firms or political organizations. It manifests itself in an acceptance of some risk of harm from opportunism, a willingness to absorb some costs to signal a preference for cooperation, and a propensity to engage in costly retaliation against opportunists.

---

[24] Eric A. Posner & John C. Yoo, note 1 *supra*, at 50.

[25] Helfer and Slaughter argue that an exclusive focus on prominent multilateral tribunals misses the emergence in recent years of many regional judicialized bodies endowed with the capacity to address disputes rising under particular international regimes. Laurence R. Helfer & Anne-Marie Slaughter, *Why States Create International Tribunals: A Response To Professors Posner and Yoo*, 93 CALIF. L. REV. 899, 910–17 (2005). With the exception of the ECJ and the ECHR, which we discuss later, the tribunals they list either lack direct enforcement powers, have not attracted much business, or both. Eric A. Posner & John C. Yoo, note 9 *supra*, at 964–67. We will discuss the question of why states would create international tribunals without expecting them to contribute to international law enforcement in the next chapter.

Distinguishing a preference for reciprocity from straightforward retaliation can be difficult. Even if it does not have this preference, a participant in a repeat play game rationally would punish its counterparty for opportunistic behavior whenever the punishment would discourage future defections. A reciprocity preference reinforces that inclination by leading some persons to assume the costs of retaliation even when the possibility of future iterations of the same game is low or uncertain. When we see retaliation, then, we cannot always be sure whether it constitutes further evidence of a preference for reciprocity. We must look for other factors indicating that the retaliating person accepts costs out of proportion to benefits to adduce the independent operation of the preference.

The quantitative evidence of extensive retaliation in WTO DSB dispute selection that we discussed earlier thus does not establish that users of that tribunal manifest a preference for reciprocity. But anecdotal evidence embodied in case studies does suggest the independent operation of a preference for reciprocity as a factor motivating the selection of disputes. In choosing our anecdotes, we concentrate on the EC-US relationship. If one were to treat the EC as a single entity for trade purposes, then these two collectivities account for a significant plurality of world exports and imports.[26] Thus any tendencies exhibited by these two economic superpowers in their dealings with each other are important, even if they were not representative of other international relations.

The economist Wilhelm Kohler has modeled EC-US trade disputes as a cooperative game where each side engages in proportionate defections from their GATT obligations as a means of both signaling updated preferences and inducing reciprocity by the other side.[27] The model justifies engaging in costly retaliation as a means of making cooperative adjustments to initial obligations that have become too costly for one state to honor fully. Full validation of this model is impossible at present, because there have been too few disputes between the United States and the EC to permit rigorous quantitative analysis. The anecdotal evidence embodied in case studies, however, does suggest the

---

[26] Excluding intra-EC trade, in 2002 the European Community accounted for 19 percent of the world's merchandise exports, and the United States for 14 percent. The figures for imports were 18 percent and 23 percent, respectively. Again excluding intra-EC trade, in that year EC merchandise exports to the United States constituted 24 percent of its total, and U.S. merchandise exports to the European Community constituted 20.8 percent of its total. If one were to treat the ten new members that joined the European Community in 2004 as if they already had joined in 2002, these percentages would increase significantly. For WTO statistical trade tables, see http://www.wto.org/english/res_e/statis_e/its2003_e/its03_bysubject_e.htm (last visited May 11, 2005).

[27] Wilhelm Kohler, *The WTO Dispute Settlement Mechanism: Battlefield or Cooperation?* 4 J. INDUSTRY COMPETITION & TRADE 317 (2004).

independent operation of a preference for reciprocity as a factor motivating the selection of disputes.

Consider several prominent cases. Soon after the WTO DSB went into effect, the United States decided to challenge two somewhat peripheral aspects of the EC's extensive protection of its market for food. The first, the *Bananas Regime* case, involved trade preferences for bananas produced in former European colonies to the detriment of those grown by U.S.-owned companies in Central America.[28] Unlike conventional protection, the EC rules did not favor local producers, and unlike conventional victims, the United States produced none of the goods subjected to discrimination. The second case, *Meat Hormones*, involved an EC ban on all meat obtained from animals whose growth had been stimulated by specified hormones.[29] The ban applied to European and foreign producers alike and reflected widely held, although scientifically unproven, fears about the possible health consequences of ingesting this meat.

The choice of these two matters as trade disputes raised eyebrows. On the one hand, neither seems to implicate important U.S. economic interests. The banana producers subject to European discrimination, although based in the United States as a matter of corporate governance, grew and packaged their product elsewhere. Consumer preferences in Europe (which embrace cigarettes and irradiated milk but generally are hostile to food additives) made it unlikely that properly labeled hormone-treated beef would capture many sales. On the other hand, the European regulatory concerns seemed conventional enough. Discriminatory trade preferences for targeted developing countries is a standard practice in North-South relations, and mollifying consumer fears about food products, whether grounded in science or not, seems a normal incident of democratic politics. One wonders what the United States meant to suggest about the broader international trade regime by selecting these issues for formal dispute resolution.

Besides offering a vigorous, if ultimately unsuccessful, defense of its practices, the European Community also responded with reciprocal claims against the United States. One in particular is striking for its complete lack of real economic consequences. In *United States – Anti-Dumping Act of 1916*, the European Community challenged an old statute that provided for a private action by victims of dumping.[30] As interpreted by the courts, this enactment added nothing to the rules and remedies applicable to predatory pricing, whether domestic or international, under U.S. antitrust law. As a formal matter, however, the

---

[28] European Communities – Regime for the Importation, Sale, and Distribution of Bananas, AB-1997–3.

[29] European Communities – Measures Concerning Meat and Meat Products (Hormones), AB-1997–4.

[30] United States – Anti-Dumping Act of 1916, AB-2000–5, -6 (2000).

antidumping law seemed to permit private enforcement of a body of rules applicable exclusively to imports.[31] The European Community argued that the 1994 Antidumping Code forbade such discrimination.

The fact that in all the instances the WTO DSB upheld the complaint and rejected the status quo may suggest that both the European Community and the United States were going after low-hanging fruit, namely regulations that clearly violated GATT rules but had no clear counterparts in their own systems. But this does not explain the case selection, as each dispute presented real costs and little benefits.[32] Each threatened to antagonize an important trading partner and thus invited costly responses, but none involved a claim where a WTO DSB victory would translate into any substantial economic advantage. A first cut, then, might lead to a conclusion that the decisions to initiate these disputes were irrational.

Further reflection, however, suggests that a preference for reciprocity may explain what happened. For both the United States and the European Community, the subjects of the disputes had a context. EC restrictions on agricultural products do harm U.S. producers, but they have a more significant impact on international trade generally. European regulation of food products reflects the Common Agricultural Program (CAP), a subsidies program for domestic producers that constitutes the largest item in the Community's budget and generates most of the charges of corruption in the Community's administration. The barriers to agricultural imports required by the CAP cost developing countries amounts far in excess of the foreign aid budgets of the Community and its member states and have proven an enduring obstacle to progress in multilateral trade liberalism.

Private enforcement of competition law in the United States rankles the European Community in much the way that EC agricultural regulation irritates the United States. The whole idea of private control over public law strikes Europeans as inexplicable, and the application of U.S. competition rules, with their emphasis on dispersion of private decision making, has resulted in sixty years of European protest and reaction. Many states have enacted blocking statutes to prevent their governments and courts from assisting U.S. antitrust litigation, and some have adopted "clawback" laws to recapture punitive damages assessed by U.S. courts against their nationals. This hostility to private enforcement coexists with a willingness to pursue government-to-government

---

[31] Ironically, several years after the WTO DSB expressed its disapproval of the 1916 Act, a private plaintiff actually won damages under the statute against a foreign firm. Goss International Corp. v. Tokyo Kikai Seisakusho, Ltd., 321 F. Supp. 2nd 1039 (N.D. Iowa 2004), aff'd, 434 F.3rd 1081 (8th Cir. 2006).

[32] Fritz Breuss, *WTO Dispute Settlement in Action: An Economic Analysis of Four EU-US Mini-Trade Wars*, 4 J. INDUSTRY COMPETITION & TRADE 275 (2004).

cooperation, as exemplified by 1995 and 1998 agreements between the U.S. Justice Department and the EC. What seems especially to bother the Europeans is the difficulty of reaching stable agreements with the United States about competition, given the inability of the government to bind private plaintiffs and courts.

The U.S. attacks on the bananas regime and the beef hormone rules, seen in this light, represent an effort to identify problems that appear symptomatic of broader European noncooperation with multilateral trade rules and at the same time seem especially perverse given the slight economic stakes for U.S. producers. The European response was symmetrical: The Community identified a U.S. legal regime that had no direct economic importance but seemed to embody what to Europeans seems a larger U.S. problem. Both the United States and the EC engaged in costly attacks (in the sense that the likely advantages seem dwarfed by the possible detriments) to identify noncooperative behavior by the other (in the case of the U.S. disputes) and a willingness to behave reciprocally (in the case of the EC response).

This minuet involving peripheral disputes may explain direct cooperation in areas of greater moment to the two entities. Consider subsidies for civil aviation, implemented in the EC through direct payments to Airbus and in the United States through a combination of government procurement and tax preferences directed at Boeing. If any economic sector might be suitable for clever government implementation of strategic trade theory, civil aviation is it. Economies of scope and scale work to push the industry toward monopoly, which in turn gives governments a rational reason to support a national champion.[33] But international trade law, which rests largely on old-fashioned theories about comparative advantage and gains from trade, bars such governmental support. The 1994 Uruguay Round Agreement on Subsidies and Countervailing Measures in particular would seem to forbid exactly the governmental assistance that strategic trade theory predicts should be forthcoming. The United States and the EC thus face a dilemma: Each can ignore the other's strong incentives to subsidize the industry and act as if the GATT rules barring government subsidies to export industries were to apply, or reach an accommodation that effectively forestalls WTO supervision of their bilateral competition to assume dominance of the industry.

[33] STRATEGIC TRADE POLICY AND THE NEW INTERNATIONAL ECONOMICS (Paul R. Krugman ed. 1986); Elhanan Helpman & Paul R. Krugman, MARKET STRUCTURE AND FOREIGN TRADE – INCREASING RETURNS, IMPERFECT COMPETITION, AND THE INTERNATIONAL ECONOMY (1985); Avinash K. Dixit & Victor Norman, THEORY OF INTERNATIONAL TRADE (1980); Paul R. Krugman, *Is Free Trade Passé?* 1 J. ECON. PERSP. 131 (1987); Kelvin Lancaster, *Intra-industry Trade Under Perfect Monopolistic Competition*, 10 J. INT'L ECON. 151 (1980); Paul R. Krugman, *Increasing Returns, Monopolistic Competition, and International Trade*, 9 J. INT'L ECON. 469 (1979).

The story does not yet have an ending, but events to date are consistent with a preference for reciprocity. In October 2004, the United States took the first step toward seeking a WTO DSB determination on the legality of EC support for Airbus. The European Community simultaneously triggered the WTO DSB process to attack U.S. support for Boeing. At that point, both entities backed away and began negotiating. They reactivated their reciprocal claims before the WTO DSB in May 2005, but this step did not end the negotiations. As long as these talks continue and the two sides delay any action by the WTO DSB, it remains possible to see this episode as an instance of two competitors looking for mutual accommodation. At the same time, the parallel legal claims – each of which has a high probability of success – gives each the possibility of punishing the other for noncooperation, at the cost of probably having its own subsidies condemned.

## Summary

Some international agreements simply identify obligations and leave it to the parties to behave cooperatively or not. Others use tribunals to clarify the obligations and to determine whether particular behavior qualifies as cooperative or not. In both instances, however, enforcement rests on choices made by the parties and (in the case of reputation) interested observers, rather than by an independent enforcement body. These choices, however, need not lead to a breakdown of cooperation. As our earlier chapters indicate, these informal enforcement mechanisms have their counterparts in private relationships that can coordinate complex and valuable cooperative behavior.

## Formal Enforcement

Among international law scholars, some doubt exists about the possibility of formal enforcement of international obligations. International bodies, so the argument goes, lack the resources to sanction lawbreakers. They have no institutions comparable to the sheriff, the police, a prison system, or the military to ensure that others obey their decisions. They depend instead on the willingness of states, or at least of domestic institutions such as national judiciaries, to fulfil their commands, and states always remain free not to cooperate. Nation states thus retain control over the enforcement process, even when they surrender control over the meaning of international law to independent bodies such as the WTO DSB or the ICJ.[34]

---

[34] Scholars who otherwise disagree about everything seem to have this belief in common. *Compare* Anne-Marie Slaughter, A New World Order 185 (2004), *with* Eric A. Posner & John C. Yoo, note 1 *supra*, at 17–18.

We believe this argument is mistaken at two levels. First, it is factually wrong. Some, although not many, international entities do possess something equivalent to the enforcement powers of an independent domestic court. Second, not all kinds of national cooperation are alike. In states with effective separation of powers and an independent judiciary, which is to say throughout the rich world and in a portion of the developing world, giving domestic judges the power to enforce international law means that enforcement will proceed regardless of the views of the government and legislature. In these instances, international law enforcement works like domestic enforcement.

## INTERNATIONAL LAW ENFORCEMENT INSTITUTIONS

It is technically correct that there do not exist any fully independent international law enforcement institutions. Rather, international organs must rely on the resources provided to them by states to enforce their orders. But several tribunals have access to enforcement resources on essentially the same terms that domestic courts have to sheriffs and their ilk. That is to say, these tribunals operate on the understanding that there exist dedicated assets – either financial or institutional – on which they can draw without the mediation of national political authorities to induce compliance. In theory, resistance is a possibility, just as hypothetically a sheriff may refuse to execute a domestic court's judgment.[35] But in most cases disbursement of the resource is a ministerial, not a discretionary, function. We describe the most prominent instances here.

### European Court of Justice and Its Descendants

The European Court of Justice (ECJ) is responsible for legal enforcement of the Treaty Establishing the European Community.[36] It can hear a wide range of challenges to EC law, including those brought by private persons.[37] In particular, the ECJ can decide at the behest of a private person, as well as of EC organs or member states, whether the law of a member state complies with EC law.[38]

---

[35] Lest this possibility seem entirely hypothetical, one should recall that in some countries newly arrived to modern legal arrangements, local authorities systematically refuse to execute domestic judicial judgments. The Russian case has received the most attention. Kathryn Hendley, *Business Litigation in the Transition: A Portrait of Debt Collection in Russia*, 38 LAW & SOC'Y REV. 305 (2004). In addition, as the notorious Marc Rich case illustrates, the subjects of a judicial decision can engage in self-help to evade the consequences. *See* In re Grand Jury Subpoenas Dated March 9, 2001, 179 F. Supp. 2nd 270 (S.D.N.Y. 2001).

[36] Consolidated Version of the Treaty Establishing the European Community, art. 220. The Court of First Instance, a subordinate body to the ECJ, assists in this function. *Id.*

[37] *Id.* arts. 230, 234.

[38] *Id.* arts. 226, 227, 234; van Gend en Loos v. Nederlandse Administratie der Belastingen, Case 26/62, [1963] E.C.R. 1; Costa v. Enel, Case 6/64, [1964] E.C.R. 585.

The enforcement powers of the ECJ rest on three complementary provisions. Article 228 of the EC Treaty gives the court the power to impose fines on states that fail to comply with their obligations under EC law. Article 244 obligates each of the member states to adopt legislation providing for the enforcement of the money judgments of the ECJ against private persons.[39] Finally, the ECJ and national courts both understand Article 234 as imposing on national courts an obligation to enforce judgments of the ECJ regarding EC law, much in the manner that state courts in the United States must respect the mandates of the federal courts.[40]

Buttressing these legal commitments is an important practical reality. The European Community dispenses a considerable amount of money, largely through the Common Agricultural Policy and developmental assistance channeled through the various Structural Funds and the Cohesion Fund. It never has threatened to withhold payments as a means of enforcing its judgments, and scholars do not agree as to whether it has the legal authority to do so.[41] But its control over such large amounts of money hints at least at an implicit threat toward scofflaws, and may explain why those states fined by the ECJ for failure to observe their legal obligations have promptly paid.[42]

The success of the ECJ in turn has spawned several imitators in the developing world. The Court of Justice of the Andean Community, set up in 1979, the Central American Court of Justice, effectively established in 1991, and the Court of Justice for the Common Market of Eastern and Southern Africa, created in 1993, all permit private initiation of disputes and issue orders that, by the terms of the relevant Treaty, member states are obligated to treat as if they were domestic court judgments. Similar bodies are on the drawing boards but have not yet opened for business.[43]

---

[39] For member-state liability in damages for breaches of EC law, see Francovich v. Italy, Cases C-6/90, 9/90 [1991] E.C.R.-I 5357; Brasserie du Pêcheur S.A. v. Germany, Joined Cases C-46, 48/93, [1996] E.C.R. I-1029. Article 256 is bolstered by the Brussels Convention on Jurisdiction and the Enforcement of Judgments in Civil and Commercial Matters, 1998 OJ (C 27) 1, to which all member states now adhere and which makes court judgments issued in one state relatively easy to enforce in all the others. *See also* Council Regulation (EC) No. 44/2001 of 22 December 2000 on Jurisdiction and the Recognition and Enforcement of Judgments in Civil and Commercial matters, 200 OJ (C 325) 33.

[40] *Compare* Costa v. Enel, Case 6/64, [1964] E.C.R. 585, *with* Martin v. Hunter's Lessee, 14 U.S. (1 Wheat.) 304 (1816).

[41] *Compare* Trevor C. Hartley, CONSTITUTIONAL PROBLEMS OF THE EUROPEAN UNION 109 (1999), *with* Maria A. Theodossiou, *An Analysis of the Recent Response of the Community to Non Compliance with Court of Justice Judgments: Article 228(2) E.C.*, 27 EUR. L. REV. 25, 40 (2002).

[42] For a detailed review of the compliance of states with ECJ judgments, see Carl Baudenbacher, *The Implementation of Decisions of the ECJ and of the EFTA Court in Member States' Domestic Legal Orders*, 40 TEX. INT'L L.J. 383 (2005).

[43] For an analytical list of regional tribunals (not limited to regional common market agreements), see Laurence R. Helfer & Anne-Marie Slaughter, note 25 *supra*, at 912–13.

*European Court of Human Rights*

The ECtHR enforces the European Convention on Human Rights (with various amendments), to which forty-five of the forty-six members of the Council of Europe (including all twenty-five of the EU members) adhere.[44] Since 1998, private persons have had direct access to the ECtHR. Before then, the European Commission on Human Rights screened complaints. The jurisdiction of the ECtHR matches the scope of the Convention, which contains capacious language that functions very much like the due process and equal protection clauses of the Fourteenth Amendment of the U.S. Constitution. In 2004, the ECtHR rendered 626 merits judgments, including 14 by its Grand Chamber, and in 589 cases it found a violation of the Convention. More than a quarter of the violations involved Turkey, but every member of the European Union except Denmark, Slovenia, and Sweden lost at least one case on the merits during the year.[45]

Article 46 of the European Convention provides that signatories shall "abide" by the judgments of the ECtHR and that a committee of the foreign ministers of the Council of Europe's members will supervise the implementation of all ECtHR judgments. In practice, this language has not led to a uniform practice of self-executing judgments, much as the authority of the UN Security Council to see to the enforcement of ICJ judgments has not led to their self-execution.[46] However, Article 41 also provides that the ECtHR has the authority to give "just satisfaction" to persons where the domestic law of an injuring state does not allow full reparation. The ECtHR has understood this language as permitting it to issue money judgments to compensate victims of Convention violations, something it did eleven times in 2004.[47]

Technically speaking, nothing in the European Convention makes ECtHR just-satisfaction judgments self-executing, in contrast to the clear language of Article 244 of the Treaty on the European Community. National legal systems must implement these decisions, which take the form of money awards against the sovereign. But national practice appears to have treated payment as fairly automatic. European human rights advocates decry the tendency of some governments not always to implement ECtHR decisions by changing general

[44] Council of Europe, Convention for the Protection of Human Rights and Fundamental Freedoms as amended by Protocol No. 11, E.T.S. No. 155. Monaco is the only member of the Council of Europe not to accept this instrument.

[45] COUNCIL OF EUROPE, EUROPEAN COURT OF HUMAN RIGHTS – SURVEY OF ACTIVITIES 2004 (2005).

[46] For description of enforcement of ECtHR judgments, see DINAH SHELTON, REMEDIES IN INTERNATIONAL HUMAN RIGHTS LAW 154–56 (1999); THE EXECUTION OF STRASBOURG AND GENEVA HUMAN RIGHTS DECISIONS IN THE NATIONAL LEGAL ORDER (Tom Barkhuysen, Michiel van Emmerik and Piet Hein van Kempen, eds., 1999).

[47] COUNCIL OF EUROPE, EUROPEAN COURT OF HUMAN RIGHTS – SURVEY OF ACTIVITIES 2004 (2005).

legislation or policy, but governments pay out Article 41 awards as a matter of course.[48]

Because the execution of Article 41 awards depends ultimately on the cooperation of national authorities, one might argue that the ECtHR does not provide an example of formal enforcement of international law. In theory, governments might refuse to pay, and we simply do not know whether any national court would regard itself as under an obligation to enforce these judgments absent government consent. But this reservation of domestic sovereignty is insignificant. National governments sometimes drag their feet before paying an Article 41 award, but as far as we can determine no state has ever refused to honor a just satisfaction judgment, and delay results in interest charges. The clarity of the obligation, combined with the implicit linkage between compliance with the European Convention and attaining or retaining membership in good standing in the European Union, in effect nullifies whatever discretion to resist that states retain. Rather, national control over ECtHR money judgments amounts to an empty formality.

## International Criminal Courts

At the conclusion of World War II, the victorious allies set up two multinational tribunals, the International Military Tribunal (IMT) in Nuremberg and the International Military Tribunal for the Far East (IMTFE) in Tokyo, to consider the criminal liability of the principal military and political leaders of Germany and Japan. Some but not all of the accused were convicted and hanged, and the occupying powers (and later the German government) proceeded to conduct their own proceedings against smaller fry. The onset of the Cold War impeded further efforts to develop the law relating to war through international tribunals, but some see the symbolic achievement of these first tribunals as enormous.

The end of the Cold War presented the opportunity to revive international criminal tribunals. The first instances – the International Criminal Tribunal for the Former Yugoslavia (ICTFY) at the Hague and the International Criminal Tribunal for Rwanda (ICTR) at Arusha, Tanzania – resembled Nuremberg and Tokyo, in that the responsible international authority – the UN Security Council – established each body after the conflict that had generated the alleged crimes had ended. Unlike the earlier tribunals, however, the constituting power

---

[48] See note 46 supra; John M. Scheib, Enforcing Judgments of the European Court of Human Rights: The Conduit Theory, 19 N.Y. Int'l L. Rev. 101 (1997); John Cary Sims, Compliance Without Remand: The Experience under the European Convention on Human Rights, 36 Ariz. St. L.J. 639 (2004).

did not already have effective control over all the potential defendants. As a result, their mandate has been both more open ended and contingent than those of the IMT and the IMTFE. Their power to indict new accused continues indefinitely, but the tribunals cannot actually proceed against anyone without the cooperation of the state in which an indicted person resides. Once a person has come within their custody, however, these tribunals have essentially the same power to determine guilt and to punish as did the IMT and the IMTFE, except that they lack the authority to impose capital punishment.

During the 1990s an international effort led by the United States sought to create a permanent International Criminal Court (ICC) to replace the practice of ad hoc creation of tribunals in the wake of humanitarian catastrophes. In 1998 an international conference produced a Statute for this body, and the instrument went into force in 2002. The ICC has the authority to prosecute and punish a prescribed list of violations of international humanitarian law. Like the ICTFY and ICTR, it cannot impose capital punishment. Although, as of June 2005, ninety-nine states had acceded to the Statute, most great powers have not. Of the nine states currently known to possess nuclear weapons (including Israel, which has not officially acknowledged its status as a nuclear power), only France and the United Kingdom adhere to the Statute. The United States in particular has gone to great lengths to ensure that its subjects not fall within the ICC's potential jurisdiction.[49]

Counting the ICC as an instance of formal enforcement involves some debatable judgments. One well could argue that the prosecutor's discretion to reject a petition to act means that private persons do not have effective access to the tribunal. Moreover, the continued opposition of the United States, China, and Russia (not to mention India, Israel, North Korea, and Pakistan) casts a shadow, to say the least, over the ICC's capacity to function at all. On the other hand, private persons do have the authority to petition the prosecutor to act, and the prosecutor in turn must answer only to the court, and not to any states, individually or collectively (putting aside the Security Council's authority, which it can exercise only collectively, to delay prosecutions). Moreover, once the court obtains jurisdiction over an accused and issues a judgment, the fulfilment of its order is fairly automatic, as it depends only on the ongoing cooperation of the jailing state. On balance, and recognizing the closeness of the case, we are

[49] Criticism of the opposition of the United States to the ICC tends to overlook the quieter, but no less adamant, refusal of other superpowers to cooperate with the institution. For an analysis of obstacles under Russian law to the participation of the Russian Federation, for example, see Bakhtiyar Tuzmukhamedov, *The ICC and Russian Constitutional Problems*, 3 J. INT'L CRIM. JUSTICE 621 (2005).

inclined to treat the ICC, but not the earlier international criminal courts, as embodying formal enforcement.

## United States – Iran Claims Tribunal

When Iranian radicals seized the U.S. embassy in Tehran in 1979 and took the staff hostage, the United States responded by freezing all Iranian assets within its jurisdiction. The Algiers Accords, which resolved this standoff, obligated the United States to pay these funds to the Bank of England as an escrow agent as consideration for the return of the hostages. The Accords also created the U.S.-Iran Claims Tribunal as a tribunal for resolving outstanding commercial disputes between the two countries and each other's citizens. The British bank in turn used $1 billion of the Iranian assets to fund a security account for payment of awards made by the Tribunal. The Bank used some of the funds in its possession to replenish the security account and eventually transferred the remaining balance to Iran. Once the Tribunal took up work in the Hague, the Nederlandsche Bank N.V. assumed administration of the security account.[50]

Although its caseload has dwindled, the Tribunal remains in operation more than a quarter century after the cut off for disputes over which it has jurisdiction. It has awarded $2 billion to claimants. In terms of volume and value of the claims resolved under its auspices, it represents one of the most impressive experiments in international adjudication in modern history.[51]

What gives the Tribunal its credibility and attraction as a forum is, for U.S. claimants, the availability of the security account to ensure satisfaction of awards and, for Iranian claimants, access to the well developed treaty-based procedures for national enforcement of foreign arbitral awards. Under the Accords, a successful U.S. claimant receives payment through an order trans-mitted from the Tribunal to the Central Bank of Algeria, which in turn instructs the Nederlandsche Bank N.V. to transfer funds to the Federal Reserve Bank of New York. The New York bank deducts a user charge and pays out the balance to the claimant. In one instance, the New York bank refused to pay the claim because it discovered that the claimant had fraudulently concealed his identity as an Iranian national, but otherwise payment has been as straightforward as enforcement of a domestic court judgment.[52]

---

[50] The texts of the various instruments that make up the Algiers Accords are reprinted in CHARLES N. BROWER & JASON D. BRUESCHKE, THE IRAN-UNITED STATES CLAIMS TRIBUNAL 674–725 (1998).

[51] Id. at 657–59.

[52] Federal Reserve Bank v. Williams, 708 F. Supp. 48 (S.D.N.Y. 1989). The Supreme Court ruled that the user fee charged by the Bank did not constitute a compensable taking under the Fifth Amendment. United States v. Sperry Corp., 493 U.S. 52 (1989).

Iranian claimants do not enjoy quite as automatic an enforcement mechanism, but they still have effective recourse for their tribunal awards. The United States is a party to the United Nations Convention on the Recognition and Enforcement of Foreign Arbitral Awards, which it has implemented through domestic legislation.[53] Accordingly, U.S. courts must enforce arbitral awards that comply with the Convention. Litigation to enforce Tribunal awards generally has succeeded.[54] The U.S. courts, however, retain the authority to determine whether an award complies with the Convention, and on several occasions have modified or refused to enforce an award for this reason.[55]

By the terms of its creation, the Tribunal deals with only a definite set of commercial disputes, bounded by time as well as subject matter. Its proponents argue that its decisions constitute a body of customary international law with enduring significance, but this claim expresses ambition more than authority.[56] What the Tribunal indisputably represents is a strong ex ante commitment by states to an independent and powerful dispute-resolution process and the institutional characteristics that make such a commitment credible.

## Investor Protection Arbitration

The legal protection of foreign investors has concerned capital-exporting countries at least since American independence. Articles 5 and 6 of the 1783 Treaty of Paris, which ratified the successful outcome of the American Revolution, committed the United States to restore the confiscated property of British subjects and not to engage in new confiscations; Article 4 obligated the United States not to impede the collection of lawful debts.[57] Frustrated by the impediments to fulfilling these obligations posed by the structure of the Confederation, the United States reconstituted itself into the current federal republic five years later. The newly created federal courts became the principal mechanism for enforcing the Treaty's protections.[58]

---

[53] Convention on the Recognition and Enforcement of Foreign Arbitral Awards, 21 U.S.T. 2517, T.I.A.S. No. 6997; 9 U.S.C. §§201–07 (2001); 28 U.S.C. §2414 (2001).

[54] The lead case upholding the argument that the New York Convention applies to Tribunal awards is Ministry of Defense of the Islamic Republic of Iran v. Gould, Inc., 887 F. 2nd 1357 (9th Cir. 1989).

[55] See Ministry of Defense of the Islamic Republic of Iran v. Gould, Inc., 969 F.2nd 764 (9th Cir. 1992) (modifying award to the extent it required violation of U.S. criminal statute); Iran Aircraft Industries v. Avco Corp., 980 F.2nd 141 (2nd Cir. 1992) (refusing to enforce award because tribunal denied losing party a meaningful opportunity to present its claim).

[56] For the claim, see CHARLES N. BROWER & JASON D. BRUESCHKE, note, at 644–48.

[57] Definitive Treaty of Peace, Great Britain-United States, September 3, 1783, 8 Stat. 80, T.S. No. 104.

[58] Ware v. Hylton, 3 U.S. (3 Dall.) 199 (1796); Hopkirk v. Bell, 7 U.S. (3 Cranch) 454 (1806); Martin v. Hunter's Lessee, 14 U.S. (1 Wheat.) 304 (1816). A 1794 treaty between Great Britain and the United States created an international commission mechanism to settle claims by subjects of the two states against the other sovereign. Treaty of Amity, Commerce, and Navigation (Jay Treaty), Great

During the nineteenth century and the first half of the twentieth, enforcement of investor protection obligations depended largely on sovereign espousal. After an investor had suffered a loss, its state would bring military, economic, or political pressure against the offending state to obtain compensation. On occasion the states would refer the dispute to a tribunal, which would offer an opinion on the existence and extent of liability. For example, after Mexico expropriated the property of U.S. investors in the course of its revolution, the two countries established a commission to determine Mexico's obligation.[59] The two countries settled the dispute through a subsequent treaty that arranged for an interstate payment.[60] The United States then distributed the funds it received to the claimants.[61]

In the years after World War II, the need to develop an ex ante legal framework for investment disputes became more pressing. Decolonization expanded the number of independent states that served as hosts for foreign capital and created a context that undermined the moral authority of property rights. At the same time, flows of capital exports, especially from the United States, grew considerably. One early structure, embodied in a 1948 Friendship, Commerce, and Navigation Treaty between the United States and Italy, designated the International Court of Justice as the tribunal to hear claims brought by one state as a result of the other's expropriation.[62] Like prewar practice, this mechanism excluded affected investors from the dispute resolution process and gave

Britain-United States, Nov. 19, 1794, 8 Stat. 116, T.S. No. 105. In practice the commission responsible for addressing the rights of British subjects failed to work, and eight years later the United States paid a lump sum settlement to Great Britain, which in turn disbursed the money to the claimants. Convention Regarding Articles 6 and 7 of the Jay Treaty, Great Britain-United States, Jan. 8, 1802, 8 Stat. 196, T.S. No. 108.

[59] Convention for the Reciprocal Settlement of Claims, United States-Mexico, Sep. 8, 1923, 43 Stat. 1730, T.S. No. 678; Special Claims Convention for the Settlement of Claims of American Citizens Arising from Revolutionary Acts in Mexico from November 20, 1910, to May 31, 1920, United States-Mexico, Sep. 10, 1923, 43 Stat. 1722, T.S. No. 676.

[60] Convention Providing for En Bloc Settlement of Special Claims, United States-Mexico, Apr. 24, 1934, 49 Stat. 3071,T.S. No. 878;Convention Respecting Claims, United States-Mexico, Nov. 19, 1941, 56 Stat. 1347, T.S. No. 980.

[61] U.S. law regarded the decisions of international claims tribunals during this period as lacking in direct effect. Any rights that an individual had to receive compensation derived from legislation authorizing the distributions of funds received by the United States, rather than from the decision to transfer funds to the United States based on some tribunal's finding of liability. Act of Mar. 3, 1863, ch. 92, §9, 12 Stat. 765, 767, *codified at* 28 U.S.C. §1502; La Abra Silver Mining Co. v. United States, 175 U.S. 423 (1899); United States v. Blaine, 139 U.S. 306 (1891); United States v. Weld, 127 U.S. 51 (1888); Alling v. United States, 114 U.S. 562 (1885); Great Western Insurance Co. v. United States, 112 U.S. 193 (1894); Frelinghuysen v. Key, 110 U.S. 63 (1884).

[62] Treaty, Protocol, and Additional Protocol Respecting Friendship, Commerce and Navigation, United States-Italy, Feb. 2, 1948, 63 Stat. 2255, T.I.A.S. No. 1965. In one instance the parties have invoked this treaty to submit a dispute to the ICJ. Case Concerning Elettronica Sicula S.p.A. (United States v. Italy), [1989] I.C.J. 15.

no formal enforcement power to the designated tribunal. But by selecting in advance a permanent body to address anticipated disputes, the Treaty moved in the direction of formalization and legalization of the obligation to protect foreign investors.

In the 1950s European countries, led by Germany, embraced and expanded the model found in the United States-Italy treaty.[63] They negotiated bilateral investment treaties (BITs) to clarify the obligation of a host state to respect investors' rights and to design a formalized dispute resolution process. Under these treaties, a state accused of expropriating an investment belonging to a national of the counterparty state agreed to specific rights of compensation and due process. In the event that one side regarded the other as defaulting on its obligation to investors, the aggrieved state (but not its investors) could initiate arbitration, typically under the auspices of the ICJ.[64]

The Convention on the Settlement of Investment Disputes between States and Nationals of Other States, signed in 1965, provided a more institutionally developed structure for these cases. It established the International Center for the Settlement of Investment Disputes (ICSID), a body affiliated with the World Bank, to manage these arbitrations. Of greater significance, it opened the door to investor-initiated enforcement and obligated signatory states to enact domestic laws to enable judicial enforcement of ICSID arbitral awards.[65] Host states and investing companies began to incorporate a reference to ICSID dispute settlement in their contracts with each other. In the 1980s, the United States and the United Kingdom began entering into BITs that took advantage of the ICSID enforcement mechanism.[66]

---

[63] The first was Treaty for the Promotion and Protection of Investments, Federal Republic of Germany-Pakistan, Nov. 25, 1959, U.N.T.S. 6575.

[64] *See* RUDOLPH DOLZER & MARGRETE STEVENS, BILATERAL INVESTMENT TREATIES 129–56 (1995). According to this source, 38 of the 80 BITs negotiated from 1959 to 1969 had Germany as a party. *Id.* at 267–69.

[65] Convention on the Settlement of Investment Disputes Between States and Nationals of Other States, Mar. 18, 1965, 17 U.S.T. 1270, T.I.A.S. No. 6090, 575 U.N.T.S. 159. As of May 2005, 155 states had signed this treaty, 142 of which had completed the ratification process. For the list, see http://www.worldbank.org/icsid/constate/c-states-en.htm (last visited Oct. 3, 2005). The United States, after adopting the Convention, implemented its obligations through a statutory enactment enabling courts to enforce ICSID awards. Pub. L. 89–532, Aug. 11, 1966, 80 Stat. 344, *codified at* 22 U.S.C. §§1650, 1650a (2001). For U.S. practice regarding this obligation, see Karaha Bodas Co., L.L.C. v. Perusahaan Pertambangan Minyak Dan Gas Bumi Negara, 364 F.3rd 274 (5th Cir. 2004) (enforcing Swiss award against Indonesian state petroleum company); Maritime Intern. Nominees Establishment v. Republic of Guinea, 693 F.2nd 1094 (D.C. Cir. 1982) (agreement to submit disputes to ICSID arbitration does not constitute a waiver of sovereign immunity in a subsequent enforcement proceeding).

[66] The first BIT that incorporated a reference to ICSID to permit independent investor claims was that between the Netherlands and Indonesia. Agreement on Economic Co-operation, July 7, 1968, Neth.-Indon., 799 U.N.T.S. 13 (terminated July 1, 1995). *See also* RUDOLPH DOLZER & MARGRETE

With the 1988 U.S.-Canada Free Trade Agreement (NAFTA), the United States took the additional step of embedding the basic investor rights of BITs into a trade agreement.[67] Chapter 11 of the North American Free Trade Agreement, the direct descendent of Chapter 16 of the 1988 pact with Canada, consummated this approach by committing Canada, Mexico, and the United States to ICSID arbitration of investment claims.[68] The NAFTA obligations in turn have generated a welter of litigation, including several controversial decisions ordering compensation for the costs of economic regulation, as opposed to outright seizure of assets. As of January 2006, investors have brought fifteen claims against Mexico, fourteen against the United States, and twelve against Canada. Of the eleven arbitral decisions on the merits, Canada and Mexico were found guilty of violating their obligations under Chapter 11 in two instances each and were ordered to pay compensation. In one additional case, Canada paid a significant out-of-court settlement to an investor after an ICSID tribunal had expressed agreement with the victim's legal theory.[69] Litigation in the U.S. domestic courts superseded two cases brought against the United States by giving the investors satisfaction, albeit on domestic grounds rather than through enforcement of NAFTA Chapter 11.[70]

The collaboration of injured investors, ICSID arbitration tribunals, and compliant domestic courts in the enforcement of NAFTA Chapter 11 has generated some controversy. Critics of economic liberalization have depicted NAFTA institutions as controlled by large businesses interested in unraveling the regulatory state. In 2001 the NAFTA Free Trade Commission, a body comprising the parties' trade ministers, issued an interpretation that appeared to second-guess prior tribunal decisions. But these reservations have not discouraged the United States from entering into similar commitments. In particular, Chapter 10 of the recently adopted Central America-Dominican Republic-United States Free Trade Agreement largely copies NAFTA's Chapter 11, and in particular provides for private enforcement of investor rights through ICSID arbitration.

The tribunals established by the various investment treaties, in particular those operating under the ICSID regime, do not constitute a permanent judicial

STEVENS, note 64 *supra*, at 130–56. The first British treaty to do so was Agreement for the Promotion and Protection of Investments, U.K.-Jordan, Oct. 10, 1979, 1203 U.N.T.S. 35. The first such treaty to which the United States was a party was Treaty Concerning the Reciprocal Encouragement and Protection of Investments, U.S.-Egypt, Sep. 29, 1982, Treat. Doc. 99–24.

[67] United States-Canada Free-Trade Agreement, Ch. 16, Jan. 2, 1988, H.R. Doc. 100–216 (1988), 27 I.L.M. 281 (1988).

[68] North American Free Trade Agreement, Ch. 11, Dec. 17, 1992, H.R. Doc. 103–159 (1993), 32 I.L.M. 605, 639 (1992).

[69] David A. Gantz, *Potential Conflicts Between Investor Rights and Environmental Regulation Under NAFTA's Chapter 11*, 33 GEO. WASH. INT'L L. REV. 651, 665–66 (2001).

[70] Hemp Industries Ass'n v. Drug Enforcement Admin., 333 F.3rd 1082 (9th Cir. 2003).

institution comparable to the appellate body of the WTO DSB, the ICJ, the ITLOS, the ECJ, or the ECtHR. Rather, legal experts make themselves available to serve as arbiters, subject to party selection after a dispute arises. The default selection rule, embodied in Articles 37(2)(b) and 38 of the 1966 ICSID Convention, allows each side to pick an arbiter and then expects them to agree on a third; if the parties do not complete their selection within 90 days, the chairman of ICSID will choose for them. But the ex post aspect of appointment to investment tribunals does not necessarily mean that these bodies lack the capacity to produce strong enforcement. One might assume, along with Professors Posner and Yoo, that parties will select arbiters based in part on predictions about how they will decide in the particular case, and that arbiters will have some incentive to conduct themselves in a manner that will lead to future appointments.[71] But the magnitude of this incentive is debatable. A party's preference for an array of arbitral outcomes may not conform to a normal distribution, and potential arbiters may systematically attach greater significance to incentives other than future arbitral appointments.[72] Accordingly, the capacity of parties to use their selection power to constrain tribunal decision making has definite limits.

In all other respects, investment dispute tribunals have significant formal enforcement power. Aggrieved investors, rather than their governments, have unconstrained discretion to initiate cases and to block compromise settlements. This maximizes the tribunal's ability to resolve the specific legal issues specified in investment protection agreements, undiluted by contextual factors that might distract a national government. As a result of the ICSID Convention, conversion of arbitral awards into money payments rests in the hands of local courts that generally operate free of local political constraints. The tribunals, in short, come close to the model of independent domestic courts that exemplifies formal legal enforcement.

*ICANN Arbitration.* The Internet Corporation for Assigned Names and Numbers (ICANN) is a private nonprofit company incorporated under Virginia law that administers the domain-name system that undergirds the Internet. Computers recognize numeric addresses for particular locations on the Internet, but humans need verbal cues to remember numeric place names. Binding a domain name to a valuable trademark enhances the value of the domain name but also can harm the trademark. This basic problem has led to

[71] Eric A. Posner & John C. Yoo, note 1 *supra*, at 21. *See also* Eric A. Posner, *Arbitration and the Harmonization of International Commercial Law – A Defense of* Mitsubishi, 39 VA. J. INT'L L. 647 (1999).
[72] It seems plausible, for example, to model the incentives of arbiters as including general resume-burnishing to advance along a diversified set of international law career paths. Aberrant activity along one dimension, such as idiosyncratic arbitral decision making, might lead to greater opportunities in other areas, such as academia or politics.

a unique system of international determination and enforcement of domain name ownership.[73]

At first, the ICANN system assigned domain names on a strict first-come, first-served principle, which abetted the vice of "cybersquatting." Malefactors would register a domain name that overlapped with someone else's brand, and then would either sell the name to the mark holder or exploit the domain name in a manner that harmed the trademark. In 1999, ICANN responded to the problem by adopting a mandatory arbitration process, to which registrants owners had to assent as a condition of obtaining or maintaining a domain name. Persons complaining that a domain name infringed a preexisting trademark can invoke this process. It entails a panel of arbiters, selected from a list maintained by ICANN, reviewing the written submissions of the parties. ICANN in turn implements the panel's ruling by deregistering any domain name found to infringe a trademark. This sanction operates independently of any national authority, political or judicial, and results in the immediate nullification of the domain name as a means of attracting Internet traffic.[74]

ICANN arbitration has a fairly small scope, but the rights it determines have considerable value. The fact that the same entity that administers the domain-name assignment system also runs the arbitration process ensures swift and highly effective enforcement. That national courts might reach different conclusions than do ICANN panels does not detract from the effectiveness of arbitration. Under U.S. law, for example, a separate, judicially enforced right to challenge cybersquatting exists, and Congress has directed the courts to give no weight to the findings of ICANN panels.[75] But the high cost of litigating a case in a U.S. court, compared to the very low cost of ICANN arbitration, ensures that judicial review of ICANN determinations occurs only infrequently.

*Private International Commercial Arbitration*

ICANN arbitration is simply an extreme manifestation of a general pattern in international commerce, namely the displacement of nationally administered law by international arbitration. Because ICANN administers a natural monopoly, its arbitration process has become a take-it-or-leave-it term in all domain-name registration contracts. But in many contexts commercial

---

[73] For a general treatment, see Jack L. Goldsmith & Tim Wu, WHO CONTROLS THE INTERNET? ch. 3 (2006).

[74] On the ICANN dispute-resolution system, see http://www.icann.org/dndr/udrp/uniform-rules.htm (last visited July 6, 2005).

[75] Anticybersquatting Consumer Protection Act (ACPA), Pub. L. No. 106–113, §3001 *et seq.*, 113 Stat. 1501 A-545 (codified in scattered sections of 15 U.S.C.). On the independence of judicial enforcement of this statute from ICANN dispute resolution, see Barcelona.com, Inc. v. Excelentisimo Ayuntamiento de Barcelona, 330 F.3rd 617 (4th Cir. 2003)(disregarding ICANN ruling and exonerating alleged cybersquatter).

partners habitually write arbitration clauses into their contracts, even when
they have access to legal systems with strong courts that enjoy a reputation for
honesty and effectiveness.

Scholars have devoted inordinate attention to certain aspects of international
commercial arbitration, in particular to the question of whether the decisions
of these arbiters stands as a distinct body of law, the proverbial *lex mercatoria*.[76]
We sidestep these issues to focus on one salient aspect of this institution. What
strikes us as important about the proliferation of international arbitration and
the corresponding willingness of national courts to defer to this process is
the apparent preference of sophisticated contracting parties to avoid national
legal systems altogether as a means of dispute resolution. Arbitration seems
important not for what it is so much as what it is not.[77]

Many reasons exist for parties to contract out of national dispute resolution. Independent of the rules of decisions that courts might apply to the cases
before them, litigation entails significant costs, both directly (think of legal
fees and the burdens of pretrial discovery) and through delay. But in at least
some instances, arbitration might mean access to different substantive rules,
with reduced decision maker discretion and more predictable outcomes. The
letters of credit issued by banks to support international documentary sales
of goods, for example, typically include both an arbitration clause and a term
incorporating the Uniform Customs and Practice for Documentary Credits
(UCP), an industry-produced set of standard contractual terms. A committee
of the International Chamber of Commerce, a nongovernmental organization
organized by commercial interests, drafts periodic revisions of the UCP, and
another component of the Chamber provides arbitration services. Some evidence suggests that the bundle of UCP terms and international arbitration
reflects the preferences of both the sellers and buyers of international letters of
credit, who value both the greater clarity of the UCP and the willingness of the
arbiters to apply these terms in a predictable manner.[78]

Complementing these private preferences to opt out of national dispute
resolution is a willingness of national courts to cooperate with this choice.
An international treaty, the Convention on the Recognition and Enforcement of Foreign Arbitral Awards, undergirds this practice, although it does

[76] For a summary of the debate, *see* Lex Mercatoria and Arbitration (Thomas E. Carbonneau ed.
1990).
[77] For development of this point, *see* Robert E. Scott, *The Rise and Fall of Article 2*, 62 LA. L. REV.
1009 (2002). *See also* Saskia Sassen, LOSING CONTROL? SOVEREIGNTY IN AN AGE OF GLOBALIZA-
TION (1999) (describing international commercial arbitration as an instance of diminished national
sovereignty).
[78] Paul B. Stephan, *The Futility of Unification and Harmonization in International Commercial Law*, 39
VA. J. INT'L L. 743, 780–84 (1999).

not mandate the preference for arbitration that the courts have displayed. For the last two decades, the Supreme Court of the United States in particular has signaled its strong support for private choices to submit disputes to international arbitration, even in instances where issues of public regulatory law are present.[79] Particularly striking is *Vimar Seguros y Reaseguros S.A. v. M/V Sky Reefer*, a case that held that arbitration of a statutorily mandated contract term did not constitute a prohibited diminution of the mandatory term's effectiveness.[80]

Other national judicial systems similarly seem disposed to allow sophisticated contractual parties to choose arbitration, particularly in the context of international transactions.[81] The problem that bothers some critics of the U.S. decisions – that submission of questions of public law to private arbitration undermines the public policies at issue – does not exist to the same degree in most other countries. Rather, the overwhelming majority of other legal systems, unlike the United States, restrict or forbid the enforcement of public law through private litigation, whether in the courts or through arbitration. For these countries, it follows that shrinking the domain of private litigation has lesser policy ramifications.

## Domestic Courts

Because judicial enforcement of domestic law provides the template for formal enforcement of any legal rule, we must consider how domestic courts employ their resources for international law enforcement. In some but by no means all jurisdictions, the judiciary enjoys considerable independence from national political authorities. Consequently, courts have the capacity, if not necessarily the inclination, to hold both governments and powerful private interests to obligations derived from sources external to the domestic legal system.

Some definition and description of this mechanism may be helpful. The capacity to enforce international rules depends primarily on the extent of the judiciary's discretion to choose among legal sources for the rules that it will apply. At one extreme, this discretion may rest on a constitutional commitment, either explicit or implicit, that cannot be limited through normal lawmaking. The existence and scope of such commitments normally are controversial,

---

[79]  Mitsubishi Motors Corp. v. Soler Chrysler-Plymouth, Inc, 473 U.S. 614 (1985) (upholding arbitrability of agreement between car manufacturer and dealer even though dealer asserted claim under antitrust laws).

[80]  518 U.S. 528 (1995).

[81]  *See* David Joseph, JURISDICTION AND ARBITRATION AGREEMENTS AND THEIR ENFORCEMENT 200–08 (2005).

but prominent examples exist. National courts in the European Union regard
themselves as bound to enforce Community law against national governments,
and the Supreme Court of the United States has flirted with the idea that its
discretion to interpret the Eighth Amendment's ban on "cruel and unusual punishment" comprises the incorporation of certain international rules.[82] Alternatively, a national lawmaker may enact legislation that refers to international
rules and directs courts to enforce them, always with the implicit reservation
that subsequent legislation may withdraw this authority. Thus, Congress in
1991 enacted a statute authorizing private suits to compensate victims of extrajudicial killings in violation of international law, the British Parliament in 1998
directed British courts to enforce the European Convention on Human Rights,
and, more debatably, the Supreme Court in *Sosa v. Alvarez-Machain* discovered
a command from Congress, mostly undetected during two centuries, to develop
a body of international tort law. Finally, courts might look to international law
for rules that fill gaps in legislation. Such interstitial uses of international law,
like legislative references, are subject to subsequent legislative overruling, but
courts also can choose to abandon them on their own initiative in the face of
reflection and experience.

These developments have spawned a vast literature, with which for the most
part we do not wish to engage.[83] Instead, we note, in order to rebut, two broad
claims about these developments that underlie, at least implicitly, some of the
scholarly debates. On the one hand, some maintain that domestic courts never
truly apply international law, but rather pick and choose among potentially
applicable rules in a manner dominated by domestic jurisprudential, political,
and methodological considerations. The absence of any body that can coordinate what domestic courts do with international law bolsters this claim. For
ease of exposition, we will call this the *misnomer objection*: Domestic courts
never stray very far from their domestic roots.

On the other hand, prominent scholars have argued that judges have
developed a sense of international solidarity that links them to their foreign
counterparts and to some extent separates them from domestic politicians and
officials. This solidarity explains why courts would expend domestic judicial

[82] For the EU case, see Karen Alter, *The European Union's Legal System and Domestic Policy: Spillover or Backlash?*, in LEGALIZATION AND WORLD POLITICS 105 (Judith Goldstein, Miles Kahler, Robert O. Keohane, & Anne-Marie Slaughter, eds. 2001); Paul B. Stephan, *Accountability and International Lawmaking: Rules, Rents and Legitimacy*, 17 Nw. J. INT'L L. & BUS. 681, 705–06 (1996–97); J. H. H. Weiler, *The Transformation of Europe*, 100 YALE L.J. 2043 (1991). For the uses of international law in interpreting the Eighth Amendment, see Roper v. Simmons, 543 U.S. 551 (2005).

[83] For a useful summary of the state of the debate in the United States, see *Agora: The United States Constitution and International Law*, 98 AM. J. INT'L L. 42 (2004).

resources to enforce international rules. This global jurisprudence supposedly functions something like the traditional Anglo-American common law, providing judges with a store of rules as well as a culture cum methodology for selecting which rules to apply.[84]

Both these observations begin with an indisputably correct insight and then overstate what follows from the uncontestable claim. Consider, for example, *A. v. Secretary of State*, the House of Lords decision that struck down portions of the Anti-Terrorism, Crime and Security Act 2001 on the grounds that they transgressed British obligations under the European Convention on Human Rights.[85] As part of proposing the 2001 Act, the British government issued an order purporting to exercise its power under the Convention to derogate from its obligations during emergencies. The House of Lords, exercising its authority under Human Rights Act 1998 to apply the European Convention to subsequently adopted parliamentary enactments and governmental orders, ruled that the derogation order was disproportionate to the threat that Islamic fundamentalists presented to the United Kingdom. Accordingly, the Lords held that the 2001 Act, which singled out foreign nationals for indefinite detention as suspected international terrorists, was unlawful.

In one sense, *A. v. Secretary of State* rested on domestic law, namely the 1998 act of Parliament that enlists the British courts in the enforcement of the European Convention on Human Rights. Moreover, Lord Bingham's opinion seems to blend European and British law and discussed British and ECtHR precedents as consistent and interrelated. At bottom, however, the opinion rested mostly on the court's understanding of how the ECtHR interpreted the Convention. The narrative posture of the decision was that of an agent, not a peer engaged in dialogue.

Nor does the decision express a sense of transnational judicial solidarity. The court noted that there existed a body of fraternal jurisprudence regarding the standards for treating resident foreigners during an international emergency, namely decisions of the Supreme Court of the United States. But the House of Lords, while noting that these cases existed, felt no compunction to follow them or even use them as an interpretive tool for teasing out the meaning of the rather abstract terms of the Convention. The focus was clearly and specifically on the decisions of the ECtHR, what international lawyers would call *lex specialis* rather than any kind of general law.

---

[84] The foremost proponent of this argument is Anne-Marie Slaughter. *See* Anne-Marie Slaughter, A NEW WORLD ORDER (2004). For a reformulation of the claim and a critique, see Paul B. Stephan, *Process Values, International Law, and Justice*, 23 SOCIAL PHIL. & POL'Y 131 (2006).

[85] A. v. Secretary of State, [2005] 2 W.L.R. 87 (H.L.).

Much the same can be said of U.S. practice. Consider first the *Sosa* decision mentioned earlier. The case rests on a provision first enacted as part of the 1789 Judiciary Act that defined the jurisdiction of the then federal district courts. Among the cases that these courts could hear were "all causes where an alien sues for a tort only in violation of the law of nations or a treaty of the United States."[86] In a nutshell, the statute left open the question whether Congress intended "a tort... in violation of the law of nations" to refer to preexisting common law that federal courts could apply to a case otherwise properly before them (e.g., cases in admiralty or where there existed diversity of citizenship between the parties), or whether Congress indirectly meant to designate the "law of nations" as a species of federal law that federal courts could construct and apply on their own. Authorities on the law of federal courts have tended to favor the first approach, while international human rights advocates have favored the second.[87] The majority opinion in *Sosa* split the difference by simultaneously proclaiming that the statute had a "strictly jurisdictional nature," but that "Congress intended the ATS to furnish jurisdiction for a relatively modest set of actions alleging violations of the law of nations."[88] The Court did not make clear what fell into the "modest set" of actions that came within the domain of federal courts, other than to specify that the interest at issue in *Sosa* – the right not to be subjected to arbitrary seizure by government agents – fell without.

Like *A. v. Secretary of State*, *Sosa* has as its foreground the interpretation of a domestic legislative provision. But also like the British case, the statute in question constitutes (or at least was interpreted as constituting) the domestic courts as a medium for channeling a particular body of international law for purposes of its enforcement. And again like the British case, the Supreme Court reached this outcome without any appeal to parallel determinations by peer judicial bodies in other countries.

Consider finally what is easily the most controversial instance of international law enforcement by domestic courts, namely, constitutional incorporation. The use of international law as a means of elaborating on the meaning of the Constitution remains problematic in the United States and elsewhere, but two recent Supreme Court decisions deserve mention. *Rasul v. Bush*, one of the trilogy of

---

[86] Judiciary Act, ch. 20, 9, 1 Stat. 73, 77 (1789), *subsequently codified at* 28 U.S.C. §1350 (2001).

[87] One of us submitted a brief in the Supreme Court arguing for the federal-courts interpretation. Brief for Professors of International Law, Federal Jurisdiction and the Foreign Relations Law of the United States as *Amici Curiae* on Behalf of Petitioner, Sosa v. Alvarez-Machain, No. 03-339 (Jan. 23, 2004) (Paul B. Stephan, counsel of record).

[88] Sosa v. Alvarez-Machain, 542 U.S. 692, 713, 720 (2004).

2004 cases dealing with judicial review of the detention of suspected terrorists, suggests that foreign nationals held by the government outside of U.S. territory enjoy some kind of constitutional protection.[89] How the Constitution operates in this context remains a very open question, but the Court seemed to envision the elaboration of such rights through reference to international human rights norms.[90] The move opens the way for U.S. judges, exercising the discretion that Justice Souter described in the quote at the beginning of this chapter, to bring the hodgepodge of state practice, unenforced multilateral treaties, and normative claims that human rights law comprises into the Constitution.[91]

The second significant decision is *Roper v. Simmons*, the case where a majority of the Supreme Court held that the Eighth Amendment's prohibition of cruel and unusual punishment forbids the execution of persons who were minors at the time they committed their crime.[92] Justice Kennedy's opinion for the Court made several arguments in support of this result, one of which is the Court's perception of an international consensus against this practice. Kennedy noted that the United Nations Covenant on the Rights of the Child forbade the execution of juvenile offenders and attached no significance to the fact that the United States for that reason had refused to adopt that instrument.[93] By cloaking international law in the Constitution, the Court could cast aside the express objections of the U.S. political branches to the rule at issue.

It might appear that any exercise of constitutional interpretation, no matter how infused with international law, must represent an instance of domestic

---

[89] Rasul v. Bush, 542 U.S. 466, 480 n. 15 (2004). The suggestion is subtle, resting as it does on a reference to Justice Kennedy's concurring opinion in *United States v. Verdugo-Urquidez*, 494 U.S 259, 277–78 (1990), which in turn was speculative rather than definitive. At least one court has embraced the suggestion. In re Guantanamo Detainee Cases, 355 F. Supp. 2nd 443 (D.D.C. 2005). *Contra*, Khalid v. Bush, 355 F. Supp. 2nd 311 (D.D.C. 2005). For fuller discussion, *see* Paul B. Stephan, *Constitutional Limits on the Struggle Against International Terrorism: Revisiting the Rights of Overseas Aliens*, 19 CONN. L. REV. 831 (1987).

[90] For an article preceding *Rasul* that anticipated this move, *see* Rosa Ehrenreich Brooks, *War Everywhere: Rights, National Security Law, and the Law of Armed Conflict in the Age of Terror*, 153 U. PA. L. REV. 675 (2004).

[91] On the historical and intellectual ties between, on the one hand, the overseas enforcement of the U.S. Constitution by courts on behalf of aliens and, on the other hand, the development of international human rights law, *see* Paul B. Stephan, *Courts, the Constitution, and Customary International Law – The Intellectual Origins of the Restatement (Third) of the Foreign Relations Law of the United States*, 43 VA. J. INT'L L. 33 (2003).

[92] Roper v. Simmons, 543 U.S. 551 (2005).

[93] *Id.* Kennedy also relied on the similar prohibition of the International Covenant on Civil and Political Rights, Dec. 19, 1966, 999 U. N. T. S. 171, and dismissed as irrelevant that the United States, in ratifying that instrument, expressly reserved its application to the juvenile death penalty and more generally had conditioned its accession to the Convention on its unenforceability within its domestic legal order.

lawmaking rather than of international law enforcement. A state's constitution reflects its particular historical and cultural circumstances as well as the specific settlements that its framers reached. But constitutional interpretation, as practiced by the contemporary Supreme Court, ranges far beyond an inquiry into history or original meaning, and has become, as least for a shifting majority of justices, essentially a means of marrying judicial authority to good policy. In this context, constitutional lawmaking can become a vehicle for domestic international law enforcement, freed of checks from the other lawmaking branches.

Our point about the inconclusiveness of the evidence about domestic international law enforcement can be broadened. Because the practice of invoking international law by national courts has changed dramatically in recent years and also has become highly controversial, we confront a moving target. We think it sufficient to observe that the practice exists, that its extent (both present and potential) is uncertain and disputed, and that some important courts do seem to accept the role of agents designated to enforce rules generated by processes operating externally to national political decision making. Because the practice of domestic courts remains unsettled, the real issues are prospective and normative rather than descriptive and positive. We will turn to these considerations in Chapter 7.

## Summary

Informal enforcement of international law is extensive and pervasive. As this chapter illustrates, however, formal enforcement, carried out either by independent domestic courts or by bodies that have powers comparable to that of international courts, has grown significantly in the last few decades. We now turn to the question of whether the enforcement patterns that we have observed conform to our model of optimal international law enforcement.

# 6 THE CHOICE BETWEEN FORMAL AND INFORMAL ENFORCEMENT

Against the force of such considerations, we find respondents' countervailing arguments quite unpersuasive. Their basic contention is that United States courts could make a significant contribution to the growth of international law, a contribution whose importance, it is said, would be magnified by the relative paucity of decisional law by international bodies. But given the fluidity of present world conditions, the effectiveness of such a patchwork approach toward the formulation of an acceptable body of law concerning state responsibility for expropriations is, to say the least, highly conjectural. Moreover, it rests upon the sanguine presupposition that the decisions of the courts of the world's major capital exporting country and principal exponent of the free enterprise system would be accepted as disinterested expressions of sound legal principle by those adhering to widely different ideologies.

> Banco Nacional de Cuba v. Sabbatino, 376 U.S. 398, 434–35 (1964) (Harlan, J.)

Without doubt there are great interests of society which justify withholding the coercive arm of the law from these duties of imperfect obligation, as they are called; imperfect, not because they are less binding upon the conscience than those which are called perfect, but because the wisdom of the social law does not impose sanctions upon them.

> Mills v. Wyman, 20 Mass. (3 Pick.) 207, 210 (1825) (Parker, J.)

IN THIS CHAPTER, WE DEMONSTRATE THAT MOST, IF NOT ALL, contemporary practice of international law enforcement conforms to predictions generated by the model of optimal enforcement that we developed in Chapter 4. In particular, as we demonstrated in the previous chapter, the framers of international law do not rely only on the moral or inspirational force of their commands, but employ a variety of devices to induce compliance. International law employs a mixture of informal mechanisms (retaliation, reputation, and a preference for reciprocal fairness) and formal enforcement (cases brought by private interested parties before an independent tribunal that has the authority to impose sanctions). In this chapter, we show that states usually employ formal enforcement where we predict they would, and informal mechanism otherwise.

To elaborate, our positive model of optimal international law enforcement leads to three hypotheses:

(1) States and other actors will rely on informal mechanisms for international law enforcement whenever applying the rules requires information that cannot be verified by an independent observer except at a high cost and where effective and verifiable proxies for that information are not readily available to an independent observer.

(2) States and other actors will rely on formal mechanisms enforcing international rules – hard law – where three conditions are satisfied: (a) the law represents a response to a collective action problem, (b) the rules can be applied by looking to verifiable information (or low-cost proxies), *and* (c) the parties' interactions are complex and their sequence is opaque.

(3) Where international lawmaking rests on voluntary choices, states will resist the adoption or extension of international rules where there exists substantial uncertainty about the kinds of enforcement mechanisms that will be adopted.

We will unpack each of these claims and then marshal the evidence that supports them.

The first claim supposes that the governmental representatives that produce international law can appreciate ex ante that information necessary for application of a rule will be unverifiable. This means that these representatives can anticipate both what information will be necessary and whether states can prove the validity of that information to a third party at an acceptable cost, even after taking into account proxy mechanisms such as allocating burdens of proof. The claim also supposes that these representatives would not prefer formal enforcement if that would result in applications of the rule that reduce social welfare.

As we will show, much of what constitutes international law comprises conditional obligations where state officials have private knowledge of whether the conditions have been satisfied. For example, many international commitments contain a proviso permitting a state to default where not doing so would threaten its national security.[1] Implicit in such a standard is an assessment by a

---

[1] Article XXI of the General Agreement on Tariffs and Trade provides: "Nothing in this Agreement shall be construed . . . to prevent any contracting party from taking any action which it considers necessary for the protection of its essential security interests . . . taken in time of war or other emergency in

state of what level of risk to its national security it will tolerate to pursue some other desirable objective. As long as a risk exists, however slight, the calculus turns on a subjective assessment of these considerations by a state's political leadership. Although the leadership's actions can signal something about its tolerance for risk, the underlying calculus necessarily must remain opaque, if only to leave potential adversaries off balance.

The second claim identifies the conditions under which we should expect to find formal enforcement, and hence hard law. It supposes, as in the first claim, that government representatives can anticipate both what information will determine the application of a rule and that information's verifiability. It is more rigorous than the first claim, in that it contends that states will invest in the cost of formal enforcement only to forestall the risk of opportunism by other actors. In other words, it applies only if states seek cooperative solutions to complex collective action problems.

The second claim also supposes a capacity to make an ex ante cost-benefit assessment of competing enforcement mechanisms. As we demonstrated in Chapter 3, contract theory rests on the assumption that the law can alter the incentives parties face to respond opportunistically to the cooperative actions of participants in a common project. Chapter 4 showed that, at least in certain contexts, formal enforcement and informal enforcement mechanisms are rivals. This fact compels the architect of international law rules to make choices even when the obligations that they create rest on verifiable information. Unambiguous rules, for example, lend themselves to moral clarity, a feature that enhances informal enforcement. Similarly, a relationship that has no clear end point and substantial value to all participants can rely on retaliation to police compliance, even if the rules involve easily verifiable information. The second claim thus suggests that formal enforcement should be exceptional, not typical. We would expect to see formal enforcement, therefore, only where the interactions of the parties are complex and lack transparency. In such cases, third-party arbiters can police opportunism better than the parties themselves.

Finally, the third claim reflects the assumptions of the other two, and in particular the assertion that formal and informal enforcement are potential rivals. It further supposes that the decision to create an international obligation

international relations . . . " Article XIV*bis* of the General Agreement on Trade in Services, Article 73 of the Agreement on Trade-Related Aspects of Intellectual Property Rights and Article 2102 of the North American Free Trade Agreement have identical language. Article 2.2 of the Agreement on Technical Barriers to Trade stipulates that states may employ technical standards that fulfill its "national security requirements." The Treaty Establishing the European Community contains multiple derogations from its general obligations to permit parties to undertake measures justified on grounds of public security.

depends on expectations about enforcement. In particular, we assume that international actors, in deciding whether to adopt or extend a norm, take into account the costs and benefits of the anticipated enforcement mechanism. In the limiting case in which a rule represents only a slight improvement over the status quo, actors would adopt the rule only if they were confident that enforcement would be sufficiently effective to generate a welfare surplus (that the cooperating parties could then share). If international actors anticipate poor enforcement choices, therefore, they may withdraw from the cooperative opportunity altogether.

Uncertainty about enforcement exists if actors cannot predict whether their expectations about enforcement will be realized. Actors, depending on context, might prefer either formal enforcement or informal mechanisms. On the one hand, a state might avoid investing in a cooperative regime if it does not have confidence that formal enforcement bodies will do their job. One explanation for the relatively small impact of investment treaties on stimulating direct investment, for example, is that investors doubt the ability of arbitral bodies to fulfil their mandate under these treaties.[2] On the other hand, a state also may shy away from a commitment altogether if it believes both that informal mechanisms would provide the optimal enforcement structure and that there is a substantial risk that formal enforcement will be adopted and thereby weaken the informal regime. In other words, bodies charged with formal enforcement of international rules pose a threat to the adoption of new rules promoting cooperative goals if actors anticipate that the enforcement agency will fail to impose sanctions when required, *or* that it will impose formal sanctions in contexts where only informal mechanisms would achieve greater compliance at a lower cost.

Our task, then, is to evaluate the evidence that supports these claims and confirms their underlying assumptions. In Chapter 5, we surveyed the various international law enforcement mechanisms that exist in the contemporary world. A review of contemporary practice regarding the enforcement of

---

[2] On the weak correlation between treaties and investment inflows, see U.N. Conf. on Trade and Dev, Bilateral Investment Treaties in the Mid-1990s, U.N. Doc. UNCTAD/ITE/IIT/7 (1998); Mary Hallward-Driemeier, Do Bilateral Investment Treaties Attract FDI? Only a Bit . . . and They Could Bite (World Bank, Working Paper No. 3121, June 2003); Tom Ginsburg, *International Substitutes for Domestic Institutions: Bilateral Investment Treaties and Governance*, 25 INT'L REV. L. & ECON. 107 (2005); Jennifer Tobin & Susan Rose-Ackerman, Foreign Direct Investment and the Business Environment in Developing Countries: The Impact of Bilateral Investment Treaties (May 2005). For evidence suggesting some positive correlation between adherence to an investment treaty and attraction of investment, see Eric Neumayer & Laura Spess, Do Bilateral Investment Treaties Increase Foreign Direct Investment to Developing Countries? (Nov. 2004); Jeswald W. Salacuse & Nicholas P. Sullivan, *Do BITs Really Work? An Evaluation of Bilateral Investment Treaties and Their Grand Bargain*, 46 HARV. J. INT'L L. 67 (2005).

international law reveals the widespread use of informal mechanisms and a modern trend toward formal enforcement. We now consider how well these practices fit our arguments. We consider three factors that our theory identifies as relevant: verifiability; complex interdependence in the production of social welfare; and the effects on primary behavior of uncertainty about enforcement. Each factor has a significant role in explaining international law enforcement.

## VERIFIABILITY

The model of optimal enforcement developed earlier predicts that parties will resist having formal enforcement turn on information that is not verifiable to a disinterested third party except at an unacceptably high cost. Beneath this straightforward proposition lies considerable complexity. Ingenious use of proxies, such as burden-of-proof rules that screen out particular kinds of errors, can reduce the cost of determining the existence of conditions that otherwise might seem unverifiable. But, at the end of the day, the existence of private information can confound formal dispute resolution and drive parties to informal enforcement.

## EXAMPLE 1: ARMS CONTROL

The threat of expensive and dangerous weapons presents a classic collective action problem. Arms races are often wasteful. Everyone would be better off avoiding investments in new weapons that produce no net benefits once one accounts for adversary responses. To the extent that new technologies are necessary only to respond to their use by others and that implementation can be observed and regulated, cooperation can enhance social welfare. At the same time, everyone has an incentive to chisel on the agreement to obtain relative gains over adversaries.

The twentieth century saw many arms control agreements, including the Washington Naval Treaty, the Geneva Protocol on chemical weapons, the various agreements between the Soviet Union (and then Russia) and the United States on nuclear weapons, the Test Ban Treaty, the Treaty on the Nonproliferation of Nuclear Weapons, and the Treaty on Conventional Armed Forces in Europe (CFE Treaty). The literature on their import and compliance is vast. What interests us, out of the many fascinating problems they present, is the agreements' enforcement structure.

Without exception, modern arms control agreements use exclusively informal enforcement mechanisms. Some have formalized monitoring and reporting rules to facilitate verification, but none ever has authorized an independent tribunal directly to punish rulebreakers. Activists have attempted to bring arms control issues before the ICJ and domestic courts, but no serious threat to implement formal enforcement has materialized. The ICJ has limited itself to platitudes about the legality of using nuclear weapons; domestic courts have used doctrines based on judicial capacity to ward off these efforts.[3] Even the sometimes detailed and particular verification obligations, such as the elaborate inventory reporting rules of the CFE Treaty, rely entirely on reputational sanctions, along with prospects of future dealings and a presumed preference for reciprocity, for their enforcement.

Contract theory explains why we observe only informal enforcement of these treaties. Arms control decisions rest on two sets of issues, the risks presented by other states' technological breakthroughs and the likelihood of a state implementing a breakthrough itself. Informed choices depend heavily on private information, including a state's current research program, its capacity to convert laboratory discoveries into production capabilities, and the significance to it of exposure to risks that other states may present. Each assessment requires a command of technological issues, a comprehensive knowledge of economic capabilities, and sophisticated if ultimately subjective political instincts, in every case informed by data that everyone involved seeks to keep as secret as possible. Even more, each factor involves guesses about the future as much or more as reconstruction of observable events.

Nor does it seem feasible to construct proxies that could be verified but would capture the underlying factors in arms control treaties. Technological change and its implications cannot easily be reduced to verifiable formulas, especially when the essential inquiry involves projections into the future. It is scientific breakthroughs that threaten to overthrow arms control regimes, yet it is exactly the nature of scientific revolutions that they cannot be anticipated except at the most abstract level.

Conversely, the informal enforcement mechanisms that arms control agreements typically employ do seem reasonably effective. Bilateral arms control fits into a structure of future dealings with a risk of retaliation, and multilateral systems also have reputational effects. Further, both kinds of agreement allow parties to demonstrate a preference for reciprocity. For example, the arms control regimes that characterized the U.S.-Soviet relationship from the early 1960s to the end of the Soviet Union evidenced high levels of reciprocity and became increasingly extensive over time.

---

[3]  *E.g.*, Advisory Opinion on the Legality of the Threat or Use of Nuclear Weapons, [1996] I.C.J. 226; United States v. Kabat, 797 F.2nd 580 (8th Cir. 1986) (illegality of nuclear weapons under international law not a defense in prosecution for physical attacks and trespass on federal military base).

Of course, arms control during the twentieth century is not a story of unblemished success. The Washington Naval Treaty in its own way created a false sense of confidence, akin to what the Soviet Union derived from the Molotov-Ribbentrop Pact. But whatever failings that the various agreements may have had, it is difficult to believe that formal enforcement could have cured them.

EXAMPLE 2: ENVIRONMENTAL LAW

In the last few decades, states have framed significant multilateral environmental agreements, the most recent and ambitious of which are the United Nations Framework Convention on Climate Change, its Kyoto Protocol, and the complementary (or perhaps competing) Asian-Pacific Partnership on Clean Development and Climate. The analytics of these agreements track those applicable to arms control. In many contexts, environmental issues entail collective action where individual states have an incentive to shirk. If, hypothetically, every state in the world but the United States were to reduce greenhouse gases, the United States would get the (presumed) benefit of reduced global warming at no economic cost. For these agreements to work, then, some enforcement mechanism is necessary. But, as with arms control, no international agreement addressing environmental issues has employed formal enforcement.[4]

Problems of third-party verification may explain why international environmental agreements do not use formal enforcement. Like arms control, environmental regulation involves forward-looking assessments of the effects of technological change informed by an economic assessment of prospective benefits and costs and a political sense of the possible. The element of deliberate secrecy is not as important as in arms control, but private information, such as trade secrets and closely held commercial data, often is critical to assessing a state's response to environmental agreements. As a result, verification problems would plague any effort to write international environmental rules that a third party would enforce.

To be sure, national governments face a verification problem when they adopt environmental laws, to which they respond either by delegating the rulemaking to a specialized agency or by periodic updating of the rules through authorized political decision makers. But even domestic laws rarely if ever provide for full formal enforcement. Rather, a government decision maker usually has a monopoly over enforcement power, subject to judicial review. The explanation

---

[4] As with arms control treaties, the courts generally have rejected efforts to create formal enforcement of international environmental law. *E.g.*, Flores v. Southern Peru Copper Corp., 343 F.3rd 140 (2nd Cir. 2003) (dismissing suit contending that environmental damage constituted an international law violation).

for this feature, we believe, flows from contract theory: The error costs of private enforcement would exceed the benefits in motivating socially productive behavior.

Environmental cooperation also exposes a significant contrast in the institutional structure of public policy implementation at the domestic level and through international cooperation. A domestic policy maker can deal with technological and economic uncertainty through a combination of agency delegation and frequent updating of the limits on the agent's discretion. In an international context, agent delegation is still available, but supervision and revision of the agent's mandate is much more costly. In the absence of an international legislature that employs something other than a unanimity rule for its decisions, states are understandably reluctant to delegate much discretion to international agents.[5] And the lack of such an agent means that a potentially efficacious solution to the verifiability problem in international environmental law is unavailable.

## Example 3: Trade

In classical economic theory, free trade is desirable even when a state extracts no reciprocal concessions for its lower tariffs. The benefits to consumers from import competition always outweigh the costs to domestic producers from lost business. Were this model comprehensive and correct, trade liberalization would not constitute a collective action problem. Rather, lower barriers to imports would represent a convergence of preferences that states could reach unilaterally.

But the classical model has at least two serious deficiencies. First, it fails to account for goods that, in technical terms, have increasing returns to scale, that is goods that, for a producer, are more profitable to make as the level of production increases. Traditionally economists spoke of natural monopolies; contemporary jargon refers to positive network externalities. Local utility grids, computer operating systems, and advanced aircraft design all serve as examples: A single producer usually can deliver these goods more efficiently than can multiple producers.

Second, structural aspects of democratic decision making make it difficult for public choices to reflect optimal public welfare. A whole science of public choice has developed to explain why systematic distortions in the decision making process persist. One of the best documented is the disproportionate

---

[5] Paul B. Stephan, *Courts, Tribunals and Legal Unification – The Agency Problem*, 3 Chi. J. Int'l L. 333 (2002).

influence of domestic producers in shaping political choices, relative to the power of consumers to have their preferences taken into account. Simplifying greatly, producers tend to face lower organizational costs when expressing their preferences; consumers, who tend to be dispersed and heterogenous, face higher costs and therefore are less effective politically.[6]

Under these conditions, trade liberalization can become a collective action problem. First, states face pressure to accede to the monopoly position of each other's producers, which in turn requires trade-offs and compensation. Second, states need to strike bargains with domestic producers in the form of expanded export opportunities to compensate for the cost of import competition. In both instances, these bargains are open to chiseling, and the risk of noncompliance will deter states from reaching optimal bargains.

States have made bilateral reciprocal trade concessions for centuries. The GATT, negotiated in 1947, ushered in the multilateral trade liberalization system that grew into the WTO. Neither the various instruments constituting the GATT system nor any other bilateral nor multilateral trade agreement involving trade (as distinguished from investment) has provided for formal enforcement. NAFTA has an unusual mechanism for internationalizing the enforcement of certain domestic import duties: Importers or domestic competitors dissatisfied with the application of national antidumping duty and countervailing duty law can invoke the reviewing power of ad hoc arbitral tribunals, rather than that of domestic courts. But, at least in theory, these tribunals apply only domestic law and do not directly enforce any of the provisions of the relevant international agreement.[7]

It is tempting to repeat our analysis of arms control and environmental agreements to explain the lack of formal enforcement in these trade pacts. Like these other subject areas, trade concessions involve forward-looking guesses about macroeconomic trends and technological innovation in particular

---

[6]  Vilfredo Pareto, MANUAL OF POLITICAL ECONOMY 379 (Ann S. Schwier & Alfred N. Page eds. & Ann S. Schwier, trans., 1971) (1927). For later work developing the same point, see Dennis C. Mueller, PUBLIC CHOICE II 238–42 (1989); Mancur Olson, THE LOGIC OF COLLECTIVE ACTION: PUBLIC GOODS AND THE THEORY OF GROUPS 143 (Rev. ed. 1971); Anne O. Krueger, *Political Economy, International Trade, and Economic Integration*, 82 AMER. ECON. REV. 109 (1992); Wendy Tacaks, *Pressures for Protectionism: An Empirical Analysis*, 19 ECON. INQUIRY 687 (1981).

[7]  We say "in theory" because in some instances the panelists seem willing to incorporate the terms of NAFTA directly in domestic law in order to overturn domestic administrative decisions. The clearest example of this practice is *Softwood Lumber Products from Canada*, No. USA-CDA-2002-1904–2 (2005), a decision on the correct methodology for calculating the margin of dumping that conflicts directly with *Corus Staal BV v. Department of Commerce*, 395 F.3rd 1343 (Fed. Cir. 2005). For the argument that the panel system is inconsistent with U.S. constitutional law, see Jim C. Chen, *Appointments with Disaster: The Unconstitutionality of Binational Arbitral Review under the United States-Canada Free Trade Agreement*, 49 WASH. & LEE I. REV. 1455 (1992).

industries, rather than the fixing of discrete historic facts. There exist two confounding factors, however. First, the modern trend in trade law is to create a dispute resolution mechanism, either a standing tribunal or an arbitration process, to address conflicts. These mechanisms do not have enforcement power, but they do generate neutral observations about the merits of disputes. Second, one important element of trade law – "national treatment," the principle that a state will not discriminate against imports in its rules and regulations – has a counterpart in the laws of the United States and the European Community. In these latter venues, both common markets rather than simply liberalized traders, the judiciary directly enforces this principle. If tribunals have jurisdiction to address disputes, even though they cannot enforce their decisions, can we really say that verifiability problems exist? Moreover, why does "national treatment" present verifiability problems when adopted in the GATT, when the U.S. and European courts find it possible to enforce it?[8]

The answer to these questions, we believe, rests partly on the fundamental point that verifiability operates as a continuum rather than as a binary categorization. Even if the underlying issue – here, whether local rules and regulations impose unacceptable costs on the functioning of a common market – contains too many imponderables to submit to a third party, easier-to-prove proxies can be constructed that do a reasonably good job of capturing what the rule seeks to do. But the choice of proxy has substantive consequences, as any deviation from perfect mimicry entails the risk of either overinclusiveness or underinclusiveness. Deciding which risk to take requires a judgment about the strength of the preference for national treatment relative to other policy concerns, such as safety, protection of local culture or the environment, and tolerating regulatory experiments. The framers of an international regime might find it desirable to make a choice, but they need not if they regard the loss of formal enforcement as an acceptable price for greater flexibility in balancing these competing policy goals.

Consider how the ECJ implements national treatment under the Treaty of Rome. Article 28 prohibits "quantitative restrictions" (a technical term that comprises bans) and "measures having equivalent effect" on imports from other members. Article 30 qualifies this flat rule by permitting restrictions "justified on grounds of public morality, public policy or public security; the protection of health and life of humans, animals or plants; the protection

---

[8]  In theory, the regional common market courts in Latin America and Asia that resemble the ECJ also have the authority to address this question and enforce their decisions with direct sanctions. As a practical matter, however, the work of these bodies does not yet support a conclusion about their effective capacity.

of national treasures possessing artistic, historic or archaeological value; or the protection of industrial and commercial property," subject to the caveat that any restriction "shall not, however, constitute a means of arbitrary discrimination or a disguised restriction on trade between Member States." To a lawyer, the obvious questions are what constitutes an "equivalent" effect, what is "arbitrary" as opposed to rough justice, and how to unmask a "disguised" restriction. The answer to each requires the use of some rule of thumb that then presents the risk of overenforcing Article 28 at the expense of Article 30, or vice versa. The ECJ's solution, at least with health and safety regulation, is to use the regulatory judgments of the producer's country as a baseline and to regard more demanding standards in importing countries as presumptively an impermissible disguised trade barrier.[9]

The Commerce Clause of the U.S. Constitution raises similar issues. By its terms, that provision only allocates regulatory jurisdiction over interstate commerce to the national government, but the Supreme Court long has understood it to contain an implicit constraint on state and local regulation that interferes with the national common market. The inevitable questions are what counts as interference, what kinds of local preferences can justify such interference, and how to offset the cost of interference versus the cost of frustrating local preferences. One proxy, evident in the first Supreme Court decision to address the issue, would forbid only explicit discrimination, such as singling out a national institution for a special tax.[10] Another variant, which the Court has used more recently, involves a lower threshold for deciding if a burden on interstate commerce exists and substantial skepticism about state justifications.[11] Our point, again, is: (1) formal enforcement substitutes a more easily verifiable rule as a proxy for the hard-to-verify standard; (2) a range of proxies are available; and (3) the choice among proxies implicates a substantive judgment about regulatory capacity and the risks of protectionism.

The necessity of using proxies and the policy judgments entailed in choosing among them explain why the WTO and similar trade regimes use the intermediate enforcement mechanism of third-party dispute resolution without formal

---

[9] For fuller discussion, see Francesca Bignami, *The Challenge of Cooperative Regulatory Federalism after Enlargement* in LAW AND GOVERNANCE IN AN ENLARGED EUROPEAN UNION 97 (George Bermann & Katharina Pistor, eds., 2004).

[10] M'Culloch v. Maryland, 17 U.S. (4 Wheat.) 316 (1819) (invalidating tax on national bank). For Justice Scalia, although perhaps not for any other Justice, this test remains the only legitimate proxy. West Lynn Creamery, Inc. v. Healy, 512 U.S. 186, 210 (1994) (Scalia, J., concurring).

[11] Complete Auto Transit, Inc. v. Brady, 430 U.S. 274 (1977) (announcing three-factor test); American Trucking Assns., Inc. v. Scheiner, 483 U.S. 266 (1987) (announcing internal consistency test). For fuller discussion of U.S. commerce clause jurisprudence and optimal rules for common markets, see Frank H. Easterbrook, *Antitrust and the Economics of Federalism*, 26 J.L. & ECON. 23 (1983); Saul Levmore, *Interstate Exploitation and Judicial Intervention*, 69 VA. L. REV. 563 (1983).

enforcement. As we argue in Chapter 3, informal enforcement mechanisms depend on clarity about both the obligation itself and either party's actions taken in response to the other's compliance with it. National treatment commitments in trade agreements, we have observed, entail complex if not imponderable determinations. A tribunal decision has the effect of replacing an unverifiable standard with a clear issue. A decision requires someone to do something or determines that nothing need be done, and observers then only have to determine whether the parties have complied with that decision. By creating clarity, the dispute resolution process promotes informal enforcement. At the same time, the absence of formal enforcement both allows informal enforcement mechanisms to function and leaves the parties greater flexibility to resist substantive policy making made through a tribunal's proxy choice.

Consider, for example, *United States – Standards for Reformulated and Conventional Gasoline*, the first decision of the WTO Appellate Body.[12] The WTO DSB determined that a U.S. environmental regulation that imposed stricter standards for the phasing out of fuel additives on imported gasoline than on domestically refined products constituted impermissible discrimination against an imported good. The Clinton Administration, determining that it could issue new regulations without going back to Congress, chose to comply with the WTO DSB; a domestic court confirmed this choice.[13] The primary effect of the WTO decision was to clarify that a particular exercise of regulatory discretion violated a general principle of GATT law and to provide the domestic regulator with a justification for an alternative exercise of that discretion. Secondary effects included bolstering the reputation of the United States as a law-abiding state and of the WTO DSB as an effective propounder of GATT law, enabling the United States to signal a preference for reciprocity, and forestalling retaliation by the trading partners of the United States.

Note that the United States could comply with the decision because the WTO DSB used a fairly narrow proxy for discrimination – it focused on the facial and clearly disadvantageous discrimination of the regulation. If the WTO DSB had used a surprising and substantively more ambitious standard, such as forbidding any regulation more stringent than that imposed by the country of production, the United States might have borne the costs of defiance, with a collateral harmful effect on the reputation of the WTO DSB. The United States might have justified such defiance as principled and forward looking. If the WTO DSB had the authority to impose direct sanctions, however, the United

---

[12]   AB-1996–1.
[13]   George E. Warren Corp. v. EPA, 159 F.3rd 616 (D.C. Cir. 1998).

States could have resisted only by refusing to honor a demand for payment. It never is easy to explain what a refusal to pay money represents beyond greed.

This example raises a parallel question, however. If dispute resolution processes such as the WTO provide the clarity needed for informal enforcers, why would formal enforcement (i.e., the direct imposition of sanctions pursuant to ex ante rules) *ever* be optimal? One answer is that informal dispute resolution – such as the WTO DSB – has an inherent limitation. Affected parties face no sanctions if they choose not to participate and decline to reveal clarifying information. Thus, as we discuss in subsequent examples, whenever the complexity of the transaction is interdependent and thus not initially observable to a third party, an informal arbiter has no mechanism for compelling the information that will permit it to "get the facts." In such a case, the key features that we associate with formal enforcement – private standing and the capacity to impose sanctions for noncompliance – become vitally important.

## Example 4: Vital State Interests

Many treaties contain a formulation that relieves a party of its obligations in cases where profound state interests are implicated. At the start of this chapter, we mentioned trade agreements, which invariably excuse noncompliance where a party believes itself faced with serious security concerns. The precise standard varies, from "essential security interests" (GATT Art. XXI and NAFTA Art. 2102) to "public security" (EC Treaty Art. 30) to "public policy" (Convention on the Recognition and Enforcement of Foreign Arbitral Awards Art. 5(2)[b]). What treaties typically reserve, however, is the capacity of a party to place important state interests above its international commitments.

Enforcement of these profound-state-interests provisions varies significantly and in ways that are consistent with our theory. We see three approaches to assertions of state interest: self-judging, which allows a state to avoid both formal enforcement of an obligation and tribunal review of its action; tribunal review with no formal enforcement; and tribunal or judicial determination with formal enforcement. The choice of approach depends enormously on the context.

Both the GATT and NAFTA contain apparently explicit commitments to self-judging of an essential security interest. Both instruments allow a party to invoke what "*it considers necessary* for the protection of its essential security interests . . . taken in time of war or other emergency in international relations" as a reason for suspending almost all of its obligations.[14] The United States

---

[14] Emphasis supplied. The GATT also allows invocation of this defense for actions "relating to traffic in arms, ammunition and implements of war and to such traffic in other goods and materials as

has invoked this language twice, once when the Sandinista regime used the old GATT dispute resolution system to challenge U.S. trade sanctions and later when the EC initiated WTO dispute settlement to attack the Helms-Burton legislation punishing persons who engaged in certain business relations with Cuba. Neither case produced a resolution of the issue, although academic commentators have argued against the self-judging aspects of these provisions.

In the context of both the GATT and NAFTA, the debate over the capacity of a dispute resolution authority to determine independently the existence of at least some elements of essential security interests seems somewhat beside the point. Assume, for example, that a WTO tribunal announced that it could decide whether an "emergency in international relations" existed, even if it could not determine what constituted an essential security interest. Because such a tribunal lacks formal enforcement power, its ruling, at most, would facilitate informal enforcement of GATT obligations. Yet a self-judged claim would implicate exactly the same enforcement structure. Other WTO members could tell for themselves, without any assistance from experts, whether a state of international emergency existed, and could not fully assess what a WTO party might regard as a threat to its vital interests. Faced with uncertainty about the character of the claim, parties would determine, based on information available to them, whether the assertion is plausible. If so, they would be inclined to give the asserting party a pass; if not, they might retaliate and shun, meanwhile updating their estimation of that state's reputation. Thus when a state asserts essential security interests to justify a general policy, such as measures targeted at another state, only informal enforcement applies, whether the assertion is self-judged or not.

But when a measure targets a particular individual, perhaps by seizing a bank account or blocking a transfer of property, different considerations apply. The juxtaposition of state power and discrete private interests presents a risk of arbitrary and discriminatory force, concentrated on an actor who may lack the capacity to defend itself. Rarely is a particular firm or individual in a position to threaten a state's security, but states easily can crush private actors. Moreover, the presence of a discrete victim makes it easier to isolate a verifiable issue. When the question to be decided is not whether a state may undertake a measure but, rather, whether it must pay compensation, an arbiter can more easily focus on discrete and determinable questions. A victim need not challenge the general validity of a public policy to demonstrate that a particular application bears no

---

is carried on directly or indirectly for the purpose of supplying a military establishment." NAFTA extends the defense to regulation of services and technology transfer.

relation to the stated purpose and that it accordingly triggers an obligation to make a money payment.

Two instances of formal enforcement of international law illustrate this point. First, BITs that provide for individual investor enforcement anticipate juxtapositions of general policies and individual interests. These treaties typically contain language holding a host state harmless for policies motivated by "protection of its own essential security interests."[15] When states invoke this provision to justify an expropriation, arbitral panels have considered themselves entitled to assess whether the state's actions fell within its terms. Consider a recent ICSID arbitration of a claim against Argentina for changing the rules under which a privatized natural gas utility could calculate its tariff. The panel rejected Argentina's argument that deteriorating economic conditions constituted a crisis implicating essential security interests. It noted that Argentina and the United States intended the treaty protections to continue to operate during times of economic difficulties and asserted that it had the capacity to determine whether Argentina had invoked its "essential security interests" pretextually to avoid scrutiny of an attack on a foreign investor.[16] Determining that Argentina had done this, the arbiters issued an award for money damages.

To appreciate how formal enforcement under these circumstances conforms to our model, one must recall that the question to be decided is not whether a state may undertake a measure, but rather whether it must pay compensation. The parties must address issues about the character of the state actions and its effect on the claimant, but not whether the overall social benefits of the action exceed its costs. Cabining the dispute in this way limits the dispute to issues that are more likely to be verifiable.

As in BITs, the Convention on the Recognition and Enforcement of Foreign Arbitral Awards puts states under a general obligation to compel a money payment to satisfy a foreign award, but excuses that duty when enforcing the award would violate that state's public policy. Were public policy to be equated with the exact terms of the local legal order, claimants could obtain enforcement of an arbitral award only in instances where a local court would have reached the same outcome (procedural issues such as jurisdiction over the respondent aside). But for the most part judges have read the public policy proviso narrowly.[17] On the few occasions where the U.S. courts have invoked

[15] Treaty Concerning the Reciprocal Encouragement and Protection of Investment, U.S.–Argentina, Nov. 14, 1991, Art. XI, Treaty Doc. 103–2.

[16] CMS Gas Transmission Co. v. Argentine Republic, ¶ 354, ICSID Case No. ARB/01/8 (May 12, 2005).

[17] E.g., TMR Energy Ltd. v. State Property Fund of Ukraine, 411 F.3rd 296 (D.C. Cir. 2005) (rejecting Ukraine's claim that enforcing arbitral award would violate public policy because underlying contract

public policy as a ground for not enforcing a foreign arbitral award covered by the Convention, the award typically required something more than a cash payment, such as a transfer of technology regulated by federal law.[18]

The same analysis applies to these decisions. Enforcing an arbitral award typically involves a money transfer, not necessarily an endorsement of the legal theory that led to the award. Limiting the public policy proviso to cases where either a cash payment would violate positive law (such as a duly authorized freeze on payments to a particular recipient) or the award requires something more than a payment frees courts from having to confront issues that may present serious verification problems.

EXAMPLE 5: HUMAN RIGHTS

Human rights law is a product of the post–World War II era, although its antecedents go back to the birth of the state system. In the last quarter-century it has become a consuming interest of that portion of the legal academy that does international law. Much of the discussion, however, has been about the body of human rights law that has not been reduced to treaty commitments, but rather exists, in the eyes of many, as an immanent system of rules and norms that enjoys the status of customary international law. We will consider the customary international law of human rights later in this book, but here we will focus on the enforcement mechanisms found in express human rights instruments.

One element of our theory is that international law enforcement matters most as a response to a collective action problem. A preliminary question, then, is whether human rights law ever involves the joint production of collective welfare. As a general matter, a state's treatment of its own subjects does not induce other states to behave opportunistically. If one state tortures its subjects, for example, other states have no greater reason to torture their own.[19] Put differently, the benefits that accrue to a society from honoring certain norms of decency and humanity do not diminish or grow as a result of the behavior of

---

violated Ukrainian prohibition of bankruptcy preferences); Karaha Bodas Co., L.L.C. v. Perusahaan Pertambangan Minyak Dan Gas Bumi Negara, 364 F.3rd 274 (5th Cir. 2004) (rejecting Pertamina's claim that the arbitral award constituted a violation of the international law doctrine forbidding punishment for honoring applicable government demands); Fotochrome, Inc. v. Copal Co., Ltd., 517 F.2nd 512, 516 (2nd Cir.1975) (enforcement of foreign arbitral award against bankrupt debtor does not violate public policy against discrimination among creditors).

[18] Ministry of Defense v. Gould, Inc., 969 F.2nd 764 (9th Cir. 1992) (not enforcing award to the extent it required a technology transfer that would have violated federal export control regime, but honoring claim for damages).

[19] For elaboration of the point, see Jack L. Goldsmith & Stephen D. Krasner, *The Limits of Idealism*, 132 DAEDALUS 47 (2001).

others. To recast the point in economic terminology, human rights can best be understood as a private good, arising in the context of particular relationships between states and those subject to their power, rather than as a jointly produced commodity.

But this point, although generally correct, does not apply to all human rights obligations. Consider the Treaty of Westphalia that ended the Thirty Years' War and, in a sense, gave birth to international human rights.[20] That Treaty obligated the signatory sovereigns to respect the rights of religious minorities, but not just for humanitarian reasons. The Protestant and Catholic sovereigns in effect both gave and took hostages, in the sense that the treatment of one's religious minority could be linked to that of the other's. Each religious camp presumably would have preferred to abuse the outsiders within their midst, and were deterred from doing so by a competing preference not to see their coreligionists in other lands abused. In other words, in some contexts human rights commitments present a collective action problem, namely, when rulers of one state for whatever reason have internalized the well-being of the subjects of other sovereigns.

Note that this point is more limited than the broad claim that the suffering of anyone amounts to an injury to us all. We appreciate the moral imperative that calls on humans to respect the basic needs of all our fellow humans. But the tendency of humans to differentiate among others in terms of their sympathies, identifying with the triumphs and sufferings of some groups more than others, is both a fundamental part of human nature and, some would argue, morally defensible in itself.[21] Accordingly, people react differently to the abuse of some groups more than others, depending on the degree of identification that they experience. Where identification is great, a collective action problem exists; where it is weak, the analytics of joint production and opportunism do not apply with the same force.

A different collective action problem arises when the particular human rights abuse by its nature involves externalized harms. The law of war crimes involves actions that harm outsiders, in the sense that adversaries are the principal victims. What distinguishes genocide from more conventional atrocities, for example, is that actors wielding something like state power single out a group for extinction because of fixed attributes that are perceived as categorically distinguishing the victims from their tormentors. Any state or group that faces a future threat of violence by others has some reason to invest in deterring such actions, but everyone has an incentive to let others bear the cost of deterrence.

[20] For a fuller discussion of the Treaty and its significance, see Stephen D. Krasner, SOVEREIGNTY: ORGANIZED HYPOCRISY (1999).
[21] Jack L. Goldsmith, *Liberal Democracy and Cosmopolitan Duty*, 55 STAN. L. REV. 1667 (2003).

The presence or absence of a collective action problem explains why many treaty-based human rights regimes do not employ formal enforcement but that the European regime and, more speculatively, the International Criminal Court, does. Consider first the function of the ECtHR. By the time of the 1999 revision of the European Convention's enforcement mechanism, it had become clear that adherence to human rights rules was a necessary, if not sufficient, condition for accession to the European Union and that this gatekeeping work had become a principal function of the ECtHR regime. For states aspiring to become fully European, treatment of their subjects was a good proxy for how they would treat the outsiders to whom they would play host within a common market.

The International Criminal Court presents a more complicated case. First, we count it as an instance of formal enforcement only because the regime does not give states an express veto over its decisions to act, but at present a number of states, most importantly the majority of nuclear powers that have not assented to the Statute of Rome, have considerable practical capability to obstruct its functions. Second, as we noted earlier, nothing stops the ICC from exercising self restraint in a way that would limit its jurisdiction to cases referred to it by the Security Council or otherwise through great power consensus. Finally, because it has not yet conducted any trials and has issued only one set of arrest warrants, any discussion of its function necessarily is speculative.

In the spirit of speculation, however, we do note that the instances in which the ICC may act according to the express terms of the Rome Statute (cases of crimes against humanity, genocide, and war crimes) all involve injuries that are likely to fall on outsiders. The potential crime of aggression, which awaits a further treaty for its definition but which the ICC in the future might prosecute, clearly involves externalized violence. Thus, the ICC's formal enforcement power, to the extent it exists, is consistent with the optimal enforcement model.

Verification issues provide another, somewhat weaker explanation of the different enforcement strategies of the European human rights regime and other treaty-based bodies of international human rights law. The multilateral instruments that set out human rights norms without creating a strong enforcement mechanism – the United Nations Charter and the Declaration of Human Rights, the various multilateral covenants, and regional covenants such as those for the American States and Africa – for the most part state the obligation as conditional or relative, relying on capacious adjectives such as "arbitrary" (bad) or "reasonable" (good). Others forbid particular kinds of discrimination, a standard that, if not constrained in some way, opens up a wide field of inquiry to justify or to condemn particular instances of similar or dissimilar treatment. In other cases of an absolute commitment, such as the prohibition of torture, the definition of the proscribed conduct is sufficiently loose to permit an implicit cost-benefit calculus.

Moreover, the multilateral instruments typically contain general qualifying provisions that can serve as a basis for a blanket immunization of state practice. For example, Article 1 (1) of the Covenant on Civil and Political Rights, one of the first multilateral instruments crafted by the United Nations, proclaims the right of self-determination that allows all peoples to "freely determine their political status and freely pursue their economic, social and cultural develop-ment." Throughout the Cold War, the Soviet Union and its camp followers relied on this language to insulate their repressive practices from international scrutiny.

If a full range of conditions – political, social, economic, and cultural – are available to define and limit the implementation of human rights obligations, justifying any particular definition or limit becomes exceedingly difficult. To determine whether a state has honored its obligation, the dispute resolution body must assess not only historical events – what happened to the victim – but also the context, in the broadest sense of the word. For the same structural reasons that compliance with arms control, environmental, and trade obliga-tions generally are unverifiable, then, such human rights also are not readily amenable to third-party determination.

With the European human rights regime, by contrast, it is possible to see the gradual development of constraints on the reference to political and social context in order to enable a less obstructed focus on the individual interests at issue. Early on, the Strasbourg Court articulated the concept of "margin of appreciation," the notion that it would take a generous view of the efforts of states to comply with their obligations under the Convention. This approach had the effect of imposing a fairly high burden on anyone seeking to challenge a state practice and thus excluded a wide range of cost-benefit inquiries from the judicial process. At the same time, the gradual convergence of the politi-cal, economic, and social systems of the members, especially apparent by the end of the 1990s, had the effect of eliminating claims of exceptionalism as a result of extraordinary circumstances. Moreover, as certain standards of prac-tice become more widespread, those countries that deviated from them stuck out more. Outliers become easier for the Court to characterize as violators.

Finally, we note that the ICC provides complicated confirmation of the claim that verification matters in determining whether formal enforcement is invoked. The ICC's jurisdiction requires not only a finding that one of the proscribed crimes has occurred, but also that no state with jurisdiction over the crime is willing or able "genuinely to carry out the investigation or prosecution."[22] The assessment of the genuineness of a state's willingness to proceed, we suspect, is inherently unverifiable, although we concede the possibility that the ICC over time might develop verifiable proxies that further the general purposes of the statute. On the one hand, the assignment to the ICC of the authority to make these determinations may be seen as undermining the claim that the verifiability of an issue is a precondition to formal enforcement. On the other hand, the resistance of the United States and others to the ICC, based exactly on this consideration, indicates that verifiability does matter.

### EXAMPLE 6: PROPERTY RIGHTS

Property rights constitute a subset of human rights that has a distinct and extensive international protection through formal enforcement. This entails interests traditionally protected by domestic legal systems and traded commercially in market-oriented societies. Both BITs and multilateral trade regimes that provide for investment protection, such as the European system, NAFTA, and CAFTA, include formal enforcement to protect these rights. ICANN and the international arbitration regime based on the Convention for the Recognition and Enforcement of Foreign Arbitral Awards also use formal enforcement to safeguard commercially valuable property. Indeed, the only instances of which we are aware where international law protection of property rights does not entail formal enforcement are those multilateral human rights instruments that cover mostly nonmarket interests such as personal dignity and due process, but also mention property in passing.

This extensive use of formal enforcement to promote international protection of property is consistent with information theory and the problem of verifiability. Third-party arbiters can invoke ancient concepts of commercially traded property and a rich vocabulary of legal doctrines addressing questions of definition and dimension of property rights. This vocabulary suggests proxies that tribunals easily can appropriate to address property disputes.

Consider, for example, arbitration of domain name names under ICANN auspices. A challenge to a registered name involves, as a legal matter, two main questions: What state's law should apply to the dispute, and whether, under the relevant law, the registered name encroaches on a legally protected intellectual property interest. Both inquiries are easily manageable under conventional legal approaches, even if the answers are not ineluctable, and there is no good reason to expect the disputants to expect anything other than these conventional materials to apply.

---

[22] Rome Statute of the International Criminal Court art. 17(1)(a).

## Summary

The choice between formal and informal enforcement of international agreements does turn to a great extent on the verifiability of the conditions on which a finding of violation must rest. Some regimes have addressed this problem by selecting proxies that permit verification at a lower cost and that exclude high-cost aspects of otherwise multifaceted issues. The choice of proxy to a large extent determines the nature of the underlying obligation, however. In many instances, the parties to international cooperative regimes appear to have chosen informal enforcement precisely to put off the substantive decision implied by a choice of a verifiable proxy that may not motivate the desired primary behavior.

## Complex Interdependence

In addition to verifiability, another condition conducive to formal enforcement of a legal norm is the extent to which obligations are complex and interdependent. Informal enforcement depends on the ability of both parties and disinterested observers to discern, at a reasonable cost, whether or not someone has complied with an obligation. The need to retaliate may explain and justify noncompliance, but a claimed right to retaliate may be opportunistic. The more difficult it becomes to distinguish noncompliance *in support of* informal enforcement (e.g., retaliation for an earlier defection by the counterparty) from opportunistic noncompliance, the greater the need for third-party dispute resolution. Put simply, the harder it becomes for interested parties and casual observers to call fouls, the greater the value that a disinterested expert can add.

To be sure, in many contexts a referee can call fouls without having any power to sanction. For example, in most sporting contests one can imagine the referee merely announcing fouls and letting the parties rely exclusively on informal mechanisms to insure mutual compliance. Giving referees sanctioning power in such environments may speed the contest along for the spectators, but it is not essential to the maintenance of a cooperative equilibrium. This is not the case, however, with complex international commitments. The actions of each state actor are, at least to some extent, not observable by third parties. Where some of the key information is private (how did you respond to the earlier actions of your counterparty?), the referee must be endowed with the power to impose sanctions for nonrevelation of information critical to determining the facts of the matter. Thus, when actions are both complex and hidden from others, but where they can be revealed and verified, a formal enforcement regime will improve the parties' incentives to cooperate fully in achieving their collective goals.

As this discussion indicates, however, complex interdependence is a necessary, but not a sufficient, condition for formal enforcement. If an issue cannot be verified to a third party at an acceptable cost, the added value of a disinterested expert vanishes. Conversely, if an issue is verifiable but also has sufficient clarity to permit low-cost monitoring by interested parties and casual observers, the expert cannot contribute much. Thus, we expect to find formal enforcement where 1) information is verifiable and 2) when a legal obligation entails interdependency.

We find the strongest confirmation of our thesis in the joint European common market and human rights regimes. The European Convention on Human Rights and the European Community have different origins and different membership, but, as we noted earlier, increasingly they have turned to a common purpose. They seek to advance European integration that has political and social, as well as economic, dimensions. This linkage, as much the product of historical accident (particularly the collapse of the Soviet-dominated East) as of design, means that in Europe, compliance with both the EC's economic rules, particularly the nondiscrimination principle at the heart of a common market, and the European Convention's human rights norms has become interdependent. In this situation, a state that represses dissent or fails to honor basic norms of due process not only threatens the welfare of its own subjects, but impairs its ability to participate in a system of economic cooperation based on some degree of individual liberty.

The problem of interdependence also illuminates why we find formal enforcement of national treatment rules in strong common market regimes but not in looser multilateral trade agreements. Trade liberalization as such typically involves nothing more than incremental economic adjustments. As we noted earlier, in some instances it presents no collective action issues at all, because the costs as well as the benefits of liberalization can fall proportionately rather than unevenly. The creation of a common market, at least on the European model, requires something more. A common market regime anticipates and to some extent drives migration of the factors of production, both capital and labor. This entails a far more substantial uprooting than simply allowing greater import competition. Success in this venture in turn depends on reducing the risk that the migrating producer will face unanticipated hostility on relocation.

We do not contend that this observation fully explains everything we know about international agreements. For example, one might suppose that free trade agreements also aspire to a level of economic integration comparable to that sought by common markets, at least when they involve neighbors with strong economic ties. But neither NAFTA nor CAFTA uses formal enforcement to bolster the national treatment rules they apply, even though they do use such mechanisms to protect investor rights. Instead, they rely on an intermediate mechanism of ad hoc arbitration with access limited to states and no formal enforcement authority.[23] Perhaps, as these regimes mature, we will see something closer to formal enforcement extended to protect importers, and not just investors, from arbitrary discrimination.

Still, the general conformity of contemporary practice to our theory's predictions is reassuring. Where we find formal enforcement, we observe: (a) the use of proxies to manage verification problems; (b) complex interdependence among the relevant obligations; and (c) an inability to observe directly the responses of individual actors to the actions of others in pursuit of cooperative goals. That states have not yet exploited all feasible opportunities for optimal collective action does not seem nearly so great a difficulty for our theory.

## UNCERTAINTY ABOUT ENFORCEMENT MECHANISMS

Our last claim is that enforcement risk can deter the creation of international rules and norms. If parties with the capacity to create international law face uncertainty about what enforcement mechanism will apply because of an inability to anticipate how tribunals might act to expand or restrict formal enforcement, they may decline to create an obligation rather than run the risk that enforcement costs will exceed any welfare gains. This means that, in cases where formal enforcement is welfare enhancing but the parties for some reason cannot create the appropriate sanctioning authority, they may elect to forego otherwise desirable collective action. Similarly, the risk of formal enforcement crowding out effective informal mechanisms may deter collective action in cases where informal enforcement alone would create a social welfare surplus.

Of course, documenting actions that have not taken place presents severe difficulties. We never can be sure why a law was not adopted, much less why it was enacted at one time rather than another. Rather than attempt a systematic review of the evidence, then, we resort to case histories that are concededly anecdotal and selective. Nonetheless, the stories are suggestive. They involve important topics about which a substantial body of international law exists – human rights, trade, criminal justice, and European integration. Each illustrates

---

[23] For the saga of ongoing U.S. resistance to a NAFTA Chapter 20 adjudication involving barriers to Mexican trucks, see *Secretary of Transportation v. Public Citizen*, 541 U.S. 752 (2004).

our claims and is consistent with our theory, even if together they do not constitute proof of its validity.

## HUMAN RIGHTS AND CIVIL RIGHTS IN THE UNITED STATES

Our first case history involves the evolution in the United States of norms forbidding racial discrimination. This is of course one of the most important stories of the last sixty years, a great, still unfolding and deeply contested narrative that goes to the heart of the American identity.[24] Concerns about international law played only a small part of the story, but they did exist. Their role in these critical developments, however marginal, is instructive.

The intersection of the U.S. civil rights movement and international law can be traced to the founding of the United Nations. Movement leaders both supported the new organization and argued that its mission, which embraced decolonization, necessarily included the dismantling of racial segregation in the United States. References to the UN Charter, and then the 1948 Universal Declaration of Human Rights, began appearing in the arguments that civil rights groups directed to both public opinion and the U.S. courts.[25] A few progressive state courts embraced the linkage between international law and a ban on segregation, which required these judges to assert their authority to interpret and enforce the UN Charter. Other judicial decisions suggested that the claim might be premature, but did not foreclose the possibility that international law could be a lever for undoing racial segregation.[26] At that moment, greater reliance on international-agreement-based judicial decisions to advance civil rights seemed a likely prospect.

Lawmakers in the United States responded to this pressure by seeking to eliminate the coercive force of its international commitments. During the early 1950s, Senator John Bricker introduced versions of a constitutional amendment that would have barred treaties from having any effect on domestic law, absent implementing legislation. Although the amendment addressed a general concern about the incorporation of international law into the domestic legal system, it clearly was prompted by the fear that U.S. membership in the United Nations could give domestic judges a means to effect legal change without the

---

[24]  The most recent, and in our view the best, account to date is Michael J. Klarman, FROM JIM CROW TO CIVIL RIGHTS – THE SUPREME COURT AND THE STRUGGLE FOR RACIAL EQUALITY (2004).

[25]  *See* Mary L. Dudziak, COLD WAR CIVIL RIGHTS: RACE AND THE IMAGE OF AMERICAN DEMOCRACY 43–64 (2000); Michael J. Klarman, note 24 *supra*, at 182–84.

[26]  Sei Fujii v. State, 217 P.2nd 481, 218 P.2nd 595 (Cal. Dist. Ct. App. 1950), *vacated*, 242 P.2nd 617 (Cal. 1952); Kenji Namba v. McCourt, 185 Or. 579, 204 P.2nd 569 (Or. 1949); Perez v. Lippold, 32 Cal.2nd 711, 198 P.2nd 17 (Cal. 1948).

participation of the two political branches. Although segregationists supported Bricker, so did many others who were neutral toward or opposed to segregation. For example, Bricker's effort won the support of the American Bar Association and at one point came within a single vote of clearing the Senate by a two-thirds majority.[27]

The Eisenhower Administration eventually fended off this movement to amend the Constitution, but only by promising to use its own powers to insulate the U.S. legal order from any U.S. international commitments. The Administration represented to Congress that it would not enter into any international agreement that had domestic law reform as its purpose.[28] To implement this pledge, the Administration began a practice, which has continued to the present, of conditioning U.S. adherence to agreements affecting domestic civil rights on the subsequent enactment of domestic legislation.[29]

Some scholars have sought to dismiss the Bricker Amendment episode by emphasizing its connection to the defense of segregation, thereby suggesting that only bigotry explains the opposition to coercive invocation of international law by the domestic courts.[30] This connection is part of the story, but fails to do justice to the complex dynamic surrounding the use of international law in the battle against U.S. racial segregation. First, the controversy survived *Brown v. Board of Education*'s definitive blow against segregation in 1954. Secretary of State Dulles gave the final pledge to Congress that held off the push for a constitutional amendment a year after *Brown* came down, and some version of the proposal remained under consideration in the Senate until 1957.[31] Second, and more importantly, the range of support for the Bricker Amendment far exceeded that for segregation. Some important part of the U.S. legal establishment separated the issues by supporting both the ending of segregation and some quarantine of international law from the U.S. legal system.

---

[27] Duane Tananbaum, THE BRICKER AMENDMENT CONTROVERSY – A TEST OF EISENHOWER'S POLITICAL LEADERSHIP (1988); Curtis A. Bradley, *Foreign Affairs and Domestic Reform*, 87 VA. L. REV. 1475 (2001).

[28] *See* 32 DEP'T STATE BULL. 820 (1955) (statement of Secretary of State Dulles that United States would not join multilateral treaties pertaining to human rights); Curtis A. Bradley, *The Treaty Power and American Federalism, Part II*, 99 MICH. L. REV. 98, 122–23 (2000); Curtis A. Bradley & Jack L. Goldsmith, *Treaties, Human Rights, and Conditional Consent*, 149 U. PA. L. REV. 399, 413 (2000).

[29] Curtis A. Bradley & Jack L. Goldsmith, note 28 *supra*, at 410–23.

[30] Louis Henkin, *U.S. Ratification of Human Rights Treaties: The Ghost of Senator Bricker*, 89 AM. J. INT'L L. 341, 348–49 (1995).

[31] In the view of contemporaries, the Supreme Court decision that undermined the Amendment supporters was not *Brown*, but *Reid v. Covert*, 354 U.S. 1 (1957), which assuaged fears that a Senate-approved treaty might indirectly amend the Constitution. DUANE TANANBAUM, note 27 *supra*, at 211–14.

As a matter of history, most progress toward dismantling the legal basis of segregation (which at some level of abstraction could be described as a cooperative effort to comply with the obligations of the UN Charter) took place after Dulles reassured the Congress that the Administration would not use international law to pursue domestic reform. The Civil Rights Act of 1957, the sending of federal troops to Little Rock, the Kennedy Administration's mobilization of the Civil Rights Division of the Justice Department, and the civil rights legislation of the mid-1960s all unfolded against a backdrop of no coercive international obligation. The domestic courts acquired an enlarged arsenal to use against racial discrimination, but none involved the UN Charter or any other international agreement.

We do not mean to suggest, of course, that fear of the domestic judges acting in tandem with the United Nations was all that prevented the United States from confronting the legal structure of segregation sooner than it did. Our point is simply that many in the U.S. establishment who supported civil rights did not want international norms to intrude into the process. For roughly a decade, some doubt existed as to whether the legal obligations derived from UN membership could be formally enforced through domestic courts. Once the Eisenhower Administration eliminated (or at least reduced to an acceptable level) this uncertainty, a minor but nonetheless real impediment to civil rights progress was removed.

## DOMESTIC ENFORCEMENT OF INTERNATIONAL TRADE LAW

A similar, if lower profile, episode involves the GATT. President Truman signed this agreement in 1947, relying on the authority of the Trade Agreements Act of 1934. Neither the 1934 Act nor the 1947 Agreement expressly addressed the issue of implementing legislation, but a handful of courts and slightly more commentators argued that a rule of direct effect should apply. State courts in particular implemented GATT's national treatment rule even though no federal statute required them to do so.[32] Congress responded passively, inserting into each subsequent trade bill language to the effect that the legislation should not

---

[32] Cases striking down legislation as inconsistent with GATT obligations include Territory of Hawaii v. Ho, 41 Haw. 565 (1957); Baldwin-Lima-Hamilton Corp. v. Superior Court, 208 Cal. App. 2nd 803, 25 Cal. Rptr. 798 (Dist Ct. App. 1962). For the commentators, see Ronald A. Brand, *The Status of the General Agreement on Tariffs and Trade in United States Domestic Law*, 26 STAN. J. INT'L L. 479 (1990); Robert E. Hudec, *The Legal Status of the GATT in the Domestic Law of the United States*, in THE EUROPEAN COMMUNITY AND GATT 187 (Meinhard Hilf, Francis G. Jacobs, & Ernst-Ulrich Petersmann, eds., 1986); John H. Jackson, *The General Agreement on Tariffs and Trade in United States Domestic Law*, 66 MICH. L. REV. 260 (1967); Note, *The United States Participation in the General Agreement on Tariffs and Trade*, 61 COLUM. L. REV. 505 (1961).

be seen as either endorsing or rejecting the proposition that the GATT had direct effect in U.S. law.[33]

During the decades that formal enforcement of the GATT in the United States remained an open question, international trade liberalization efforts concentrated on tariff reduction and the elimination of transparently discriminatory barriers to imports. Beginning with the Tokyo Round Agreements of 1979, however, the GATT regime began to extend to more subjects and to threaten a greater range of domestic policies. The Tokyo Agreements represented a turn toward combating disguised discrimination, which typically involves the appropriation of a valid regulatory objective as a (more or less) pretextual basis for barring imports. The growth in extent and complexity of the international economy compelled this move. But, as our discussion of international trade law earlier indicates, discouraging disguised discrimination presents a greater risk of interfering with legitimate public policies. Inevitably the policy maker must choose between over- and underenforcement of the nondiscrimination norm.

When confronted with this dilemma, the United States responded by clarifying that there would be no formal enforcement of the more controversial aspects of the new GATT agreements.[34] Roughly a decade later, when approving the next major multilateral trade agreement, Congress took a more comprehensive approach. The 1993 NAFTA, which took shape in the shadow of the Uruguay Round negotiations and in significant respects reflected them, provided the first occasion for Congress to state explicitly that the domestic courts could not engage in independent enforcement of any part of the agreement without separate legislative authorization.[35] The following year, Congress applied exactly the same conditions to the Uruguay Round Agreements, which superseded as well as extended the 1947 GATT.[36]

Neither the human rights nor the GATT case study proves that the United States displayed a more cooperative attitude toward potential partners in multilateral agreements because it was free of the threat of coercive enforcement by independent domestic courts. We recognize that other factors might explain

---

[33] Act of June 16, 1951, §10, 65 Stat. 75, *codified at* 19 U.S.C. §1366 (2001); Act of Aug. 7, 1953, §103, 67 Stat. 472; Act of July 1, 1954, §3, 68 Stat. 360; Trade Agreements Extension Act of 1955, 69 Stat. 162, *codified at* 19 U.S.C. §1351 (a)(1)(A) (2001); Act of Aug. 20, 1958, P.L. 85–686, §10, 72 Stat. 680.

[34] *See* Trojan Technologies, Inc. v. Commonwealth of Pennsylvania, 916 F.2nd 903, 908 (3rd Cir. 1990), *cert. denied*, 501 U.S. 1212 (1991) (discussing 1979 Agreement on Government Procurement).

[35] North American Free Trade Agreement Implementation Act, §102, *codified at* 29 U.S.C. §3312 (2001). The Act does carve out a small role for judicial enforcement of the Agreement, but only in cases where the U.S. government (and not private parties or other governmental bodies) seeks to enforce the Agreement against itself or state or local governments. *Id.* §102(b)(2), (c)(2).

[36] Uruguay Round Agreements Act of 1994 §102, *codified at* 29 U.S.C. §3512 (2001)

both the periods of cooperation and the earlier resistance to international commitments. We still find it instructive that, in these two disparate areas and at two different times, U.S. efforts to exhibit cooperative compliance with its international obligations coincided with strong measures to discourage formal enforcement.

## THE VIENNA CONVENTION ON CONSULAR RELATIONS AND THE INTERNATIONAL CRIMINAL COURT

Greater flows of people across state borders increases the likelihood that foreigners will find themselves in trouble with the authorities. During the 1960s the United States led an effort to establish minimum standards for the treatment of foreign citizens arrested for crimes. The Vienna Convention on Consular Relations, which went into force in 1969, obligates all parties, when arresting a subject of another party, to notify the arrestee "without delay" of his right to contact the consul of his state.[37] Notification enables the notified state both to keep track of its subjects and, presumably, to lend assistance to the arrested person.

In the United States, compliance with the Vienna Convention notification requirements has been uneven at best. Most arrests involve local and state police, rather than federal agents, and many of these arresting officers seemingly do not know of their duty to notify foreign citizens of the right to contact a consul. People who did not receive proper notice in turn have sought three different kinds of relief. Those who made incriminatory statements after arrest have sought to suppress that evidence in their criminal trials, making an analogy to the famous *Miranda* decision.[38] At least one victim has brought a tort suit for

---

[37] Vienna Convention on Consular Relations, art. 36(1)(b), April 24, 1963, 21 U.S.T. 77, 596 U.N.T.S. 261.

[38] Miranda v. Arizona, 384 U.S. 436 (1966) (requiring exclusion of postarrest statements unless arrestee receives specific warnings). The cases that have rejected an attempt to derive an exclusionary rule from the Vienna Convention include United States v. Ortiz, 315 F.3rd 873 (8th Cir. 2002); United States v. Minjares-Alvarez, 264 F.3rd 980 (10th Cir. 2001); United States v. Jimenez-Nava, 243 F.3rd 192 (5th Cir. 2001); United States v. Page, 232 F.3rd 536 (6th Cir. 2000); United States v. Lawal, 231 F.3rd 1045 (7th Cir. 2000); United States v. Cordoba-Mosquera, 212 F.3rd 1194 (11th Cir. 2000); United States v. Li, 206 F.3rd 56 (1st Cir. 2000); United States v. Lombera-Camorlinga, 206 F.3rd 882 (9th Cir. 2000); State v. Sanchez-Llamas, 338 Ore. 267, 108 P.3rd 573 (Ore.), *cert. granted*, 126 S. Ct. 620 (2005); Ramirez v. State, 279 Ga. 569, 619 S.E.2nd 668 (Ga. 2005); Conde v. State, 860 So.2nd 930 (Fla. 2003); State v. Navarro, 260 Wis.2nd 861, 659 N.W.2nd 487 (Wis. App. 2003); People v. Preciado-Flores, 66 P.3rd 155 (Colo. App. 2002); People v. Griffith, 334 Ill. App. 3rd 98, 777 N.E.2nd 459 (Ill. App. 2002); State v. Martinez-Rodriguez, 131 N.M. 47, 33 P.3rd 267 (N.M. 2001); State v. Jamison, 105 Wash. App. 572, 20 P.3rd 1010 (Wash. App. 2001); Garcia v. State, 117 Nev. 124, 17 P.3rd 994 (Nev. 2001); Rocha v. State, 16 S.W.3rd 1 (Tex.Crim.App. 2000); Kasi v. Commonwealth, 256 Va. 407, 508 S.E.2nd 57 (Va. 1998).

damages.[39] And a number of people convicted of capital crimes and sentenced to death have argued that the absence of consular guidance led to an inadequate defense that should invalidate their sentence. This last class of cases interests us here, because the ICJ has placed its authority behind the claim.

The Vienna Convention has an Optional Protocol, which recognizes the "compulsory jurisdiction" of the ICJ with respect to "[d]isputes arising out of the interpretation or application of the Convention . . . "[40] The United States invoked this provision in 1979 in response to the Iranian seizure of the U.S. embassy staff in Tehran and ultimately obtained a decision of the ICJ condemning (but taking no action regarding) the Iranian action.[41] Beginning in 1998, several countries in turn invoked their rights under the Convention and its Optional Protocol to bring the United States before the ICJ. In each case, they challenged capital sentences imposed on their nationals. The fact patterns were similar in each case: The local arresting authorities had failed to inform a foreign subject of his right to contact his consul, the arrestee was convicted of a capital crime and sentenced to death, and the arrestee first learned of and asserted his right to contact his consul only after the conclusion of trial and his sentencing.

In its first case, the ICJ requested the United States not to carry out the sentence pending its review of the claim, but the United States declined to intervene in the State proceedings, leading to the convict's execution.[42] In the second, the ICJ ordered the United States not to carry out the execution of a German national pending its resolution of a similar claim, but again the United States failed to prevent the State from carrying out the sentence. In that proceeding the ICJ subsequently determined that the Vienna Convention obligated the United States to conduct a hearing on the question of whether the failure to notify an arrestee of his rights had prejudiced his trial and thereby invalidated his sentence.[43] Finally, Mexico brought a claim involving fifty-one of its citizens currently on death row in various States. In (for once) a timely fashion, the ICJ ordered the United States to conduct judicial hearings to determine whether any of the designated convicts

---

[39] Jogi v. Voges, 425 F.3rd 367 (7th Cir. 2005) (damages available under 28 U.S.C. §1350); Standt v. City of New York, 153 F. Supp. 2nd 417 (S.D.N.Y. 2001) (allowing suit under 42 U.S.C. §1983).

[40] Optional Protocol to the Vienna Convention on Consular Relations Concerning the Compulsory Settlement of Disputes, art. I, April 24, 1963, 21 U.S.T. 325, 596 U.N.T.S. 487.

[41] Case Concerning the Diplomatic and Consular Staff in Tehran (United States v. Iran), 1980 I.C.J. 3.

[42] Vienna Convention on Consular Relations (Paraguay v. United States), [1998] I.C.J. 426; Breard v. Greene, 523 U.S. 371 (1998) (declining stay to postpone execution after ICJ request).

[43] LaGrand (Germany v. United States), [2001] I.C.J. 104; Federal Republic of Germany v. United States, 526 U.S. 111 (1999) (denying stay of execution after ICJ order).

had been prejudiced by the violation of his Vienna Convention notification right.[44]

Several of the fifty-one named Mexican citizens sought postconviction relief on the basis of the ICJ decision. No court embraced the argument that the ICJ interpretation of the Vienna Convention was binding on U.S. courts, although an Oklahoma court in one instance granted the requested relief.[45] The Supreme Court granted certiorari to consider the issue in a case coming from Texas. In response, the U.S. government repudiated the Optional Protocol with respect to future disputes, rejected the ICJ's interpretation of the Vienna Convention, defended the decision of the federal courts not to intervene in these cases, but announced that it nonetheless wished Texas to provide the judicial hearing that the ICJ had believed necessary. The Supreme Court, in a five-four vote, then dismissed the case.[46]

We can see these developments as elements of an unfolding dialectic, with the ICJ seeking to harden its authority to interpret and apply the Vienna Convention and the U.S. government becoming increasingly apprehensive that the Supreme Court would collaborate in this effort. The outcome was the denunciation of the treaty on which the ICJ's authority rested. In taking this step, the government did not react to any new judgment by the ICJ but, rather, to the Supreme Court's decision to review an uninterrupted string of lower court decisions refusing to give effect to the ICJ interpretation. The risk that the treaty denunciation eliminated thus was not greater postconviction rights for aliens but, rather, the prospect of federal court enforcement of ICJ decisions.

Perhaps it goes without saying that we cannot prove that the threat of federal court enforcement of ICJ judgments motivated the U.S. repudiation of the Optional Protocol. Perhaps the United States wanted only to punish the ICJ for its decisions and would have found the outcome of the dispute intolerable even without domestic court enforcement. The timing of the action, however, is highly suspicious: It occurred in the midst of the Supreme Court's deliberations and at a time when no new cases were pending before the ICJ. The United States

---

[44] Avena and other Mexican Nationals (Mexico v. United States), [2004] I.C.J. 128.

[45] Torres v. State, 120 P.3rd 1184 (Okl. Crim. App. 2005) (describing course of litigation).

[46] Medellín v. Dretke, 544 U.S. 660 (2005) (dismissing case in light of presidential position). *See also* Gomez v. Dretke, 422 F.3rd 264 (5th Cir. 2005) (staying decision on federal postconviction relief while person named in *Avena* judgment pursues a state court hearing). One of us participated as an *amicus curiae* in *Medellín*. Brief for Professors of International Law, Federal Jurisdiction and the Foreign Relations Law of the United States as *Amici Curiae* on Behalf of Respondent, Medellín v. Dretke, No. 04–5928, Feb. 28, 2005 (Paul B. Stephan, counsel of record). The Supreme Court currently is considering the question of whether U.S. courts should adopt the ICJ's interpretation of the Vienna Convention. Bustillo v. Johnson, 126 S. Ct. 621 (2005) (granting certiorari).

had endured its defeats in the ICJ well enough before then. It is difficult not to infer that this stoicism had something to do with the previous refusal of all federal courts to consider the question of implementing ICJ judgments.[47]

In sum, the United States apparently could tolerate the risk of not having its views on the Vienna Convention prevail as long as the consequence was only having to explain its refusal to implement orders of the ICJ. Once it faced a substantial risk that domestic courts might order compliance with those orders, however, the United States terminated the ICJ's future capacity to interpret the Convention. As a result, the realm of formal enforcement of a particular international obligation has shrunk, without any offsetting change in the scope of the underlying commitment.

## EUROPEAN INTEGRATION AND THE CONSTITUTIONAL TREATY

Our final case history is still unfolding. In 2004, the heads of the governments of the twenty-five EU members agreed to a Treaty Establishing a Constitution for Europe.[48] For its supporters, the Treaty represented the culmination of a half-century of European integration by providing a strong political foundation for the economic structures that have become the EC. It contained a list of basic individual rights, largely complementing those found in the European Convention on Human Rights, and expanded the scope of authority of the EC organs, especially the European Parliament and the ECJ. It represented, in sum, a first but critical effort to legalize the status of Europe as unified politically and culturally, as well as economically, through a federal structure that increasingly would resemble that of the United States.

The effort to confirm this Treaty foundered on the shores of popular consent. The Treaty could take effect only if all twenty-five states (as distinct from their governments) approved it through a domestically valid ratification process. Some states, notably Germany, chose not to submit the Treaty to the electorate for ratification, as their constitutions permitted parliamentary approval of such commitments. But most states pursued referenda. As is well known, voters in France and the Netherlands, two of the original six members of the European Economic Community, rejected the Treaty, and the United Kingdom then suspended its ratification process. Absent extraordinary upheaval, it appears that,

---

[47] Subsequent to the U.S. repudiation of the Optional Protocol, Judge Wood, writing for the Seventh Circuit, asserted that "we are of the opinion that the United States is bound by ICJ rulings in cases where it consented to the court's jurisdiction, just as it would be bound by any arbitral procedure to which it consented . . . " Jogi v. Voges, 425 F.3rd 367, 384 (7th Cir. 2005). This claim, which she acknowledged to be "controversial," implies that the express statutory authorization of judicial enforcement of arbitral awards, and not of ICJ decisions, is irrelevant.

[48] 2004 O. J. (C 310) 1.

for the foreseeable future, the Treaty as written, as well as the deep integration project it embodied, has failed.

We recognize that the politics surrounding the Treaty ratification process, as well as the general difficulty of interpreting recent events as evidence, make it impossible to draw any strong conclusions about the significance of this episode. Certainly the debates over ratification, especially those in France, focused mostly on matters of symbolism, rather than on the legal implications of the Treaty. The most frequently cited explanations for Dutch and French rejection are anxiety about Islamic immigrants and general anger at the national political establishment, even though the Treaty did not directly raise either of these issues. Commentators have referred to a tacit red-brown alliance, with the hard left and ultranationalists unified in their opposition to the Treaty. At most, then, we can make only very qualified and tentative judgments about the processes that brought about the Treaty's failure.

That said, we still find it striking that the Dutch and French voters, knowing that their choice would be decisive for the Treaty's survival (as earlier votes, and the later ballot in Luxembourg, arguably were not), opted for the status quo over a project that greatly enhanced the risk of more and harder European law. The Treaty seemed to extend the scope of community law, and therefore the enforcement power of the community organs, into areas previously considered outside the scope of the prior treaties. By seeking to strengthen the legitimacy of EC organs, it also suggested an increase in their authority. How the organs, in particular the ECJ, would implement the various human rights provisions that made up a large part of the Treaty was unclear. The status quo, in contrast, had hard law aplenty, but also left substantial room for national governments to negotiate over the implementation of their obligations. Without stronger assurances that deeper integration would not entail harder law emanating from Brussels, the voters plausibly could have chosen to remain with a not uncomfortable status quo.

## Summary

Our theory has three main positive claims: (1) that states avoid formal enforcement of international law obligations that entail high verification costs; (2) that states are most likely to choose formal enforcement in circumstances where an obligation presents low verification costs (taking into account acceptable proxies), arises within a project that has collective action problems, and entails complex interaction that defeats moral clarity; and (3) that uncertainty over enforcement may deter states from making international commitments. These claims are consistent with what we observe about the practice of international law enforcement in the contemporary world. We recognize that we have not submitted this evidence to rigorous quantitative analysis, and accordingly we cannot claim that we have proven the validity of our underlying theory. What we have done is to shift the burden of proof to those who would argue that international law enforcement does not correspond to considerations of rationality and that insights derived from analysis of private transactions have no bearing on the construction of international law. To the extent that international law is designed and made through some kind of voluntary process, its enforcement seems to reflect the same underlying pressure toward optimality under conditions of uncertainty and information asymmetry that explains private contracts. As we said earlier, these case histories do not prove our claim that uncertainty about the means of enforcement can deter cooperation, but they are broadly consistent with this critical element of our theory.

# 7 THE FUTURE OF INTERNATIONAL LAW AND ITS ENFORCEMENT

There is an elaborate regime of practices and institutions by which the United States and other nations enforce commitments inter sese or decide that, in the national interest, promises given by or to another sovereign should not be enforced in a specific case. Sometimes this is done purely for reasons of prudence, sometimes for convenience, or sometimes to secure advantage in unrelated matters. Incalculable mischief can be wrought by gratuitously introducing into this often delicate process court enforcement at the instigation of private parties. We believe that such a course is to be avoided unless it can be said that private enforcement was clearly agreed to and envisioned by the contracting States in the treaties themselves.

United States v. Li, 206 F. 3rd 56, 68 (1st Cir. 2000) (Seyla & Boudin, JJ., concurring)

IT MAY WELL BE USEFUL TO HAVE A BETTER UNDERSTANDING OF HOW THE enforcement of international law functions in the modern world, but where does that leave us? As scholars, we take some satisfaction in providing an analytically rigorous account of why, across a broad range of subjects and problems, we observe formal enforcement when we do and informal measures elsewhere. But as lawyers, we also feel under an obligation to help the policy maker – judge, legislator, or government official – who must make choices about enforcement strategies. How does contract theory help the international lawmaker?

We must start with an obvious, but perhaps controversial, point. For a policy maker to care about contract theory and its contributions to international law and its enforcement, he or she must believe that policy has something to do with increasing social welfare. We do not mean to suggest that our putative policy maker must be indifferent to other theories of justice besides welfare maximization, but, at a minium, he or she must seek to optimize the welfare effects of whatever steps are taken in pursuit of justice. Our policy maker must believe that public choices have consequences, not all of which are intended, and that it is helpful to minimize the harms, and to maximize the benefits, of those consequences, if doing so is otherwise consistent with the principles of justice that motivate the policy.

We concede that many goals that have motivated international relations in the recent past – accelerating the historical path to communism, enabling a racially superior group to fulfil its biological destiny, spreading the realm of the true faith – have had nothing to do with social welfare as we understand it. Our intuition is that, over time, such goals do not withstand evolutionary pressure very well, and that policies animated by a concern for social welfare adapt better to the challenges of a hostile and changing world. But we concede that this is an intuition, not a fact, and if it is wrong, we probably have nothing useful to say to those who exercise power and make policy.

But the existence of so many, and so many different kinds of cooperative ventures undertaken through international law reassures us that our welfare-based claims will not fall on totally deaf ears. The previous chapters document how much the goal of maximizing welfare animates current policy in so many venues. Arms control, environmental regulation, trade, human rights, and the laws of war, to pick just a few examples, have many purposes and dimensions, but the thread of joint production of social welfare appears to run through each project. It is not too great a leap to imagine that the demand for such policies will persist, and perhaps even grow.

With this behind us, we can get to the two big policy points that our analysis supports. One is that international law, bolstered with appropriate enforcement mechanisms, has the potential to help our increasingly complicated and inter-connected global population cope with the challenges before us. The second point is that uncertainty about the applicable enforcement options for existing international law regimes may deter policy makers from undertaking socially beneficial international projects. We need greater clarity about when formal enforcement will apply, which is to say that policy makers need to address the problem of enforcement risk.

In the abstract, enforcement risk is bipolar. When those responsible for formal enforcement duck their responsibilities, uncertainty arises, just as when enforcers pursue the hardening of the law without a mandate to do so. As a practical matter, however, the latter problem seems greater. The policy community, and in particular academic international law specialists, largely (although not uniformly) push for more hard law. Accordingly, current trends favor those who wish to harden the rules or norms that currently exist and to do so without the participation of the makers of these rules. Our analysis calls into question these trends, and in particular questions domestic litigation strategies designed to generate formal enforcement of various international law norms. We turn, then, to a discussion of both the possibilities and the limits of the enforcement of international law.

## Opening up New Areas of International Cooperation

A casual glance at the dozens of scholarly periodicals dedicated to international law or the many books devoted to empowering the international community suggests that we do not lack for proposals to expand international cooperation. But why do we not see even more activity at the level of policy? Typically, resistance to the more feasible of these projects comes in the form of a perceived threat to sovereignty. Opponents of more and greater international law argue for both the value of sovereignty as a basis for a population's self-governance and self-fulfilment and the unacceptability of sacrificing these benefits in pursuit of the stated objective of the international project.

These assertions about the importance of, and danger to, state sovereignty typically build on a *folie à deux* in which the proponents and critics of these projects, undoubtedly unintentionally, reinforce each other.[1] Both groups assume that international law in some sense operates like other kinds of law, in that an obligation entails something hard and binding. Both take the hardening of these commitments for granted, and assume that state commitments to cooperative objectives ultimately will be subject to formal enforcement.

Our theory separates the questions of obligation and enforcement. In particular, by choosing informal enforcement over formal enforcement, states can adjust their commitments ex post in response to updated information. By maximizing their ability to respond to new knowledge, states can reduce the perceived threat to their sovereignty that results from an ex ante commitment to rules administered by an independent body with sanctioning power. To be sure, by accepting an obligation that is enforced informally, a state finds its range of action circumscribed to the extent it values its reputation, is averse to retaliation, or prefers reciprocal cooperation. After all, our argument rests on the premise that informal enforcement has real bite. But informal enforcement does mean that a state has greater control over how it balances its obligations against other needs that later events, both expected and unexpected, may create.

---

[1]  Note the suggestion of our colleague John Setear that "it tends to be political conservatives who fear that international agreements and international institutions will erode U.S. sovereignty; paradoxically, those who are most suspicious of international law appear to believe most fervently in its power." John K. Setear, *A Forest with No Trees: The Supreme Court and International Law in the 2003 Term*, 91 VA. L. REV. 579, 674 (2005).

Lest all this seem too abstract, let us consider some concrete projects for future cooperation where some attention to enforcement mechanisms might make a difference. As teachers of contract law, we find problems of international trade familiar and congenial; others might make similar arguments in other areas. We are impressed with the claim that very simple (although politically very difficult) steps could be taken to greatly expand the size and distribution of the benefits of free trade. We mean that the rich world – the United States, the EC, and Japan, in particular – could dismantle the barriers to agricultural imports that their existing systems of farm subsidies require. The current multilateral negotiations under WTO auspices, known as the Doha Round, have this proposal as a central topic.

We realize that such a step is normatively problematic. Many in the rich world believe that local farmers preserve a way of life, a sense of connection with the past, the loss of which would rob their culture of much that makes it worthwhile. Others see the issue as one of national security: A state that cannot feed its population exposes itself to the whims of a hostile world. On the other side of the ledger, however, are claims that the developing countries can produce better agricultural products at a lower cost and can use the gains from such production to reduce poverty, not simply to make a comfortable life even better for a well-off population. It is not implausible to believe that the harm to the developing world from rules that shut out their products from the U.S., EC, and Japanese domestic markets far exceeds, in both static and dynamic terms, the value of all the foreign aid that the poor countries receive.[2] Isn't a policy choice to undo these obstacles morally as well as economically attractive?

It is not our purpose to decide this question, or even to marshal the quantitative evidence on which each side rests. Ultimately, the controversy requires politics and struggle: Even though a liberalizing policy might increase welfare and have ethical force, it inevitably will hurt some people, who legitimately might fight it. Rather, we hope to illuminate how disentangling the issue of enforcement from the question of obligation can expand the range of feasible policy choices. If fighting poverty in the developing world through greater agricultural exports is an attractive goal, but if cultural preservation and food security also matter, informal enforcement of liberalization commitments might provide the best means of balancing these objectives.

---

[2]  For an estimate by World Bank economists of the size of the benefits to currently poor countries from agricultural trade liberalization, see Kym Anderson & Will Martin, Agricultural Trade Reform and the Doha Development Agenda, World Bank Policy Research Working Paper 3607 (May 2005).

The precedent for taking down rich-country trade barriers to expand opportunities for the poor is the 1994 commitment, embedded in the Uruguay Round Agreements, to undo the system of quotas that had restricted imports of textiles into rich countries.[3] The textile industry throughout its history has demonstrated how learning-by-doing in an industry leads to a greater willingness to substitute low-skill labor for highly skilled (and compensated) workers. The great technological innovations of Britain in the eighteenth century migrated to the United States in the nineteenth, where New England mills employed lower-skill workers, many imported from francophone Canada. Then, in the United States, the mills fled New England for the South in the late nineteenth and early twentieth centuries. During the post–World War II period, production increasingly moved offshore, especially to Asia. In defiance of the letter as well as the spirit of the GATT system, the prosperous countries negotiated numerous *Multifiber Agreements (MFA)* with the new textile-producing countries. The MFA system set country-by-country, product-by-product quotas which the rich countries implemented domestically and which the poor countries agreed not to attack through the GATT.[4]

The Uruguay Round negotiations, which lasted from 1986 to 1994, envisioned a grand bargain in which the poor countries would open up their markets to the rich world's services industries and strengthen protection for the intellectual and investment property rights of capital exporters, in return for a dismantling of the quotas and other barriers that protected the rich world's domestic markets. At the end of the day, the Agreements contained very soft commitments on services and agriculture, and somewhat harder agreements to strengthen intellectual property protection and open up textile markets, softened by a ten-year phase-in period. For the ensuing decade, the rich countries played a game of chicken, not making any substantial adjustments to reflect the pending textiles obligation. On January 1, 2005, the commitment matured, and the rich countries scrambled to respond to the threatened flood of inexpensive textiles from China, India, and other developing countries.

In both Europe and the United States, the trade law concept of *safeguards* has provided the principal means of resisting the now-matured textiles obligations. This concept emphasizes both the softness as well as the constraints of trade law obligations. It permits states to derogate from their obligations in cases where sudden surges of imports cause especially great domestic harm.

---

[3]  Agreement on Textiles and Clothing, April 15, 1994, http://www.wto.org/english/docs_e/legal_e/16-tex_e.htm (last visited September 1, 2005).

[4]  For a review of this background, see Henry R. Zheng, *Defining Relationships and Resolving Conflicts Between Interrelated Multinational Trade Agreements: The Experience of the MFA and the GATT*, 25 STAN. J. INT'L L. 45 (1988).

The WTO DSB, in turn, can review safeguard measures to determine if they conform to the 1994 Agreement on Safeguards. Exporters faced with safeguards imposed by importers may retaliate, although typically they lack the economic leverage to do so. Once the WTO DSB determines that a safeguard violates the Agreement, a state has an obligation to rescind the measure, but it does not have to compensate any state whose exporters suffered harm from the illegal trade barrier.

Both the EC and the United States have invoked this right as their basis for reinstating some quotas on textiles produced in China.[5] China in turn has the right to seek WTO DSB review of these actions. But even if the WTO DSB were to determine that these actions go beyond the bounds of what the 1994 Agreement on Safeguards permits, the EC and the United States would only have to suspend the measures, and would have no duty to compensate China for the losses resulting from the illegal barriers to imports. And, as we discussed in the previous chapter, the WTO in any event cannot enforce directly any decision it makes, although it can manage the reputational and retaliatory effects of a dispute.

We do not know how the liberalization of textiles trade will play out, but it seems unlikely that the current safeguards will do anything more than delay the restructuring now under way. After some time, one suspects that cheap Asian textiles will dominate these markets, lowering the cost of low-end clothing and thus benefitting both the poorest consumers in the West and poor workers in the East. The safeguards permit an interval between the time the obligation comes into effect and the time when states will comply, but it is likely that they will only postpone the inevitable.

For critics who object to trade liberalization, the stakes in the debate over textiles are high. Some see textiles manufacturers as the epitome of exploitive capitalists.[6] They believe that any reduction in labor costs will result only in greater profits for the corporations that make these goods, and not in lower prices for consumers or higher wages for workers in the developing world. This, of course, is an empirical claim, and the incidence of gains from liberalizing textiles trade can (and will) be assessed. We note, however, that the historical record for other industries that have gone through liberalization indicates that the gains generally are not limited to the suppliers of capital.[7]

---

[5] For domestic litigation challenging the U.S. restrictions to no avail, see *U.S. Ass'n of Importers of Textiles and Apparel v. U.S. Dept. of Commerce*, 413 F.3rd 1344 (Fed. Cir. 2005). For the EC regulation that postponed enforcement of the quota to accommodate already shipped products, see Commission Regulation (EC) No. 1478/2005, 2005 O.J. (L 236) 3.

[6] *E.g.*, Naomi Klein, No Logo: Taking Aim at the Brand Bullies (1999).

[7] For a review of the claim, see Thomas A. Pugel & Peter H. Lindert, International Economics 61–76 (11th ed. 2000).

For trade liberals who believe the Uruguay Round did not go far enough, the interval between obligation and compliance might indicate a weakness of the multilateral trade regime. From the perspective of contract theory, however, the safeguards can be seen as a mechanism for managing uncertainty and adjusting ex post to an efficient outcome in which resulting gains are shared. Recall that when parties write relatively simple contracts, they face the choice between protecting investments with hard terms or anticipating future adjustments with soft terms. The first option risks a contract that may not provide for states of the world in which there is no ex post welfare surplus. If the contract fails to accommodate this problem, the parties will be motivated to take costly precautions ex ante including, at the limit, deciding to forego the cooperative project altogether. One solution is to agree to a broad standard of good faith modification of the obligation but, as we have seen, the vagueness of the standard risks moral hazard should the parties choose formally to enforce the contract. This problem is solved, as a practical matter, by anticipating future modifications of the obligation and relying on informal enforcement mechanisms to ameliorate the moral hazard problem.

Thus the promises made in 1994 to open up the markets of the rich world were implicitly conditioned on the capacity of the affected governments to minimize the pain caused by dislocation of domestic production. The decade-long adjustment period created an opportunity for threatened rich-world producers to shift their resources (including, one would hope, retraining or compensating incumbent workers), but the effectiveness of the adjustment process was subject to both macroeconomic and industry-specific contingencies. Safeguards function as a modification mechanism that allows countries that promise to reduce import barriers to take into account shortcomings in the resource allocation process. To be sure, the possibility that importing countries might impose safeguard measures may diminish the incentive for high-labor-cost producers to make the necessary adjustments, and for low-labor-cost producers to increase investment in anticipation of greater exports. Thus, the modification process stimulated by safeguards does undermine to some degree the ex ante goal of encouraging efficient investment. But the importers' power to stall and force an adjustment is not unconstrained; it functions within a regime of informal enforcement that limits the moral hazard risk that the exporters face.

The textiles story, we believe, can serve as a model for liberalization of agricultural trade. The distribution of agricultural production within the developing world is, of course, different from that for textiles, as is the technology of carriage. But in very crude terms, the issues are the same for both industries. If anything, rich-world protection for local producers is greater and more entrenched with respect to agriculture, while the potential benefits to the developing world from liberalization are larger.

As with textiles, the rich world can commit within the WTO structure to reduce the current barriers to agricultural imports. The obligation would entail both substituting import duties for the current quotas on physical quantities of permitted imported goods – a process known to specialists as *tariffication* – and choosing nonprohibitive tariff levels for these duties. A secondary issue would be the use of food standards and safety measures as a potential trade barrier. The Uruguay Round Agreements purported to deal with this issue, but the EC in particular has had great difficulty complying with the obligation.[8] The rich world would bargain for some delay in the implementation of its commitment, and would reserve the existing multilateral trade rules for safeguards and dispute resolution, or something like them.

Were the rich world states to enter into such a bargain, they would retain the flexibility to update their commitments in light of new information. A successful adjustment by rich world farmers into new lines of production would enable the liberalization of agricultural imports to proceed apace. Intransigence by these producers might lead rich world states to delay implementing their commitments, probably by imposing safeguards. Food exporting states in turn could seek compensating concessions, as GATT safeguards rules permits, or accept delay as an unavoidable cost of doing business. During this adjustment process, the trading partners of the United States, the EC, and Japan – not just developing countries, but relatively prosperous agricultural exporters such as Australia, Argentina, Canada, and New Zealand – could update their assessment of the willingness of those countries to honor their obligations and, where appropriate, increase their investments. The WTO DSB could update all concerned with information about the responses of the various parties to their commitments. Unless the rich world were to maintain a united front, concessions by one bloc would induce the others to reduce agricultural trade barriers.

We do not offer this scenario as a nirvana solution to economic conflicts. Even with updating, safeguards, and reciprocity, the rich world at the end of the day might put the interests of domestic farmers above that of maintaining a multilateral system of trade liberalization. Given a grave enough economic crisis and implacable pressures to protect farmers, the GATT DSB could go the way of the Permanent Court of International Justice, the creature of the League

---

[8] Agreement on the Application of Sanitary and Phytosanitary Measures, published at http://www.wto. org/english/docs_e/legal_e/15sps_01_e.htm (last visited Aug. 22, 2005); United States – Continued Suspension of Obligations in the EC Hormones Dispute, WT/DS320/7 (Jun. 7, 2005) (constituting panel for dispute settlement of EC claim that U S sanctions are excessive).

of Nations that failed so badly in managing the rising tide of international violence in the 1930s. It is a truism, but nonetheless true, that any commitment entails risk. The question remains which course presents the graver risk.

The status quo, one could argue, leads to an unacceptable immiserization of the developing world with potentially catastrophic consequences, of which the current terror threat is only one visible part. Because of verifiability concerns, formal enforcement of trade liberalization is likely to kill any potential deal and, in a worst case scenario, also could lead to a conflict that might destroy the multilateral trading system. If these are the choices that a policy maker faces, liberalization accompanied by informal enforcement begins to look better and better.

We offer this stylized argument for designing enforcement mechanisms for trade liberalization, but its adaptability to other issues seems obvious. Imagine, for example, an international regime established to manage a flu pandemic in advance of its emergence. To succeed, such a regime might require reporting and quarantines, including regulation of population movements across borders.[9] Would such a regime work better or worse if states faced substantial sanctions imposed by a third party for derelictions in reporting or border management? Again, our point is that international cooperation based on contingent planning and technological uncertainty lends itself to informal enforcement, and that threatening to do otherwise might thwart a valuable, perhaps even essential enterprise.

REDUCING ENFORCEMENT RISK

By enforcement risk, we mean uncertainty about what enforcement mechanisms will apply to a particular international obligation. Every commitment to formal enforcement runs a risk of enforcement slack, which is to say that the designated enforcer may fall down on its job. Symmetrically, every commitment to formal enforcement runs a risk of enforcement creep, which is to say that someone with formal enforcement capacity chooses to add new obligations to its inventory of what it enforces. Both risks are real and costly, but in a world where the general trend is toward hardening of international law enforcement, enforcement creep seems a greater problem than does enforcement slack.

We emphasize what we hope is an obvious point: The legal system should strive toward rules that produce the optimal level of risk, not those that minimize or eliminate risk altogether. Risk reduction also is costly, and should not be pursued if the cost, in terms of foregone opportunities to enhance social

---

[9]  For further discussion, see David P. Fidler, *Public Health and National Security in the Global Age: Infectious Diseases, Bioterrorism, and Realpolitik*, 35 GEO. WASH. INT'L L. REV. 787 (2003).

welfare, exceeds the benefits, also in terms of opportunities taken that otherwise would be foregone. The problem of optimizing enforcement risk thus cannot be separated from the particular project at hand, and meta-rules about when formal enforcement should apply that cut across subjects are unlikely to be useful.

Accordingly, we illustrate the problem of enforcement creep by reference to six current debates regarding specific expansions of the international law domain. Two involve proposals to bolster the autonomy and influence of existing international institutions, namely, the ICC and the WTO DSB. Two involve the use of domestic courts in the United States as enforcement agents of particular international regimes, namely the jurisdiction of the ICJ and the Geneva Conventions regulating the treatment of detainees seized during hostilities. A fifth debate involves the rules for determining the domain of treaties within U.S. law when the parties intend the instrument to have direct effect in the domestic legal order, and the last involves the recognition of a rule of customary international law – specifically, the doctrine of odious debt – to supplant traditional contract doctrines. Each illustrates how our theory can aid in the analysis of concrete and contentious contemporary issues about international law and its enforcement.

## THE INTERNATIONAL CRIMINAL COURT AND INTERNATIONAL CRIMINAL LAW

As we noted in Chapter 5, the ICC exists, but its function and future remain deeply contested. The ICC has opened several investigations but has yet to conduct its first trial. More importantly, the lack of support from significant military powers risks condemning this most ambitious of international criminal tribunals to irrelevance. Seven of the nine known nuclear powers have not acceded to the Rome Statute, and the United States in particular has extracted (some would say extorted) agreements from the United Nations and various countries to exempt its military from future ICC prosecutions for conduct in particular operations. More generally, the role of international criminal courts in enforcing norms of international humanitarian law remains controversial and uncertain. Eric Posner and John Yoo argue, for example, that if the ICC remains on its present course, "[w]ar criminals will appear before the ICC only in those rare cases where they are nationals of a defeated state whose new government seeks to acquire international legitimacy."[10]

---

[10] Eric A. Posner & John C. Yoo, *Judicial Independence in International Tribunals*, 93 CALIF. L. REV. 1, 70 (2005).

The principal debate over the ICC involves the tribunal's authority to determine for itself whether a particular conflict merits investigation for possible crimes. The issue is complex because the ICC's Statute posits two requirements for any exercise of ICC jurisdiction: The tribunal must establish both the existence of the elements of one of the specified crimes *and* the inability of any state with jurisdiction over the crime effectively to prosecute the offense itself.[11] The first test looks like a traditional legal function, but the second requires a politically charged and highly discretionary assessment.[12] In theory, the ICC's control over which cases to pursue, an essential element of formal enforcement, ensures that the application of international humanitarian law will not depend on the interests of any state, whether the sovereign or any ally of an offender. But the price of self-determined jurisdiction may be obstruction by great powers, which do not see the benefits of independent adjudication of war crimes as worth the risks posed to their military.

The fundamental problem, our model suggests, is the absence of any readily verifiable proxies for the question of whether a state has the capacity effectively to prosecute an offense. There may be a few places, such as Somalia, where no functioning criminal justice system exists, but there are precious few instances where such a clear criterion will do any work. Has a state that has made a considered decision to implement a "peace and reconciliation" process, as exemplified by post-Apartheid South Africa, lost its capacity effectively to prosecute? Should the test be applied as of the time that a crime occurs, when perpetrators may operate outside the reach of any state, foreign as much as domestic, or later, when stability has been restored? Is a refusal to hand over someone itself tantamount to effective incapacity? If not, what reasons count as justifying the refusal?

The problem with the effective capacity standard, as illuminated by these questions, is not simply that answers in particular instances may seem arbitrary. War crimes arise in politically charged environments and engage convictions passionately. Each of the great powers has its own special grievances and sense of injustice, and therefore a predisposition to believe that it may be the victim of discrimination. Ignoring these fears and trusting in the wisdom and impartiality of a new international authority seems too much to expect.

If, as we argue, the main problem with the ICC is its self-judging of its jurisdiction, then the question becomes how to contrive a solution. Simply

---

[11]  Statute of the International Criminal Court, arts.5, 17, published at http://www.icc-cpi.int/library/about/officialjournal/Rome_Statute_120704-EN.pdf (last visited September 19, 2005).

[12]  For discussion of the dispute and its implications for international law generally, see Paul B. Stephan, *Process Values, International Law, and Justice,* 23 SOCIAL PHIL. & POL'Y 131 (2006).

amending the Statute of Rome seems unlikely over the short run, given the number of states that rejected U.S. objections to self-judging at the time of the Statute's adoption. But a tacit collaboration between the ICC and the great powers might yet save the court from irrelevance.

An implicit bargain would require the ICC not to exercise its self-judging power, but instead to develop a custom of awaiting some fairly clear signal of support from the great powers before initiating a prosecution. Such a solution would require considerable self-restraint on the part of ICC officials and some signs that the great powers would use the ICC, if left free to choose. The latter requirement at least seems realistic. In the case of allegations of genocide arising out of the Darfur conflict, for example, China, the Russian Federation, and the United States, three nonsignatories to the Rome Statute that have veto power within the UN Security Council, agreed to refer a matter to the ICC for investigation.[13] Presumably the nonsignatories, a rather diverse group, went along with this decision on the theory that a predicate decision by the Security Council alleviates concerns about unfettered agency discretion.

No one can say whether this episode will become a precedent, but the possibility is intriguing. Were the ICC to let its self-judging authority wither away and limit its work to cases that come from the Security Council, it would give up the chance to apply international humanitarian law to the states with the greatest capacity to exert military force. But the court would remain available to deal with the crimes of outlier regimes that deviate from generally accepted practices in the use of organized violence and lose the capacity to shield their subjects from retribution.

Critics might respond that this solution defeats the entire concept of justice by using different war crimes standards for great powers and everyone else. This argument, however, embodies the nirvana fallacy. Throughout its history, international law has distinguished between states that matter and those that do not. Until modern times, for example, the concept of customary international law was confined to "civilized" nations, thus precluding a large part of humanity from participating in its formation. The United Nations Charter, which proclaims the concept of sovereign equality, also enshrined the principle of great power superiority through the recognition of a veto right on the part of permanent members of the Security Council. To insist now that international justice cannot be a respecter of states not only demands a break with this history, but makes it nearly impossible to maintain a permanent war crimes tribunal. The choice, as we see it, is between that presented by Posner and Yoo, where the ICC will operate only when it is not needed, namely when a new

[13]  S.C. Res. 1593, U.N. SCOR, 59th Sess, 5158th Mtg., U.N. Doc. S/Res/1593 (2005).

regime wishes to punish its predecessors, or a surrender, tacit if not express, of
the power to self-judge jurisdiction.

## Privatizing the WTO DSB

Under the GATT system that preceded the WTO, dispute settlement emerged
gradually over the course of decades. The dispute-settlement (as distinguished
from the enforcement) process became fairly formalized, but the disputes implicated mostly straightforward regulatory issues. With the WTO DSB, we got an
even more formal dispute-settlement process (but still no formal enforcement)
and, as a result of the various Uruguay Round Agreements that extended international trade law, a greater risk that environmental, health, and safety regulation would be found inconsistent with legal obligations. As a result, the
dispute-resolution process has become more controversial.

Even though the new structure has generated some reservations, several
respected commentators have proposed moving from formal dispute resolution to full formal enforcement. They see this as the next logical step in the
development of WTO law. Although they do not put it this way, the cumu-
lative effect of their proposals amounts to privatizing GATT enforcement. If
their regime were to be adopted, persons besides states could bring claims and
the WTO DSB could mete out sanctions without relying on intervening state
cooperation to give them effect.[14]

These proposals to privatize the WTO DSB are not so far fetched. The Appellate Body has embraced the principle that nongovernmental groups can make
submissions, as long as at least one party to a proceeding consents to their
participation. The United States, one of the more frequent parties before the
WTO DSB, generally has promoted public participation in its proceedings,
even in instances where a group does not support the U.S. position. These
concessions do not amount to a power to initiate and sustain a dispute in the
face of governmental opposition, but they do represent the first step toward
the sharing of control over the prosecution and defense of disputes before the
WTO DSB. As for private sanctions, in one case the United States offered, and
the EC accepted, a lump-sum payment to settle a dispute after a finding that
the United States had violated its obligations.[15] This single instance does not

[14] E.g., Gregory Shaffer, Defending Interests: Public-Private Partnerships in WTO Litigation
(2003); Andrew T. Guzman, A Compliance-Based Theory of International Law, 90 Calif. L. Rev. 1823,
1872–75 (2002); Andrew T. Guzman, The Cost of Credibility: Explaining Resistance to Interstate Dispute
Resolution Mechanism, 31 J. Legal Stud. 303 (2002); Joel P. Trachtman & Philip M. Moremen, Costs
and Benefits of Private Participation in WTO Dispute Settlement: Whose Right Is It Anyway? 44 Harv.
Int'l L.J. 221 (2003).
[15] United States – Section 110(5) of the US Copyright Act, WT/DS160/23 (2003).

quite constitute a compensation system, as the United States paid nothing for the injuries caused by its violation in the period before the WTO DSB finding. Still, this voluntary agreement to commute into a cash transfer an obligation not to violate international trade law at least points in the direction of formal enforcement.

Those who would harden WTO law by taking the right to initiate and settle claims out of the exclusive hands of governments and creating a mechanism for the payment of monetized compensation for law violations start with the premise that the WTO rules enhance efficiency. If so, greater compliance would increase joint welfare. Consider, for example, the unwinding of the textiles quotas we discussed earlier. If states had known during the ten-year transitional period that they would face sanctions for failure to make adequate adjustments in anticipation of the new regime, the rich countries might have invested more in compensating and closing the soon-to-be-redundant textile producers. When the new rules came into effect in 2005, the rich countries then would have not needed to extend their quotas, an outcome that would have benefitted both producers in the poor world and consumers in the rich world. Thus, the argument goes, hardening the enforcement of WTO rules would result not just in better compliance, but in better patterns of international trade.

Our theory suggests that these claims overlook the dynamic effect of enforcement choices on the making of international commitments. As we have noted earlier, many (although not necessarily all) of the obligations derived from the GATT and the Uruguay Round Agreements implicate issues for which verification is a serious concern. Trade issues arise across the full spectrum of commercial activity and implicate a vast range of political, cultural, and technological questions. At the same time, most involve to one degree or another technical experts bound together by a common professional identity.

These considerations indicate that wholesale adoption of private enforcement of WTO obligations might well induce less rather than more commitment to welfare-enhancing international obligations. Commitments that contemplated a deferral of an obligation to permit gradual adjustments, for example, would necessarily require an assessment of the quality of a state's effort to make that adjustment. Given the complexity of interpreting macroeconomic as well as industry-specific effects, devising mutually acceptable proxies for this compliance standard seems daunting.

At the same time, the complex interdependency of these obligations means that hard enforcement might produce significant payoffs in some areas. To the extent that WTO obligations involve a retrospective assessment of discrete transactions, as opposed to forward-looking guesses about macroeconomic trends, verifiability would diminish as a concern. The challenge then becomes

identifying discrete areas of international trade law that lend themselves to
formal enforcement.

One area that strikes us as a logical candidate for harder enforcement are the
rules governing the imposition of countervailing and antidumping duties on
imported goods. In theory these duties allow states to retaliate against unfair,
and thus actionable, practices. Improper state subsidies to encourage exports
can be countervailed by the country of importation, and firms that dump goods
as part of a strategy of predation must pay a penalty equal to the amount by
which the import price falls below a good's "normal" value. The problem, as
trade experts know, is that national law everywhere defines actionable subsidies
and the margin of dumping in such elastic terms as to convert what purports
to be retaliation for wrongful conduct into protection against competition by
low-cost producers. Recognizing the problem, the members of the WTO have
drafted and implemented agreements regulating how states administer these
duties.

The most recent of these instruments formed a part of the Uruguay Round
Agreements.[16] Speaking broadly, they do three things. First, they limit what a
state can treat as an actionable subsidy or as dumping. Second, they require
states, as a condition of imposing duties, to establish that actionable subsidies
or dumping has harmed, or threatens to harm, domestic producers. Third,
they limit the measures that states can take to retaliate. The WTO DSB has
elaborated on the meaning of these commitments in several proceedings. As
is true throughout the WTO DSB regime, however, only states have the right
to complain about another country's practices, a rulebreaking state has no
obligation to compensate for injuries caused by past illegal duties, and the only
sanction for a refusal to comply with a WTO DSB ruling is trade retaliation by
the state or states that bring a proceeding.

Would it be possible to allow importers that face countervailing or antidumping duties directly to attack them through the WTO DSB, and for the WTO
DSB to have the authority directly to impose sanctions on states found to have
violated the relevant Uruguay Round Agreement? There are obvious benefits to
such a step. States do not manipulate countervailing or antidumping regimes
to produce advantages that the beneficiaries could justify openly. It seems likely
that this kind of protection exists only if it can remain shadowy. Its elimination
almost certainly would enhance both global welfare and benefit the states that
now indulge in the practice.

[16] Agreement on the Implementation of Article VI of the General Agreement on Tariffs and Trade 1994,
published at http://www.wto.org/english/docs_e/legal_e/19-adp_01_e.htm (last visited Sep. 2, 2005);
Agreement on Subsidies and Countervailing Measures, published at http://www.wto.org/english/
docs_e/legal_e/24-scm_01_e.htm (last visited Sep. 2, 2005).

Moreover, the costs of formal enforcement are not likely to exceed these benefits. To begin with, the framers of a future agreement could limit determinations as to whether a national rule or process conforms to the Uruguay Round obligations to a retrospective assessment of particular proceedings, rather than permitting facial challenges to the mechanisms as written. This would ensure that the international body responsible for enforcing the obligations focuses on historical, verifiable events, rather than conjecturing about future consequences. They also could impose a burden of proof on those claiming that national practices violated these obligations.

One concrete reason to believe that formal enforcement of these particular WTO obligations could work is that NAFTA already does something quite similar. The NAFTA Agreement also regulates the assessment of countervailing and antidumping duties by the signatory states, imposing virtually the same rules as those found in the Uruguay Round Agreements. NAFTA Chapter 19, however, extends enforcement of these constraints by creating an international mechanism to review the decisions of national administrative agencies, and each party to NAFTA has enacted legislation that gives domestic effect to the decisions of this mechanism. In the case of the United States, for example, two administrative agencies, the International Trade Administration of the Department of Commerce and the International Trade Commission, must make certain determinations as a prerequisite to the collection of countervailing or antidumping duties. Normally, persons dissatisfied with these determinations (either importers or competing domestic producers) may appeal them to the Court of International Trade, with appellate review by the Federal Circuit and, ultimately, the Supreme Court. In the case of imports from Canada or Mexico, these courts do not review the agency determinations, and instead a binational panel of arbiters, three from the country of exportation and two from the United States, perform the review function.[17]

Extending the NAFTA international review mechanism to all WTO members, which is to say to most international trade, would be ambitious, but not inordinately so. In the case of the United States, for example, 28 percent of imported goods already come from Canada and Mexico.[18] Our proposal would require simply that the remaining 72 percent be subjected to a similar legal regime.

To be sure, the NAFTA enforcement mechanism is not an exact model for our proposal. Under Article 1904(2) of NAFTA, the binational panels are

[17] 19 U.S.C. §1516a(f)(3), (g)(7), (8) (2001). *See* American Coalition for Competitive Trade v. Clinton, 128 F.3rd 761 (D.C. Cir. 1997) (dismissing on standing grounds lawsuit claiming that Title 19 binational panel review violated various provisions of U.S. constitution).
[18] To be precise, this was the percentage of imported goods for 2004.

obligated to impose domestic law.[19] The analogy is to the federal courts system of the United States, where under the famous *Erie* doctrine federal judges are obligated to apply, and if necessary determine, State law regarding all issues that do not present a question of federal law.[20] The binational panels exist for the same reason that federal courts have diversity jurisdiction: Even holding the applicable law constant, some organs offer greater assurances of impartial application than do others.

Our proposal would go a bit further: We would obligate states to incorporate these particular aspects of their WTO obligations into their domestic law and then have an international mechanism sanction noncompliance. But we do not think this extension is significant. Rarely do states openly acknowledge that their laws are inconsistent with their international obligations, at least as of the time that they assume the obligation. Moreover, judges typically recognize a convention, known in the United States as the *Charming Betsy* canon, that obliges them to try to interpret domestic law in a manner that reconciles seemingly inconsistent rules.[21] Thus we regard the choice of an international enforcement mechanism as far more consequential than the choice of rules that this mechanism would enforce.

Our broader point is that existing proposals to privatize the enforcement of all the Uruguay Round Agreements fail to take into account the costs that formal enforcement entail and, paradoxically, make it harder to isolate those particular WTO obligations for which formal enforcement would produce net benefits. A careful assessment of the distinct obligations makes it possible to identify those obligations for which formal enforcement by an international arbiter would not create excessive costs. But unless one recognizes why formal enforcement can be costly, one cannot isolate the instances in which it nonetheless is justified.

## ICJ DECISIONS AS CREATING PRIVATE RIGHTS

In the previous chapter, we described the controversy over the validity of the several ICJ decisions regarding U.S. fulfilment of its obligations under the Vienna Convention on Consular Relations. The response to the latest ICJ decision has been mixed and is still ongoing. The President both repudiated the Optional

---

[19]  In the case of the United States, this point is reinforced by Section 102 of the North American Free Trade Agreement Act, *codified at* 29 U.S.C. §3312 (2001), which declares in essence that none of the NAFTA obligations has direct effect in U.S. law except to the extent that Congress has incorporated them by statute.

[20]  Erie R. Co. v. Tompkins, 304 U.S. 64 (1938) (in exercising diversity jurisdiction, federal courts must apply the law as they believe the relevant State would, rather than develop an independent body of federal common law).

[21]  Murray v. The Charming Betsy, 6 U.S. (2 Cranch) 64, 118 (1804) ("[A]n act of Congress ought never to be construed to violate the law of nations if any other possible construction remains...").

Protocol that gave the ICJ jurisdiction over Vienna Convention claims and asked Texas, in one case, to provide the postconviction hearing that the ICJ had ordered. The issue of the legal significance of the President's action is now before the Texas courts.

We are not interested in the particulars of the litigation currently in the U.S. court, but rather in the underlying issue it presents of the effect of ICJ orders in domestic law.[22] It appears that at some point the Supreme Court will have to consider whether U.S. courts should give effect to the orders of the ICJ in cases where the United States has acceded to that tribunal's jurisdiction. One court of appeals already has announced that "we are of the opinion that the United States is bound by ICJ rulings in cases where it consented to the court's jurisdiction, just as it would be bound by any arbitral procedure to which it consented . . ."[23] We will not dwell here on the technical dimensions of that argument. Rather, we consider whether, in light of contract theory, domestic judicial enforcement of ICJ orders arising from instruments such as the Optional Protocol will help or hinder the objectives of the Vienna Convention and other treaties like it.

To begin with, the Vienna Convention deals with a classic collective action problem. In the abstract, all states probably prefer that other states treat their subjects well and that they have a free hand when dealing with foreign criminal suspects. The Vienna Convention takes a modest, if somewhat indirect, step toward setting minimum standards in the treatment of criminal suspects. The Optional Protocol in turn designates the ICJ as a tribunal with the authority to ascertain the specifics of what the Convention requires in particular instances. The signatories to that Protocol presumably understood that the ICJ had no enforcement powers of its own. Did the decision to join the Optional Protocol nonetheless represent, as one U.S. court has suggested, a commitment by each signatory state to require its own courts to implement any decisions that the ICJ might make?

[22] As we write, the Supreme Court is considering the question of whether it should embrace the ICJ's interpretation of the Vienna Convention as, among other things, forbidding the application of a procedural default rule to foreclose post-conviction consideration of a claim under that treaty. Bustillo v. Johnson, 126 S. Ct. 621 (2005) (granting certiorari). We should disclose that in both *Medellín* and Bustillo one of us participated as an *amicus curiae* in both the Supreme Court litigation and the Texas Court of Appeal's consideration of the subsequent application for postconviction relief. Brief for Professors of International Law, Federal Jurisdiction and the Foreign Relations Law of the United States as *Amici Curiae* on Behalf of Respondent, Sanchez-Llamas v. State, No. 04-10566, and Bustillo v. Johnson, No. 05-51, Feb. 1, 2006 (Paul B. Stephan, counsel of record); Brief for Professors of International Law, Federal Jurisdiction and the Foreign Relations Law of the United States as *Amici Curiae* on Behalf of Respondent, Medellín v. Dretke, No. 04–5928, Feb. 28, 2005 (Paul B. Stephan, counsel of record); Brief for Professors of International Law, Federal Jurisdiction and the Foreign Relations Law of the United States as *Amici Curiae* on behalf of Respondent, *Ex parte* Medellín, No. AP-75,207.

[23] Jogi v. Voges, 425 F.3rd 367, 384 (7th Cir. 2005).

To use contract theory to answer this question, it is helpful to distinguish a first-order and second-order approach. As an initial matter, one might ask whether a decision to use domestic courts to enforce ICJ decisions would result in greater benefits, in terms of enhanced compliance with an obligation to cooperate, than costs, in terms of undermining informal mechanisms to induce compliance. In other words, one could ask first whether states rationally might make the commitment under consideration. A second-order issue is whether domestic courts should make this decision in the absence of either a clear signal from the domestic legislature to do so or a background practice of assuming that domestic courts generally have the obligation to enforce the orders of international tribunals.

The distinction between first- and second-order analysis is important because, in the case of ICJ decisions, the two approaches may indicate different outcomes. On the one hand, questions about what constitutes compliance with the Vienna Convention seem discrete, retrospective, and therefore generally verifiable. Moreover, the application of the Convention to particular practices entails some complexity, and the interdependency of the obligation makes it difficult to separate legitimate reciprocity from illegitimate shirking. The technical issue that divides the United States from Paraguay, Germany and Mexico, for example, is whether the Convention permits a state to apply its general rules of criminal procedure so as to foreclose a postconviction assertion of a claim that the victim of a violation failed to raise at a time when he should have known of its existence, or instead requires that a state give everyone an opportunity to demonstrate prejudice as a result of a violation no matter how lax the victim has been in asserting his Vienna Convention rights. In other words, does the Convention relieve a victim (or more precisely, the victim's lawyer) of the conventional (under U.S. practice) burden of ascertaining at some point during the criminal justice process that a violation occurred and then calling the court's attention to this fact? Arguments can be made for both sides, and to have a third party untangle this problem probably would reinforce general compliance with the Convention.

One might object that this argument provides a basis for giving the ICJ formal enforcement power, but not for deputizing national courts to enforce the ICJ's determinations. The problem is the enormous variation in the independence and authority of domestic judicial systems, leading to asymmetry in the enforcement mechanism. In the case of the Iranian hostage crisis, for example, the Iranian judges did not pretend to act as a check on the national political élite, so the ICJ ruling went completely unenforced. Why would countries with strong and independent judiciaries consent to bind themselves to formal enforcement, if more disordered states – exactly those most likely to violate the Convention's rules – would not face comparable constraints?

A sufficient response is that the Vienna Convention does the least good with respect to states that lack strong or independent courts. Access to consular officials does not help an arrestee if the local judiciary will behave as the regime's puppet. But in states with reasonably effective court systems, consular intervention may make a difference in the treatment of arrested subjects. States where the judges will enforce the Convention, in other words, are also those states where rights under the Convention are likely to matter the most.

On balance, then, a decent argument exists for creating a regime that requires local judges to implement decisions of the ICJ regarding the Vienna Convention. But this only explains why states might do this. The second-order question is whether judges should take the initiative in exercising this function, in the absence of clear signals from local lawmakers that they have this authority. Should domestic judges, those in the United States in particular, act as norm entrepreneurs to encourage other national judiciaries to take over the formal enforcement of the ICJ's decisions, or should they instead wait for further instructions?

Framed as a second-order question, the case for formal enforcement through local courts seems decidedly weaker. For example, the effort of U.S. courts to encourage other nations' courts to follow in their footsteps may or may not succeed. But a clear indication of a willingness to exercise such initiative may have harmful implications for enforcement of both the Vienna Convention and other international regimes as well.

First, a state might denounce its obligation rather than accept formal enforcement. In the case of the Optional Protocol to the Vienna Convention, for example, the United States withdrew its acceptance of ICJ jurisdiction in future cases rather than run the risk that its courts would enforce the ICJ's decisions. Once the preferred outcome – only informal enforcement of ICJ orders – became less than certain, the government chose no ICJ orders to the alternative of formal enforcement of ICJ orders.

Second and more important, the risk of formal enforcement of ICJ orders under the Optional Protocol opens up the possibility of general domestic judicial enforcement of ICJ decisions. During the Nicaraguan civil war of the 1980s, for example, the ICJ came to the conclusion that U.S. support for paramilitary forces opposing the Sandinista regime (itself the product of successful paramilitary operations) violated principles of customary international law.[24] Victims

---

[24]  Case Concerning Military and Paramilitary Activities in and against Nicaragua (Nicaragua v. United States of America), 1986 I.C.J. 14.

of the paramilitaries then sued the U.S. government in U.S. courts, seeking to enjoin the government from future actions that would violate the ICJ's order.[25] If the Vienna Convention merits formal enforcement, why not the customary rules applicable to the Nicaraguan dispute?

The problem, put broadly, is that not knowing when its domestic court will choose to enforce ICJ orders increases the enforcement risk to the United States resulting from recognition of ICJ jurisdiction, and the United States generally has a choice whether to submit a matter to the ICJ or not. Reducing this enforcement risk requires a clear specification of when domestic enforcement will occur. The best evidence of the present baseline, however, is a general practice of nonenforcement, albeit one that the Supreme Court has neither blessed nor condemned. No U.S. court (or, for that matter, any foreign court of which we are aware) has ever asserted the power to enforce ICJ decisions.[26]

In theory, a court might identify the considerations leading it to enforce ICJ orders based on the Vienna Convention and its Optional Protocol in a way that reassures lawmakers about the risk of extension to other regimes. But at present, any departure from the existing baseline of no domestic enforcement of any ICJ decisions would be destabilizing. Nothing about the Optional Protocol, at least in form, distinguishes it from any other commitment that the United States has made to recognize ICJ jurisdiction. And once a court relies on substantive distinctions, such as the significance of some international law rules relative to others, it faces the difficulty of binding future courts made up of judges with potentially different substantive preferences and values.

The U.S. experience with proposals for formal enforcement of the UN Charter during the 1940s and 1950s and of the GATT during the 1960s, recounted in Chapter 6, seems relevant here. Uncertainty about whether domestic judges would enforce these rules induced greater caution in their development. Similarly, we anticipate further U.S. retrenchment on ICJ jurisdiction, and perhaps withdrawal from other tribunal-based dispute-resolution arrangements, if domestic courts give any indication that they will act as the ICJ's enforcement agents. On balance, then, policy makers who find our theory helpful should wish for courts to wait on the political branches before finding themselves empowered to carry out the will of the ICJ.[27]

---

[25] Committee of U.S. Citizens Living in Nicaragua v. Reagan, 859 F.2nd 929 (D.C. Cir. 1988) (rejecting lawsuit on grounds that ICJ decisions have no domestic effect in U.S. law).

[26] Mark Weisburd, *International Courts and American Courts*, 21 MICH. J. INT'L L. 877 (2000). As we noted earlier, *Jogi v. Voges* 425 F.3rd 367 (7th Cir. 2005), seems to have endorsed an argument for asserting this power, but the court took no such action.

[27] We express no view on whether, in the specific instance of the *Medellín* dispute, President Bush's order constitutes a sufficient authorization on the part of the political branches. This is a matter of the domestic constitutional law of the United States, a subject on which we profess no special expertise.

## International Humanitarian Law as Private Law

A variation on the Vienna Convention problem is a treaty that obligates a state to treat individuals in a certain fashion but specifies no enforcement mechanism. Consider the background to this problem. Some international agreements clearly disavow direct domestic enforcement.[28] Others expressly call for domestic judicial enforcement, either by their own terms[29] or through implementing domestic laws.[30] Many of the agreements that expressly call for direct domestic enforcement involve private commercial transactions where the parties typically are strangers to each other, not likely to engage in repeat play and, by the nature of the transaction in which they engage, are relatively heterogenous.[31] Typically the potential losses parties face have a high variance. In these cases, informal enforcement is unlikely to be optimal.

There remain, however, a significant number of agreements where the intention of the parties is unclear. Those situations force national lawmakers, and in particular domestic courts, to articulate interpretive strategies and to construct default rules to determine the domestic effect of agreements that fail to address the issue. The controversial instances involve human rights treaties, which do not address the enforcement question explicitly, but which the United States invariably ratifies subject to a statement that the domestic courts shall not enforce the obligations contained therein.[32]

Courts and commentators tend to approach defaults from one of two directions. The *proactive approach*, as we shall term it, presumes the efficacy of domestic judicial enforcement of international agreements and puts the burden of proof on those arguing against intervention. It focuses only on capacity issues such as verifiability, asking whether an agreement contains "sufficiently

---

[28]  *See* Portuguese Republic v. Council (Case C-149/96), [1999] E.C.R. I-8395 (analyzing deliberate decision of Uruguay Round parties not to have agreements directly enforceable).

[29]  Convention for the Unification of Certain Rules Relating to International Transportation by Air, Oct. 12, 1929, 49 Stat. 3000, T.S. No. 876, 137 L.N.T.S. 11; Articles of Agreement of the International Monetary Fund, July 22, 1944, 60 Stat. 1401, 2 U.N.T.S. 39, *as amended*, 20 U.S.T. 2775; 29 U.S.T. 2203, T.I.A.S. NO. 11898.

[30]  Convention for the Unification of Certain Rules of Law Relating to Bills of Lading, Aug. 25, 1924, 51. Stat. 233, 120 L.N.T.S. 155, *implemented by* Carriage of Goods at Sea Act of 1936, 46 U.S.C. app. §§1300–1315 (2001).

[31]  For a review of international agreements involving private commercial transactions, see Paul B. Stephan, *The Futility of Unification and Harmonization in International Commercial Law*, 39 Va. J. Int'l L. 743 (1999).

[32]  For a debate on whether the treaties permit this limitation, compare Curtis A. Bradley & Jack L. Goldsmith, *Treaties, Human Rights, and Conditional Consent*, 149 U. Pa. L. Rev. 399 (2000), with Ryan Goodman, *Human Rights Treaties, Invalid Reservations, and State Consent*, 96 Am. J. Int'l L. 531 (2002), and Louis Henkin, *U.S. Ratification of Human Rights Treaties: The Ghost of Senator Bricker*, 89 Am. J. Int'l L. 341 (1995). *See also* Sosa v. Alvarez-Machain, 542 U.S 692, 728, 735 (2004) (giving effect to Senate reservation). *But see* Igartua-De La Rosa v. United States, 415 F.31d 145, 189–90 (1st Cir. 2005) (Howard, J., dissenting) (rejecting authority to impose reservations).

determinate standards" on which courts can base their actions.[33] The *bargaining approach*, as we shall call it, is exemplified by the opinion of Judges Seyla and Boudin quoted at the beginning of this chapter. It asks whether the agreement bargained for judicial enforcement. Implicit in the bargaining approach is a recognition that agreements might contain a mix of verifiable and nonverifiable conditions representing offsetting concessions, and that enforcement of only some might upset the parties' expectations and skew performance away from observable but nonverifiable conditions. It also reflects a systematic response to the problem of enforcement risk.

To appreciate the differences between these approaches, consider one class of treaties, the Geneva Conventions regarding the law of armed conflict. These instruments codify what once was called the law of war (*ius in bello*) and now is known as international humanitarian law. One in particular, governing the treatment of prisoners of war, seems to lend itself to formal enforcement: Each state needs a mechanism credibly to induce others to respect the rights of its soldiers; each has an incentive to abuse its captives in the absence of a sanction; in actual conflicts the interactions between each side in how each treats the other's soldier is complex and interactive; and the rules' requirements can be formulated in verifiable terms. The United States ratified the Prisoner of War Convention in 1955 without any express reservations about enforcement, and the Army has promulgated a regulation seeking to implement U.S. obligations under it.[34] Does either this convention or the regulation implementing it create rights that persons held as prisoners of war may assert in a U.S. court? How does our theory help in devising an answer?

As in our discussion of the Vienna Convention, the distinction between first-order and second-order analysis is useful. The proactive approach conforms to a first-order analysis. It asks whether the treaty is susceptible to legal enforcement, which translates as an inquiry into the verifiability of the rules that the treaty provides. The bargaining approach, in contrast, asks whether the decision to imply judicial enforcement in the absence of any clear signal from the treaty framers will create an enforcement risk that may have systemic consequences for treaty negotiation.

As we already have suggested, were one to ignore enforcement risk, the case for formal enforcement of the Geneva Convention on prisoners of war would

---

[33]   Carlos Manuel Vázquez, *The Four Doctrines of Self-Executing Treaties*, 89 AM. J. INT'L L. 695, 713–15 (1995) (citing cases).

[34]   Geneva Convention Relative to the Treatment of Prisoners of War, Aug. 12, 1949, 6 U.S.T. 3316; Enemy Prisoners of War, Retained Personnel, Civilian Internees and Other Detainees, Army Reg. 190–8, §§1–5, 1–6 (1997); Hamdi v. Rumsfeld, 542 U.S. 507, 549–51 (2004) (Souter, J., concurring) (discussing U.S. implementation of Geneva Convention).

seem strong. The fact that the Army seeks to incorporate the Convention's requirements into its own practices seems to resolve any doubts about verifiability. Heterogeneity counsels for third-party enforcement, especially when captives belong to informal organizations rather than traditional armies. Yet the weight of judicial authority, if not academic opinion, seems to be against judicial enforcement. No appellate court yet has found that any of the Geneva Conventions create rights that U.S. courts can enforce directly.[35]

The problem is that implying a judicial enforcement power from a treaty's silence presents greater enforcement risk, and greater potential for destabilizing the expectations of treaty makers, than would recruiting domestic courts to enforce the orders of international tribunals. Designation of an international tribunal as having compulsory dispute settlement power is still relatively uncommon, while myriad treaties address the interests of individuals in a manner that might seem to create rights. A second-order analysis thus would indicate that, as in the case of the Vienna Convention, courts should wait for better information from the political branches before treating treaties that do not address enforcement as conveying judicial authority.

To be sure, current doctrine on when U.S. courts will find judicially enforceable rights within a treaty is incoherent.[36] One might argue that no decision can increase the instability of such unsettled doctrine. But the case law is not as disorderly as the commentators' efforts to extract general principles might suggest. The results, as distinguished from the courts' explanation of the outcome, form a fairly clear pattern. Rarely does a U.S. court actually find itself authorized to enforce a treaty. In particular, no court has found any treaty codifying international humanitarian law as in and of itself creating judicially enforceable rights. Given this baseline, our theory and the second-order argument derived from it points in the direction of continued judicial restraint.

## THE DOMAIN OF THE WARSAW CONVENTION

When there is domestic enforcement of an international instrument, disagreements over the extent of the agreement's domain still can arise. If a treaty specifies an obligation and designates courts as the proper agents for sanctioning noncompliance, how seriously should courts take the question of whether

---

[35] Johnson v. Eisentrager, 339 U.S. 763 (1950) (applying earlier prisoner of war convention and finding no judicially enforceable rights); Hamdan v. Rumsfeld, 415 F.3rd 33 (D.C. Cir.) (1949 Convention not judicially enforceable), *cert. granted*, 126 S. Ct. 622 (2005); Hamdi v. Rumsfeld, 316 F.3rd 450 (4th Cir. 2003) (same), *vacated and remanded on other grounds*, 542 U.S. 507 (2004). For academic commentary, see Derek Jinks & David Sloss, *Is the President Bound by the Geneva Conventions?* 90 CORNELL L. REV. 97 (2004).

[36] Carlos Manuel Vázquez, note 33 *supra*, at 695.

the obligatory rule applies to the case before it? If a treaty's rules are otherwise suitable, should courts be cautious about extending them to transactions that do not fall within the scope of the treaty, read formally and literally?

As noted earlier, one multilateral convention that, in the view of its framers, contemplated formal enforcement by domestic courts is the Warsaw Convention on international air transport.[37] This treaty was the second modern multilateral agreement regulating the shipping industry and closely resembles its predecessor, the Hague Rules governing sea transport.[38] It stipulates some mandatory terms for carriage contracts, offers other contractual default terms that parties can reject with express provisions, and, in the United States, provides a basis for federal (as opposed to state) court jurisdiction over disputes arising from these contracts.[39]

All this may seem straightforward, but the Warsaw Convention also presents a predictable problem when a multilateral instrument attempts to regulate a dynamic, technologically changing industry. Several versions exist, separated by decades and, one assumes, each later version informed by experience under the earlier one. But the new versions supplant the older ones only to the extent that a state chooses to adhere to the latest version and denounce its earlier commitment. Unless all states act uniformly, we end up with a world where different states adhere to different versions. For many provisions, the different versions are indistinguishable, but some meaningful variation in the terms of the versions does exist.

A recent case illustrates the problem. In *Chubb & Sons, Inc. v. Asiana Airlines*,[40] the court had to decide what law governed a dispute over the misdelivery of goods shipped by international air carrier. The flight originated in South Korea and ended in the United States, presumptively bringing the transaction under the Warsaw Convention. But the United States acceded only to the 1929 version of the Convention, while South Korea had joined only the

---

[37] Convention for the Unification of Certain Rules Relating to International Transportation by Air, Oct. 12, 1929, 49 Stat. 3000, T.S. No. 876.137 L.N.T.S. 11, *reprinted in note following* 49 U.S.C. §40105 (2001).

[38] Convention for the Unification of Certain Rules of Law Relating to Bills of Lading, Aug. 25, 1924, 51 Stat. 233, 120 L.N.T.S. 155 [hereinafter Hague Rules], implemented by Carriage of Goods at Sea Act, Apr. 16, 1936, 49 Stat. 1207,46 U.S.C. app. §§1300–1315 (2001).

[39] For description and analysis of the Warsaw Convention, see Paul B. Stephan, *The Futility of Unification and Harmonization in International Commercial Law*, 39 Va. J. Int'l L. 743, 768–72 (1999).

[40] 214 F.3rd 301 (2nd Cir. 2000), *cert. denied*, 533 U.S. 928 (2001). For a later case raising similar issues, see *Avero Belgium Ins. v. American Airlines, Inc.*, 423 F.3rd 73 (2nd Cir. 2005) (Hague Protocol to Warsaw Convention did not apply to relations between Belgium and United States at time of contract; U.S. ratification of subsequent Montreal Protocol did not have the effect of ratification of separate Hague Protocol).

1955 version.[41] The court had to decide whether an agreement existed between the two countries as a result of their acceptance of overlapping but distinct obligations.[42]

A proactive approach would invoke a pro-agreement default on the theory that judicial enforcement of some obligations is preferable to no enforcement. One can find a model in §2–207 of the Uniform Commercial Code, which allows courts to make a judicially enforceable contract in cases where an offer and acceptance do not match.[43] The trial court in *Chubb* reached this result, finding that treaty relations existed between the United States and Korea as to all the terms of the two conventions that were identical. Both versions contained a low default limit on the carrier's liability for misdelivery, but only the 1929 version threw out that cap in cases where the carrier deviated from the route described in the contract. The carrier had landed in Los Angeles, although the contract had specified San Francisco, and had completed the delivery by truck, arguably increasing the risk of misdelivery. Under the trial court's analysis, the carrier enjoyed the benefit of the damages cap and, because only one version of the Convention dispensed with the cap upon deviation from the promised route, did not suffer because it had failed to perform perfectly. The proactive approach resulted in the application of international rules, but produced a contract of carriage that deviated from that provided by the version of the Warsaw Convention that the United States accepted.

On appeal, the Second Circuit took a bargaining approach, requiring something closer to the common law's mirror-image rule to limit treaty relations to instances where states had assumed identical obligations. This default implements the idea that parties might regard the total bargain as motivating performance and correspondingly consider partial enforcement as an unwanted outcome. As with our other examples, we applaud the court's willingness to employ a second-order analysis to limit the domain of a concededly effective treaty. Because the United States had endorsed a treaty that applied only to flights originating in one party and ending in another, and because South

---

[41] Protocol to Amend the Convention for the Unification of Certain Rules Relating to International Carriage by Air signed at Warsaw on 12 October 1929, Sep. 28, 1955, 478 U.N.T.S. 371.

[42] The existence of treaty relations determined both the subject matter jurisdiction of the federal court that heard the case and the substantive rules for determining liability and damages.

[43] UNIFORM COMMERCIAL CODE §2–207(3). The trial court in *Chubb* did precisely this, although it based its decision on an interpretation of the Warsaw Convention and the Vienna Convention on the Law of Treaties, May 23, 1969, 1155 U.N.T.S. 331. Chubb & Son, Inc. v. Asiana Airlines, 1998 WL 647185 (S.D.N.Y.1998). The United States was (and is) not a party to the latter instrument, although the Department of State maintains that some portions of it have the force of customary international law.

Korea was not a party to that treaty (even though it had joined a very similar instrument), a court should not use the Warsaw Convention to govern disputes such as this one. Instead, the shipper and the carrier should have to rely on the common law of contract, of which the Warsaw Convention was not a restatement, or some other version of state law.

## ODIOUS DEBT AND SOVEREIGN CONTRACTS

Our last example involves domestic judicial enforcement of customary international law. One might immediately object that because customary international law, by definition, does not result from the formal interstate bargaining process that produces treaties, a theory about contracting has nothing to say about the subject. We disagree.

We concede that analyzing customary international law presents many challenges. Because no overwhelming consensus exists about when a rule becomes customary international law – in H. L. Hart's terminology, the field lacks a rule of recognition – one cannot propose an account of the practice that some expert will not dispute. But at least one conception of customary international law is anchored in the concept of state consent, in the sense that a rule does not bind a state until some authoritative decision maker accedes to it. We limit our claim to this conception, however incomplete some might regard it.

If one accepts that customary international law results from state consent, it is not too great a stretch to conceive of domestic judges as agents with the capacity to signal that consent. A court might act as a norm entrepreneur, hoping to persuade other jurisdictions to embrace a rule that advances some desirable goal, or it might observe the emergence of a customary rule and assume that the political branches would prefer to signal cooperation rather than defection. An early and significant decision of the U.S. Supreme Court made exactly the latter argument to justify adherence to a doctrine of sovereign immunity in the absence of a statutory rule.[44] We do not dispute the authority of domestic courts to act in this fashion in cases over which they otherwise have jurisdiction.[45]

The issue remains whether federal courts should look actively for customary rules to enforce or, in most cases, fall back on other sources of law to resolve disputes before it. How does our theory help courts to choose between a quick

[44] Schooner Exchange v. McFaddon, 11 U.S. (7 Cranch) 116 (1812) (vessel belonging to French navy not subject to attachment by U.S. courts).
[45] The statement in text recognizes that some take the position that customary international law does not, simply by its status as customary international law, constitute federal law for purposes of federal court jurisdiction under Article III of the Constitution or 28 U.S.C. §1331 (2001). For the controversy, see the authorities cited in note 29 of Chapter Two.

trigger and greater caution when deciding whether to supplant domestic law with an international custom? Are there second-order issues in the choice of trigger?

We illustrate the problem with an issue that has recently emerged as significant, namely the question of odious debt. Very bad regimes can incur debts, either by contract or by violating rights for which compensation is a remedy. On occasion, the bad regimes are replaced by others, not as obviously cruel and dangerous. When this happens, under what circumstances may the new regime obtain relief from its predecessor's obligations? The case of Iraq, which incurred substantial indebtedness to foreign creditors under the Ba'athists, makes the matter somewhat pressing.

When a regime borrows on behalf of a state, several issues arise. First, does the sovereign debtor have the capacity to endow its creditors with conventional enforcement rights, including the ability to obtain arbitral awards and court judgments and to attach the sovereign's property to obtain satisfaction? Second, if the creditors can acquire these rights, can they assert them against later regimes that subsequently obtain the authority to act on behalf of the sovereign? Third, are there any circumstances in which a debt incurred nominally on behalf of a sovereign can be repudiated by a subsequent regime?

The first two of these questions generally have affirmative answers, due both to legislative developments such as the codification of the doctrine of sovereign immunity and judicial propounding of rules of state succession. As a result, a loan contracted by one regime results in legally enforceable rights that, depending on the sovereign's foreign asset holdings and foreign-source revenues, can result in meaningful recourse for creditors, and a regime change normally does not alter the creditors' rights. Only because of this does the last question become relevant.

In the aftermath of the Spanish-American War, representatives of the United States took the position that debts undertaken by Spain and secured with Cuban revenues were invalid as to the Cuban security. Spain had used the loan proceeds to pay for the suppression of the Cuban opposition on whose side the United States (at least nominally) had fought. The peace treaty that resulted reflected the U.S. position, although Spain rejected the arguments that the United States had made. Two decades later Chief Justice Taft, presiding over an arbitration between Costa Rica and the Royal Bank of Canada, revived these arguments to relieve Costa Rica from the burden of paying a debt for which a previous dictator had contracted. The evidence suggested that the dictator had converted the proceeds to his personal use.[46] Alexander Sack, an itinerant international

[46] Tinoco Arbitration (Gr. Brit. v. Costa Rica), 1 R.I.A.A. 375 (1923)

law scholar, then articulated what he understood to be a principled version of the U.S. position. According to Sack, an indebtedness incurred by a prior regime is "odious" and therefore subject to repudiation without recourse if the prior regime acted without the consent of the governed, the debt proceeds did not benefit the subjects of the regime, and the creditor had adequate notice of both these facts.[47]

Out of these rather scanty precedents has emerged what some experts claim to be a customary international law norm. During the 1990s, supporters of the effort by developing countries to rid themselves of their inherited debt burden revived the concept and suggested that international organs, including nonjudicial bodies such as the International Monetary Fund, as well as national courts ought to invoke the odious debt doctrine to relieve these sovereigns from obligations incurred by a prior regime. To date, none has done so. But the Iraqi case, with its extreme facts and geopolitical salience, might yet be the instance where the doctrine obtains some purchase.

For the odious debt concept to be anything more than a talking point in a negotiation, some body with formal enforcement authority would have to decide to apply customary international law to a dispute between a sovereign debtor and its creditors. We contemplate two contexts in which this might arise. First, some creditor transactions might fit within the scope of a bilateral investment treaty, which would give creditors access to arbitration and subsequent judicial enforcement of an arbitral award. The debtor sovereign might invoke the doctrine as a defense. Second, creditors might sue in a national court, especially in jurisdictions where a sovereign debtor had attachable assets, and the defendant sovereign debtor might ask the judge to recognize the odious debt doctrine as a rule of decision. In either instance, the adjudicator would have to choose between recognizing a customary rule and applying domestic law.

As a matter of industry practice, most formal sovereign debt contracts contain choice of law provisions that direct the adjudicator to apply either English or New York law. Involuntary debts arising from torts obviously do not present this constraint, but even English or New York courts might decide that their law includes certain rules of customary international law. As a result, both arbitral tribunals and national courts hypothetically have the authority to invoke the odious debt doctrine even when constrained by a choice of law commitment, and certainly could invoke the doctrine in cases of unliquidated tort liability.

---

[47] Alexander N. Sack, Les Effets des Transformations des États sur leurs Dettes Publiques et Autres Obligations Financières (1927). For recent commentary, see Anna Gelpern, *What Iraq and Argentina Might Learn from Each Other*, 6 Chi. J. Int'l L. 391 (2005).

Presumably, the adjudicator would decide this question against the background of domestic rules that might apply to a creditor's claim. Most contracts for sovereign debt, whether bank loans or bonds, reflect the work of sophisticated counsel and are unlikely to contain express barriers to enforcement. Both the United States and the United Kingdom have enacted statutes that bar a sovereign immunity defense to enforcement of conventional loan contracts, and the common law of both jurisdictions generally would regard a successor regime as required to meet its predecessor's legal obligations. But some parts of the odious debt doctrine have counterparts in national law. First, a debtor can argue that, under its domestic legal order, the persons who contracted for the debt lacked the legal authority to do so.[48] This *ultra vires* defense corresponds to Justice Taft's determination in the *Tinoco* arbitration that the Costa Rican dictator borrowed for his own benefit and violated various local laws to do so. Second, a creditor that colludes with a regime's agents in concealing the circumstances of a transaction, such as by paying a bribe to place a loan, presumably has committed fraud, for which rescission is a conventional remedy. What national law does *not* do, in the absence of a law forbidding the borrowing authority from undertaking the transaction, is rescind a contract where the loan contract was unwise or the uses to which the loan proceeds are put were frivolous. If most despots bother to enact domestic laws that allow them to make loans under conditions that please them, and if most creditors do not pay bribes or engage in other conduct that might be characterized as fraud, then national law at its current state of development would limit the capacity of new regimes to repudiate the debts of their odious predecessors.

As in our prior discussion, we begin with a first-order analysis. We accept as plausible the claims that making it more costly for bad regimes to borrow from international capital markets is normatively desirable, and that achieving this goal presents a collective action problem. Some might object that odiousness is in the eye of the beholder and thus not truly verifiable, but we are willing to assume that discrete and verifiable proxies can be created. For purposes of discussion, let us assume that a regime would qualify as odious only if it both completely lacked democratic accountability as a result of suppression of all forms of dissent and systematically engaged in extrajudicial violence against its citizens. Let us also stipulate that successor regimes would bear the burden of proving both that their predecessor met this test and that creditors knew

---

[48] Hazell v. Hammersmith & Fulham London Borough Council, 2 W.L.R. 372 (H. L. 1991) (debt contract unenforceable because Borough Council lacked legal capacity to enter into it); State v. Morgan Stanley & Co., 194 W. Va. 163, 459 S.E.2d 906 (W. Va. 1995) (basing judgment against broker on state customer's legal incapacity).

that they met it. Those who see the odious debt doctrine as a means to launch a broad critique of global capitalism might find this definition too confining. What it does, however, is identify those circumstances where regimes are most likely to use government resources for purposes other than benefitting the general population. For example, under this test a large portion of outstanding Iraqi debt probably qualifies as odious.

We further assume that sovereign debtors overall might prefer legal rules that isolate bad actors by discharging odious debts. A discharge rule would increase credit costs for bad regimes (because creditors would face a higher risk of a subsequent discharge), thus generating a separating equilibrium in which "good regimes" that eschewed the bad behavior would be offered lower credit rates. It is also possible that creditors might do better by specializing, with some lending to good states and others working with bad sovereigns. At present, creditors cannot capture benefits from specialization because they cannot easily differentiate between types of debtors. Notwithstanding these collective benefits, no individual creditor or sovereign debtor has an incentive to agree to a term in the debt contract that discharges odious debt. As long as odiousness vel non remains an insufficient ground for invalidating a sovereign's contract, creditors cannot reward nonodious regimes with lower interest rates. In principle, then, some widely applicable rule that discharges the debts of successors to bad regimes probably would enhance social welfare.

What, then, of second-order effects? Judicial adoption of a discharge rule, in the context of the international sovereign debt market, presents two kinds of instability problems. First, the retroactive introduction of new, unanticipated terms into long-established and widely used contracts increases legal risk generally. A court would have difficulty reassuring parties that its odious debt decision is a one-off matter, and not part of a general skepticism about sovereign debt contracts.

Second, although we stipulate that in theory a good proxy for odiousness may exist, in practice finding an acceptable proxy presents serious instability problems, especially if a court were to ground its determination on customary international law. As many before us have noted, claims about the content of customary international law, especially regarding the human rights that individuals enjoy against states, have exploded in the last quarter-century. Because these claims rest largely on the views of expert jurists rather than of politically accountable governments or legislatures, the centrifugal pressures to expand its domain are great, and the centripetal pressures essentially nonexistent. A judge seeking to consult jurists' opinion about the content of human rights law to determine what qualifies as odious would find a wealth of opinion but no clear and determinate core.[49]

The indeterminate nature of customary international law is not just a general problem, but one that affects the odious debt doctrine specifically. One can find, for example, reputable authorities who maintain that repression and murder are sufficient, but by no means necessary, to label a regime as odious. Many of the current proponents of the doctrine make arguments that echo those of the New International Economic Order of the 1970s, which challenged the capacity of postcolonial regimes ever to enter into binding commitments with powerful institutions of the developed world. Experts criticize the economic choices of any regime, especially in the developing world, that fails to address environmental concerns, the interests of indigenous peoples, or the rights of workers. If odiousness is to be determined in light of these opinions, then much of sovereign borrowing, both past and future, suffers from enforcement risk. Moreover, expanding the scope of odiousness – a process that seems inevitable if customary international law is to do the work – undercuts the supposed benefits of a separating equilibrium that the doctrine is supposed to create.

Several conclusions result from this analysis. First, either the United States or the United Kingdom reasonably might consider amending their statutory law of sovereign immunity to block enforcement of sovereign debt obligations in cases that satisfy a narrow and clear definition of odiousness. A precedent of sorts exists in the 1996 amendment to the U.S. Foreign Sovereign Immunity Act, which lifted immunity for certain acts of terrorism and other gross human rights abuses.[50] Symmetrically, the United States might extend immunity to debts incurred by prior regimes that engage in comparable misconduct. The sanctions regime of Title III of the Helms-Burton legislation, which provides a cause of action against persons who "traffick" in property seized by the Cuban government as part of its revolution but also eliminates this action once the President determines that Cuba has enjoyed a democratic restoration, also provides a model for this hypothetical legislation.[51] Our point is simply that legislation designed to implement a manageable and valuable form of the odious debt doctrine is feasible and not without precedent.

---

[49]   Curtis A. Bradley & Jack L. Goldsmith, *Customary International Law as Federal Common Law: A Critique of the Modern Position*, 110 HARV. L. REV. 816, 839–40 (1997).
[50]   Antiterrorism and Effective Death Penalty Act of 1996, §221(a)(1), Pub. L. 104–132, 110 Stat. 1214, codified at 28 U.S.C. §1605(a)(7) (2001).
[51]   Liberty and Democratic Solidarity (LIBERTAD) Act of 1996, §302(h)(1)(B), Pub. L. 104–114, 110 Stat. 788, codified at 22 U.S.C. §6082(h)(1)(B) (2001).

Second, judicial efforts to achieve this outcome in advance of any national legislation present, within the framework of our theory, substantial problems. A broad, judicially created right to repudiate odious debt could add to the costs of transition away from authoritarian and repressive regimes, because their successors would have difficulty credibly committing either to the honoring of past obligations or to not backsliding on their own human rights records. A general rise in the cost of credit to developing country sovereigns seems a more likely outcome than either the establishment of a separating equilibrium between good and bad regimes or increased pressure on lenders not to prop up dictators. The general point is that sovereign debt contracts are complex, as are the conditions under which the right to repudiate an obligation incurred by a predecessor regime will be welfare enhancing. Courts are ill equipped to craft a precise rule to govern these situations, and the alternative of a broad standard is likely to lead to moral hazard that will cause more harm than good.

## Conclusion

We do not maintain that contract theory provides a comprehensive and exclusive account of how the enforcement of international law works, much less an infallible means of resolving all questions about international law's future. Nor have we conclusively proved that our model of optimal international law enforcement has the best fit of all conceivable explanations for the enforcement practices that we observe today. Our goal in this book has been more modest, but not unimportant. We have sought to demonstrate that the general direction in the hardening of international law enforcement is broadly consistent with contract theory, and that future research into, as well as policy choices about, international law and its enforcement must now grapple with its implications.

Contract theory, broadly conceived, illuminates both why we see formal enforcement of international law and what we should consider when deciding whether and how to add to formal enforcement's tasks. This perspective directs our focus toward the factors that identify when formal enforcement is likely to produce the greatest net benefits, namely where rules represent a response to a collective action problem, entails verifiable factors, and addresses complex interactions among relatively heterogenous actors.

This method of analysis also contributes to our understanding of the optimal process for embracing formal enforcement. By distinguishing the first-order and second-order implications of a particular enforcement choice – typically, a call for courts to adopt formal enforcement ahead of any treaty or legislative command – we have suggested why formal enforcement might seem attractive and yet have serious negative consequences. The costs of more enforcement flow directly from a critical dimension of international law, namely that it rests on state consent and thus remains subject to state repudiation.

Finally, contract theory, bolstered by studies in allied disciplines, affirms the potency of informal enforcement in many, if not most, contexts where international cooperation is thought to produce welfare gains. The fact that informal enforcement is flexible, operates ex post rather than ex ante, and dispenses with a predefined sanctioning structure sometimes leads analysts, particularly legal academics, to assume that informal mechanisms are inadequate to promote beneficial collective goals. We have sought to demonstrate that these assumptions are generally unwarranted. In sum, contract theory: (a) explains the hardening of international law enforcement; (b) identifies areas where further hardening is likely to have the greatest payoffs; and (c), by explaining the pervasiveness and potency of informal enforcement, cautions against undesirable extensions of formal mechanisms. We want to emphasize these last two points. Recent uses of formal law enforcement suggest great possibilities, as the rules governing complex international cooperation come more and more to resemble conventional, reliable law as we know it in its domestic forms. At the same time, the effectiveness of international law is undermined by all-encompassing efforts to add formal enforcement to all (or most) cooperative projects. An indiscriminate hardening of international law is likely to reduce rather than enhance the very benefits that the proponents of hard international law are seeking to promote. Contract theory provides a valuable perspective to guide sensible response to each of these challenges.

# GLOSSARY

**Activity level.** Economic analysis seeks to assess the extent to which a regulation or legal rule affects the extent and nature of an activity. A legal rule imposing a sanction will have an effect on the level of the regulated activity to the extent that the cost of the sanction for engaging in the activity outweighs the *net* benefits of that activity (that is, the benefits from engaging in the regulated activity minus the benefits derived from the next best use of the actor's resources). But the rule will not affect the level of activity that the rule regulates if, for example, the cost of the sanction for violating the rule is less than the *net* benefits derived from violating the rule. To put the matter more simply, a legal rule may not have any activity-level effects if an actor has reasons to be indifferent to the rule.

**Adjustment.** In contract parlance, one party offers an adjustment to its counter-party as a means of accommodating unanticipated changes in the circumstances affecting the performance of their obligations. If, for example, the parties contract to deliver a specific quantity of a commodity at a specific price over a period of years, and if the market price of that commodity were to drop unexpectedly, the seller might offer the buyer an adjustment by allowing the buyer to take a reduced quantity of the commodity in that year. Adjustments offered as an accommodation to one's counterparty in light of unforeseen or unlikely events are to be distinguished from renegotiations sought by one party to exploit the counterparty's foreseeable vulnerability following a relation-specific investment.

**Adverse selection.** Adverse selection is a term of art derived from insurance that posits that parties with higher risks will be more likely to purchase insurance than low-risk parties and thus the "selection" of insureds is adverse to the interests of the insurer. This will lead insurers to increase the premiums charged for the insurance in question. Unless the insurer can separate parties on the basis of risk categories, the adverse selection of high-risk types will ultimately lead to a blended premium reflecting the mixed population of insureds. Thus, low risk types will be forced to subsidize those with higher risks. As applied to information theory, the concept suggests that where key attributes of individuals are not observable (say, whether employees are shirkers or not), there will be an equilibrium in which the price (or wage) offered for the service in question will reflect the pool of parties with both characteristics and a resulting cross-subsidization of one type (shirkers) by the other type (nonshirkers).

**Agency costs.** Whenever one person acts on behalf of another (a condition that applies to most forms of cooperation), there exists the possibility that the actor (in legal terms, the agent) may have reasons not to act in the best interests of the person on whose behalf she acts (the principal). Anticipating such conflicts of interest, the parties may arrange for the principal to monitor the agent (such as by requiring standardized regular reports), for the agent to offer a bond such as by voluntarily limiting her discretion to engage in certain behavior, or otherwise accept the conflicting interests as an inevitable part of the relationship. The sum of monitoring, bonding, and residual conflict-of-interests costs is called agency costs.

**Antidumping.** Dumping describes the strategy of selling goods in a market at an otherwise irrationally low price (such as below marginal cost) as a means of destroying competition and thus establishing a monopoly. As used in trade law, the term applies to importing goods at a price below that charged in some other relevant market, such as the producer's home market, even when the import price results in profits for the producer. Antidumping duties seek to offset the effect of dumping by imposing a tax on imported goods equal to the margin of dumping, that is the difference between the import price and the price of the same or similar goods in some other relevant market.

**CAFTA (Central American Free Trade Agreement).** The governments of the United States and five Central American countries plus the Dominican Republic signed CAFTA in 2004, and the U.S. Congress gave its approval the following year. This trade agreement seeks to establish duty-free trade among the parties and also sets some limits on national government regulation that might affect trade. CAFTA closely resembles the NAFTA (see later) and fits within a larger project of establishing a free trade zone within the entire Western Hemisphere.

**Collective action problem.** A collective action problem exists whenever cooperation among people is jointly beneficial but individual actors have an incentive to behave in a way that is inconsistent with their collective obligations. The famous prisoners' dilemma, used in game theory, provides a theoretical model for one common type of collective action problem.

**Complete contingent contract.** A contract that specifies all possible future contingencies that may affect the parties' performance and specifies the particular obligation of the parties for each contingency is a complete contingent contract.

Such a contract should not be confused with one that is complete in the sense that the parties' obligations are fixed for all possible outcomes, but that does not alter those obligations in the light of contingencies about which the parties might care. The latter type of contract is easy to write but is ex ante inefficient, because the parties are subject to obligations that they would prefer not to have, given certain contingencies. A complete contingent contract, by contrast, is efficient but is impossible to write (as a practical matter), given the infinite number of contingencies that might affect the value of performance under a contract.

**Contract theory model.** This book proposes an informal model of optimal enforcement of international law that is derived from what contract theorists argue is the best strategy (in the sense of optimal social value) for contract enforcement.

**Countervailing duties.** Under trade law, certain kinds of government subsidies to domestic producers (specifically those used to encourage exports) are deemed unfair and therefore subject to offset in the country of importation. The importing country achieves this offset by imposing a tax on imports equal to the amount of subsidies received. This tax is called a countervailing duty.

**Customary international law.** Many international lawyers believe that a consistent pattern of state practice that results from a sense of legal obligation produces a legal rule or norm that binds states. The functional effect of the concept of customary international law is to provide an explanation for rules of international law that do not have their foundation in a treaty. Questions of what constitutes a state practice and a sense of legal obligation, as well as the effect of customary international law in national legal systems, are very controversial.

**Discount rate.** Finance theorists and economists both think about ways of assessing the equivalence of present and future events. The discount rate is an assumed rate of return (such as an interest rate) that a present investment will earn in order to produce a future sum. More generally, it is the factor by which future events are assessed in terms of their present value. To say that a person or transaction has a high discount rate means that the future is relatively uncertain and insecure.

**EC (European Community).** The European Community (previously known as the European Economic Community until renamed by the 1992 Maastricht Treaty) is the institutionally most developed and legally most significant component of the European Union, which as of 2004 has twenty-five members. The EC has responsibility for implementing the "four freedoms" of the Treaty of Rome, namely, free flows of goods, services, capital, and people within the EU. In addition to the ECJ, it has a Commission based in Brussels, a Parliament, and a Council comprising representatives of the governments of the twenty-five members, all of which have certain lawmaking responsibilities.

**ECJ (European Court of Justice).** The European Court of Justice, based in Luxembourg, is the judicial branch of the European Community, which as of 2004 has twenty-five members. The jurisdiction of the ECJ and the legal effect of its judgments rest ultimately on the 1957 Treaty of Rome, as revised several times by subsequent treaties.

**ECHR (European Convention on Human Rights).** The European Convention on Human Rights was propounded in 1950 and took effect in 1953. Forty-five states comprising almost all of Europe now adhere to it. It sets minimum standards of human rights obligations and establishes an enforcement mechanism, principally the European Court of Human Rights.

**ECtHR (European Court of Human Rights).** The European Court of Human Rights, based in Strasbourg, is the principal enforcement mechanism for the European Convention on Human Rights. As a result of amendments to the Convention in the 1990s, private persons can sue a state directly in the ECtHR and, under the proper circumstances, receive a damages award.

**EU (European Union).** The European Union, created by the 1992 Maastricht Treaty, comprises the European Community plus two less developed mechanisms for cooperation in law enforcement and internal affairs and in foreign and security policy.

**Formal enforcement.** As we define the term, formal enforcement of a legal obligation requires the existence of an independent body to which interested persons can take complaints about noncompliance and which has the authority to mete out sanctions that take effect fairly automatically. A domestic court is the model for formal enforcement, but not the only example.

**Future interactions.** Future interactions are one of the mechanisms that provide an incentive for compliance with a legal obligation regardless of the availability of formal enforcement. If a party anticipates future interactions with someone to whom it owes an obligation and if it anticipates that the counterparty will retaliate for its failure to honor an obligation, it will take that retaliation into account in deciding whether to carry out its obligation. Future interactions thus are one way of achieving informal enforcement of a legal obligation.

**GATT (General Agreement on Tariffs and Trade).** This multilateral agreement, signed in 1947 and taking effect the following year, set a program for trade liberalization and established certain obligations on the part of the parties to each other. The Uruguay Round Agreements of 1994 reaffirmed the GATT and created a new institutional structure for implementing its goals.

**Hidden information.** Information that one party in a social interaction has and which other parties to that interaction lack is hidden. The concept is a relative one, in the sense that information may not be absolutely unavailable to other parties but may be too costly for them to obtain relative to the information's value. Typically, the term "hidden information" refers to characteristics or attributes of other parties that are costly to observe as distinct from actions taken by other parties (which is known as "hidden action").

**Hold-Up.** Hold-up involves a strategy in which one party to a cooperative endeavor seeks to exploit another party in light of the latter's relation-specific investment. The strategy entails consenting to an obligation which, if honored, would make the other party's investment profitable and then, once relation-specific costs have been absorbed, demanding a greater share of the contractual surplus.

**ICANN (Internet Corporation for Assigned Names and Numbers).** This non-profit corporation, established under Virginia law, administers the system under which numeric Internet addresses are assigned domain names. It decides what domain names are permitted and provides an arbitration mechanism for persons who wish to contest particular domain name assignments.

**ICC (International Criminal Court).** This body, created by the 1998 Rome Statute, has the authority to investigate and prosecute particular international crimes such as genocide and crimes against humanity. Its power to proceed in particular cases rests on a determination that states with jurisdiction over the charged crime are unable or unwilling to pursue a prosecution. Although most European countries adhere to the Rome Statute, the People's Republic of China, the Russian Federation, and the United States (as well as India, Israel, Pakistan, and North Korea, all thought to be nuclear powers) do not.

**ICJ (International Court of Justice).** This body, known colloquially as the World Court, was created at the same time as the United Nations as a mechanism for resolving international law disputes between states. Its jurisdiction rests on state consent, which might be expressed in a treaty or given in a particular instance after a dispute arises. It has no enforcement powers, although parties to the United Nations Charter accept the obligation to enforce its judgments.

**ICTFY (International Criminal Tribunal for the Former Yugoslavia).** UN Security Council Resolution 827, adopted in 1993, created a tribunal to investigate and prosecute international crimes occurring in the conflicts that followed the break up of Yugoslavia. It operates in The Hague and continues to hear cases. Its most prominent case was the prosecution of the former Serbian leader Slobodan Milosevic.

**ICTR (International Criminal Tribunal for Rwanda).** UN Security Council Resolution 955, adopted in 1994, established this tribunal to investigate and prosecute international crimes associated with the Rwandan genocide of that year.

**IMT (International Military Tribunal).** This organ, more popularly known as the Nuremberg Tribunal, was established by the victorious states at the end of World War II to try the most prominent Germans accused of war crimes. Other war crimes prosecutions were carried out by the allies individually as well as by the Federal Republic of Germany after its creation in 1949.

**IMTFE (International Military Tribunal for the Far East).** The Tokyo War Crimes Tribunal, created by the United States at the end of World War II, conducted war crimes prosecutions against Japanese subjects.

**Inequity aversion.** A great body of experimental evidence indicates that a substantial portion of individuals have an aversion to inequity, in the sense that they will both repay generosity from others and also will punish persons who behave unfairly, even at a cost to themselves. This characteristic explains why many people manifest a preference for reciprocity, in that they will respond to generous behavior with similar conduct and will punish opportunism even when the punishment is costly to them.

**Informal sanctions.** Informal sanctions are the means by which persons can be induced to comply with their obligations other than by formal enforcement. Social pressures such as shaming and boycotting, retaliation in the course of future interactions, and internal pressures such as inequity aversion all constitute informal sanctions.

**ITLOS (International Tribunal for the Law of the Sea).** This organ, established by the 1982 Convention on the Law of the Sea and commencing operations after that instrument went into force in 1994, decides disputes under the Convention. Most of its docket consists of challenges to the seizure of vessels, but it has jurisdiction to decide all matters governing the interpretation of the Convention when brought by a state that adheres to that instrument. Like the ICJ, it has no enforcement powers of its own.

**Joint production of social welfare.** The central focus of contract theory is the study of how people commit to cooperate in mutually beneficial activity where, individually, they have incentives to deviate from the collective objective. The product of that commitment is a welfare surplus that is then shared among the parties. Contract theory thus assumes implicitly that contracts engage public resources, including mechanisms of formal enforcement, because they advance social welfare. It further assumes that enforcement is necessary to solve the collective action problems that arise in such cooperative projects.

**MFA (Multifiber Agreements).** The GATT contains no exceptions from its general rules liberalizing trade in goods, but over the years countries that export and import textiles reached a series of accommodations that set numerical quotas on the import of textiles into the United States and Europe. The 1994 Uruguay Round Agreements contained a commitment to phase out this quota system after ten years, and this obligation took effect at the beginning of 2005.

**Misnomer objection.** One objection to the claim that domestic judges enforce international law is that these judges merely invoke international rules to obscure the domestic concerns that motivate their rulings. According to this objection, there are no (or no significant) instances of domestic judicial enforcement of international law. To the contrary, judges only invoke the rhetoric of international law to pursue domestic ends.

**Moral clarity.** This term refers to the ability of observers to determine whether someone has behaved fairly or opportunistically. The effective use of informal sanctions requires some degree of moral clarity. Third-person arbiters may be preferable as a means of addressing issues of compliance in the absence of moral clarity, although these arbiters may still face problems of verifiability and information extraction.

**NAFTA (North American Free Trade Agreement).** This multilateral agreement between Canada, Mexico, and the United States was signed in 1992 and went into effect the following year. In addition to removing tariff barriers to trade in goods among the three parties, NAFTA created several dispute-resolution mechanisms. Under the provisions of NAFTA, investors can challenge government actions that result in impermissible injuries.

**National treatment.** This term refers to the obligation of GATT parties not to discriminate between imported goods and domestic products in terms of regulation. It requires states to treat imports as if they were national products once the imported goods have cleared customs.

**Observable information.** Observable information is the opposite of hidden information. It can be detected by observers at a cost that is less than its value to the observer.

**Opportunity costs.** This term refers to the cost of foregoing an otherwise desirable activity. In deciding whether to undertake a particular course of action, an actor must take into account the value to him of alternative courses of action. Opportunity costs are to be distinguished from direct costs, that is the outlays required to undertake a particular course of action. In determining whether the benefits from an action outweighs its costs, an actor must consider both direct and opportunity costs.

**Preference for reciprocal fairness.** This concept mirrors that of inequity aversion. It reflects the empirical evidence that indicates that a substantial proportion of individuals have a preference for reciprocity, in the sense that they will repay generosity without any obligation to do so and will punish those who treat them unfairly even at a cost to themselves and when they derive no direct benefit from the punishment.

**Private information.** Private information is possessed by one or more persons engaged in a social interaction that has not or cannot be shared with other parties to that interaction. The existence of private information brings an element of uncertainty to contracting and other cooperative interactions. When private information cannot be disclosed directly, persons sometimes can signal its content by publicly absorbing costs that would be rational to bear only if certain hidden conditions were true. For example, if the quality of goods cannot be disclosed to a buyer at a reasonable cost, the seller's willingness to provide a warranty may operate as a signal of the quality of the goods.

**Private standing.** This term refers to the capability of persons who have suffered from the violation of a legal obligation to invoke the resources of an enforcement body without having to obtain the permission of a public authority.

**Publicist.** Proponents of customary international law maintain that a class of experts called publicists have the capacity to determine the existence and content of these customs. The Statute of the International Court of Justice authorizes that body to refer to "the teachings of the most highly qualified publicists of the various nations, as subsidiary means for the determination of rules of law."

**Reciprocity.** Reciprocity involves matching morally clear behavior with behavior that has the same moral quality. Cooperative, generous, and fair behavior invites reciprocal cooperation, and opportunism invites punishment.

**Relation-specific investment.** An investment in a collective endeavor is relation specific where it has greater value to the investor if used in the endeavor than if used elsewhere. Producers often must absorb costs to produce goods for specific customers. These costs constitute a relation-specific investment if the capacity to make these goods has a lower payoff were these specific customers not to purchase them.

**Renegotiation.** Renegotiation is the process by which parties seek to adjust their obligations and rights under an agreement after some uncertainty has been resolved. When renegotiation follows after a relation-specific investment, it raises the risk of **hold-up.**

**Reputation.** Reputation is one of the mechanisms for informal enforcement of obligations. To the extent third parties can determine whether a person honors her obligations or instead behaves opportunistically, that person will acquire a reputation that future persons contemplating social interaction will take into account. A reputation for compliance will lead to greater opportunities for engagement in cooperative interactions, while the opposite reputation will lead to reduced opportunities, and in extreme cases to shunning and boycott.

**Safeguards.** In trade law, a country that experiences an abnormal increase in imports may take measures to prevent this outcome, including the imposition of quotas. The GATT regulates the circumstances under which a country may impose safeguards and also authorizes the exporting country to retaliate. To some degree, however, a country that imposes a safeguard measure and then withdraws it after a determination of its illegality under the GATT may face no sanction, especially if the exporting country lacks effective retaliatory capacity.

**Sanctions, control over.** One of the fundamental distinctions between formal and informal enforcement of a legal obligation is whether a third-party tribunal has control over the sanctions that will attach to a violation of the obligation. Control is rarely absolute, because most tribunals rely on other agents to carry out its orders. But if the agent's role is ministerial rather than discretionary, as in the case of a sheriff who seizes property to enforce a judicial judgment, then the tribunal can be said to have control over sanctions. Conversely, bodies such as the ICJ and the WTO DSB, which rely wholly on the discretion of national governments whether to implement their orders, cannot be said to have control over sanctions and thus do not engage in formal enforcement of legal obligations.

**Separating equilibrium.** Where information is hidden, a signal that effectively conveys the existence of that information creates what is called a separating equilibrium. If the willingness to assume a warranty acts as an effective signal of quality, for example, then the warranty results in different market prices for high-quality and low-quality goods, even though purchasers cannot observe quality directly (except at a prohibitive cost) before purchase.

**Signals.** Signals are costly actions that the possessor of hidden information can undertake to indicate to others that this information exists. The assumption of a warranty by a seller, for example, may signal that the goods sold are of good quality, and the refusal to assume a warranty may signal that the goods are inferior.

**Standing.** Standing involves the capacity to bring a dispute to a tribunal. Some tribunals, such as the ICJ and the WTO DSB, allow only states to have standing. In domestic law, different standing capabilities are attached to different kinds of rights. In the case of corporations, for example, a limited set of rights can be enforced by shareholders through a derivative action, but others accord standing only to the designated representative body of the corporation, normally the board of directors or certain officers.

**Tariffication.** In trade law, tariffs are generally seen as less of an impediment to liberalization than are quotas, which set limits on the number of units of a good that can be imported in a given period. One strategy for liberalization, as in the case of agricultural products, is to substitute tariff barriers (taxation on import) for quotas. The term for this substitution is tariffication.

**UCP (Uniform Customs and Practice for Documentary Credits).** The International Chamber of Commerce, a private organization representing companies engaged in international commerce, has published elaborated definitions that private persons can choose to incorporate into their contracts. The UCP, one instance of these definitions, comprise terms for letters of credit issued by banks, either as a means of paying for services or to guarantee performance of an obligation.

**Uruguay Round Agreements.** Under the GATT, the parties negotiate periodically in "rounds" to liberalize their trade relations. The most recent, called the Uruguay Round because the conference commencing negotiations was held in that country, in 1994 culminated in a series of agreements, including those establishing the World Trade Organization and the World Trade Organization Dispute Settlement Body.

**Verifiable information.** Information that can be proven to a third party at a reasonable cost is called verifiable. Not all observable information is verifiable, because an observer may not necessarily be able to convince a third party at a reasonable cost that his observations are accurate. An issue that depends exclusively on verifiable information is called **contractible**, because a contract that turns on that issue can be enforced by a third party. A sophisticated understanding of verifiability must take into account various indirect methods of establishing the existence of a condition or quality, such as the use of proxies or the allocation of burdens of proof.

**WTO (World Trade Organization).** The Uruguay Round Agreements, among other accomplishments, created the WTO as the institutional structure for administering and enforcing the GATT and other multilateral trade agreements.

**WTO DSB (World Trade Organization Dispute Settlement Body).** One of the 1994 Uruguay Round Agreements created the Dispute Settlement Body. This mechanism comprises three stages: negotiations among the disputants, an arbitral procedure involving experts chosen for the particular proceeding, and review by the Appellate Body, a permanent institution attached to the WTO. Decisions of the Appellate Body are adopted by representatives of the WTO members as an official determination of the WTO. The members may not alter the decision of the Appellate Body unless a consensus, including the prevailing state, agrees to do so.

# TABLE OF AUTHORITIES

NATIONAL LEGISLATION

TREATIES AND OTHER INTERNATIONAL AGREEMENTS

SECONDARY AUTHORITIES

Kenneth W. Abbott, *Modern International Relations Theory: A Prospectus for Lawyers*, 14 YALE J. INT'L L. 335 (1989)

Kenneth W. Abbot, Robert O. Keohane, Andrew Moravcsik, Anne-Marie Slaughter, & Duncan Snidal, *The Concept of Legalization*, in LEGALIZATION AND WORLD POLITICS 37 (Judith L. Goldstein, Miles Kahler, Robert O. Keohane, & Anne-Marie Slaughter, eds. 2001)

Kenneth W. Abbott & Duncan Snidal, *Hard and Soft Law in International Governance* in LEGALIZATION AND WORLD WOLITICS 37 (Judith L. Goldstein, Miles Kahler, Robert O. Keohane, & Anne-Marie Slaughter, eds. 2001)

Bruce Ackerman, *The Rise of World Constitutionalism*, 83 VA. L.REV. 771 (1997)

*Agora: The United States Constitution and International Law*, 98 AM. J. INT'L L. 42 (2004)

Guillermo Aguilar Alvarez & William W. Park, *The New Face of Investment Arbitration: NAFTA Chapter 11*, 28 YALE J. INT'L L. 365 (2003)

George Akerloff, *The Market for "Lemons": Quality Uncertainty and the Market Mechanism*, 84 Q.J. ECON. 355 (1970)

Gar Alperwitz, ATOMIC DIPLOMACY: HIROSHIMA AND POTSDAM: THE USE OF THE ATOMIC BOMB AND THE AMERICAN CONFRONTATION WITH SOVIET POWER (1985)

Karen J. Alter, ESTABLISHING THE SUPREMACY OF EUROPEAN LAW (2001)

Karen Alter, *The European Union's Legal System and Domestic Policy: Spillover or Backlash?* in LEGALIZATION AND WORLD POLITICS 105 (Judith Goldstein, Miles Kahler, Robert O. Keohane & Anne-Marie Slaughter, eds. 2001)

José E. Alvarez, *The WTO as Linkage Machine*, 96AM.J.INT'L L. 146 (2002)

AMERICAN LAW INSTITUTE, RESTATEMENT OF CONTRACTS (1932)

AMERICAN LAW INSTITUTE, RESTATEMENT (SECOND) OF CONTRACTS (1981)

AMERICAN LAW INSTITUTE, RESTATEMENT (THIRD) OF THE FOREIGN RELATIONS LAW OF THE UNITED STATES (1987)

James Barr Ames, LECTURES ON LEGAL HISTORY(1913)

Kenneth Anderson, *Squaring the Circle? Reconciling Sovereignty and Global Governance Through Global Government Networks*, 118 HARV.L. REV. 1255 (2005)

Kym Anderson & Will Martin, AGRICULTURAL TRADE REFORM AND THE DOHA DEVELOPMENT AGENDA (2005)

Robert Axelrod, THE EVOLUTION OF COOPERATION (1984)

Kyle Bagwell & Robert W. Staiger, THE ECONOMICS OF THE WORLD TRADING SYSTEM 95–110 (2002)

THE EXECUTION OF STRASBOURG AND GENEVA HUMAN RIGHTS DECISIONS IN THE NATIONAL LEGAL ORDER (Tom Barkhuysen, Michiel van Emmerik and Piet Hein van Kempen, eds. 1999)

Carl Baudenbacher, *The Implementation of Decisions of the ECJ and of the EFTA Court in Member States' Domestic Legal Orders*, 40 TEX. INT'L L.J. 383 (2005)

David J. Bederman, *The 1871 London Declaration, Rebus Sic Stantibus and a Primitivist View of the Law of Nations*, 82 AM.J.INT'L L. 1 (1988)

Eyal Benevisti, *Customary International Law as a Judicial Tool for Promoting Efficiency*, in THE IMPACT OF INTERNATIONAL LAW ON INTERNATIONAL COOPERATION – THEORETICAL PERSPECTIVES 85 (Eyal Benevisti & Moshe Hirsch eds. 2004)

Lisa Bernstein, *Merchant Law in a Merchant Court: Rethinking the Code's Search for Immanent Business Norms*, 144 U. PA. L. REV.1765 (1996)

Lisa Bernstein, *Private Commercial Law in the Cotton Industry: Creating Cooperation through Rules, Norms and Institutions*, 99 MICH. L. REV. 1724 (2001)

Francesca Bignami, *The Challenge of Cooperative Regulatory Federalism after Enlargement* in LAW AND GOVERNANCE IN AN ENLARGED EUROPEAN UNION 97 (George Bermann & Katharina Pistor, eds. 2004)

Iris Bohnet, Bruno S. Frey, & Steffen Huck, *More Order with Less Law: On Contract Enforcement, Trust and Crowding*, 95 AM. POL. SCIENCE REV. 131 (2001)

Robert H. Bork, COERCING VIRTUE: THE WORLDWIDE RULE OF JUDGES (2003)

Robert T. Boyd & Peter J. Richerson, CULTURE AND THE EVOLUTIONARY PROCESS (1985)

Robert Boyd & Peter J. Richerson, Solving the Puzzle of Human Cooperation

Curtis A. Bradley, *Customary International Law and Private Rights of Action*, 1 CHI. J. INT'L L. 421 (2000)

Curtis A. Bradley, *The Charming Betsy Canon and Separation of Powers: Rethinking the Interpretive Role of International Law*, 86 GEO. L.J. 479 (1998)

Curtis A. Bradley, *Foreign Affairs and Domestic Reform*, 87 VA. L. REV. 1475 (2001)

Curtis A. Bradley, *The Treaty Power and American Federalism, Part II*, 99 MICH. L. REV. 98 (2000)

Curtis A. Bradley & Jack L. Goldsmith, *Customary International Law as Federal Law: A Critique of the Modern Position*, 110 HARV. L. REV. 815 (1997)

Curtis A. Bradley & Jack L. Goldsmith, *Treaties, Human Rights, and Conditional Consent*, 149 U. PA. L. REV. 399 (2000)

Ronald A. Brand, *The Status of the General Agreement on Tariffs and Trade in United States Domestic Law*, 26 STAN. J. INT'L L. 479 (1990).

Fritz Breuss, *WTO Dispute Settlement in Action: An Economic Analysis of Four EU-US Mini- Trade Wars*, 5 J. INDUSTRY COMPETITION & TRADE (2005)

Rosa Ehrenreich Brooks, *War Everywhere: Rights, National Security Law, and the Law of Armed Conflict in the Age of Terror*, 153 U. PA. L. REV. 675 (2004)

CHARLES N. BROWER & JASON D. BRUESCHKE, THE IRAN-UNITED STATES CLAIMS TRIBUNAL (1998)

Ults Martin Brown, Armin Falk, & Ernst Fehr, *Relational Contracts and the Nature of Market Interactions* 72 ECONOMICA 747 (2004)

Michael Byers, CUSTOM, POWER, AND THE POWER OF RULES:INTERNATIONAL RELATIONS AND CUSTOMARY INTERNATIONAL LAW (1999)

Lan Cao, *Looking at Communities and Markets*, 74 NOTRE DAME L. REV. 841 (1999)

LEX MERCATORIA AND ARBITRATION (Thomas E. Carbonneau, ed. 1990)

ANTONIO CASSESE, INTERNATIONAL LAW (2001)

Anupam Chander, *Globalization and Distrust*, 114 YALE L.J. 1193 (2005)

Gary Charness, *Responsibility and Effort in an Experimental Labor Market*, 42 J. ECON. BEHAV & ORG. 375 (2000)

Abram Chayes & Antonia Handler Chayes, THE NEW SOVEREIGNTY: COMPLIANCE WITH INTERNATIONAL REGULATORY AGREEMENTS (1995)

Jim C. Chen, *Appointments with Disaster: The Unconstitutionality of Binational Arbitral Review under the United States-Canada Free Trade Agreement*, 49 WASH. & LEE L. REV. 1455 (1992)

Noam Chomsky, HEGEMONY OR SURVIVAL: AMERICA'S QUEST FOR GLOBAL DOMINANCE (2003)

R. H. Coase, *The Nature of the Firm*, 4 ECONOMICA 386 (1937)

Jean Louise Cohen, *Whose Sovereignty? Empire Versus International Law*, 18 ETHICS & INT'L AFFAIRS 1 (2004–05)

Council of Europe, EUROPEAN COURT OF HUMAN RIGHTS – SURVEY OF ACTIVITIES 2004 (2005)

Anthony A. D'Amato, THE CONCEPT OF CUSTOM IN INTERNATIONAL LAW (1971)

Lori Fisler Damrosch, *The Role of the Untied States Senate Concerning "Self-Executing" and "Non-Self-Executing" Treaties*, 67 CHI.-KENT L. REV. 515 (1991)

Allison Marston Danner, *Enhancing the Legitimacy and Accountability of Prosecutorial Discretion at the International Criminal Court*, 97 AM. J. INT'L L. 510 (2003)

Charles Darwin, THE DESCENT OF MAN (1874)

Edward L. Deci, R. Koestner, & Richard M. Ryan, *A Meta-Analytic Review of Experiments Examining the Effects of Extrinsic Rewards on Intrinsic Motivation*, 125 PSYCH BULL. 627 (1999)

Avinash K. Dixit & Victor Norman, THEORY OF INTERNATIONAL TRADE (1980)

Rudolph Dolzer & Margrete Stevens, BILATERAL INVESTMENT TREATIES (1995)

Mary L. Dudziak, COLD WAR CIVIL RIGHTS: RACE AND THE IMAGE OF AMERICAN DEMOCRACY (2000)

Jeffrey L. Dunoff & Joel P. Trachtman, *Economic Analysis of International Law*, 24 YALE J. INT'L L. 1 (1999)

Frank H. Easterbrook, *Antitrust and the Economics of Federalism*, 26 J. L. & ECON. 23 (1983)

Aaron S. Edlin & Stefan Reichelstein, *Holdups, Standard Breach Remedies, and Optimal Investment*, 86 AM. ECON. REV.478 (1996)

Friedrich Engels, THE ORIGIN OF FAMILY, PRIVATE PROPERTY AND THE STATE (1972) [1884]

Tanisha Fazal, *State Death in the International System*, 58 INT'L ORG. 311 (2004)

Ernst Fehr & Armin Falk, *Wage Rigidity in a Competitive Incomplete Contract Market*, 107 J. POL. ECON. 106 (1999)

Ernst Fehr & Urs Fischbacher, *Social Norms and Human Cooperation*, 8 TRENDS IN COGNITIVE SCIENCE 185 (2004)

Ernst Fehr & Simon Gächter, Do Incentive Contracts Crowd Out Voluntary Cooperation?

Ernst Fehr & Simon Gächter, Fairness *and Retaliation: The Economics of Reciprocity*, 14 J. ECON. PERSP. 159 (2000)

Ernst Fehr, Simon Gächter & Georg Kirchsteiger, *Gift Exchange and Reciprocity in Competitive Experimental Markets*, 42 EUR. ECON. REV. 1 (1998)

Ernst Fehr, Simon Gächter, & Georg Kirchsteiger, *Reciprocity as a Contract Enforcement Device: Experimental Evidence*, 65 ECONOMETRICA 833 (1997)

Ernst Fehr & Bruno Rockenbach, Incentives and Intentions – The Hidden Rewards of Economic Incentives

Ernst Fehr & Klaus Schmidt, *A Theory of Fairness, Competition and Cooperation*, 114 Q. J. ECON. 817 (1999)

Ernst Fehr & Klaus Schmidt, *Theories of Fairness and Reciprocity – Evidence and Economic Applications*, in ADVANCES IN ECONOMICS AND ECONOMETRICS: THEORY AND APPLICATIONS, EIGHTH WORLD CONGRESS, VOLUME I, at 208 (Mathias Dewatripont, Lars Peter Hansen, & Stephen J. Turnovsky, eds. 2003)

David P. Fidler, *Public Health and National Security in the Global Age: Infectious Diseases, Bioterrorism, and Realpolitik*, 35 GEO.WASH. INT'L L. REV.787 (2003)

Vincy Fon & Francesco Parisi, *International Customary Law and Articulation Theories: An Economic Analysis*, 2 INT'L L. & MGT. REV. 1 (2006)

Thomas M. Franck, FAIRNESS IN INTERNATIONAL LAW AND INSTITUTIONS (1995)

Thomas M. Franck, *Legitimacy in the International System*, 82 AM. J. INT'L L. 705 (1988)

Bruno S. Frey & Reto Jegan, *Motivation Crowding Theory*, 15 J. ECON. SURVEYS 589 (2001)

Bruno S. Frey & Matthias Benz, Motivation Transfer Effect

Simon Gächter & Armin Falk, *Reputation and Reciprocity: Consequences for the Labour Relation*, 104 SCAND. J. OF ECON. 1 (2002)

David A. Gantz, *Potential Conflicts Between Investor Rights and Environmental Regulation Under NAFTA's Chapter 11*, 33 GEO.WASH. INT'L L. REV. 651 (2001)

Anna Gelpern, *What Iraq and Argentina Might Learn from Each Other*, 6 CHI. J. INT'L L. 391 (2005)

Tom Ginsburg, *International Judicial Lawmaking*, 45 Va. J. Int'l L. 631 (2005)

Tom Ginsburg, *International Substitutes for Domestic Institutions: Bilateral Investment Treaties and Governance*, 25 Int'l Rev. L. & Econ. 107 (2005)

Tom Ginsburg & Richard H. McAdams, *Adjudicating in Anarchy: An Expressive Theory of International Dispute Resolution*, 45 Wm. & Mary L. Rev. 1229 (2004)

Uri Gneezy & Aldo Rustichini, *A Fine is a Price*, 29 J. Legal Stud. 1 (2000)

Charles J. Goetz & Robert E. Scott, *Principles of Relational Contracts*, 67 Va. L. Rev. 1089 (1981)

Charles J. Goetz & Robert E. Scott, *Liquidated Damages, Penalties and the Just Compensation Principle: Some Notes on an Enforcement Model and a Theory of Efficient Breach*, 77 Colum.L.Rev. 554 (1977)

Jack L. Goldsmith, *Liberal Democracy and Cosmopolitan Duty*, 55 Stan. L Rev. 1667 (2003)

Jack L. Goldsmith & Stephen Krasner, *The Limits of Idealism*, 132 Daedalus47 (2001)

Jack L. Goldsmith & Eric A. Posner, *A Theory of Customary International Law*, 66 U. Chi. L. Rev. 1113 (1999)

Jack L. Goldsmith & Eric A. Posner, The Limits Of International Law (2005)

Jack L. Goldsmith & Tim Wu, Who Controls The Internet? (2006)

Ryan Goodman, *Human Rights Treaties, Invalid Reservations, and State Consent*, 96 Am. J. Int'l L. 531 (2002)

Ryan Goodman & Derek P. Jinks, *Filartiga's Firm Footing: International Human Rights and Federal Common Law*, 66 Fordham L. Rev.463(1997)

Ryan Goodman & Derek Jinks, *How to Influence States: Socialization and International Human Rights Law*, 54 Duke L. J. 621 (2004)

John Gray, False Dawn:The Delusions Of Global Capitalism (1998)

Avner Greif, *Reputation and Coalitions in Medieval Trade: Evidence on the Maghribi Traders*, 49 J. Econ. Hist. 857 (1989)

Avner Grief, *Informal Contract Enforcement: Lessons from Medieval Trade* in 2 The New Palgrave Dictionary of Economics and Law 287 (Peter Newman, ed. 1998)

Sanford J. Grossman & Oliver D. Hart, *The Costs and Benefits of Ownership: A Theory of Vertical and Lateral Integration*, 94 J. Pol. Econ.691 (1986)

Andrew T. Guzman, *A Compliance-Based Theory of International Law*, 90 Calif. L. Rev. 1823 (2002)

Andrew T. Guzman, *The Cost of Credibility: Explaining Resistance to Interstate Dispute Resolution Mechanisms*, 31 J. Leg. Stud. 303 (2002)

Andrew Guzman & Beth A. Simmons, *To Settle or Empanel? An Empirical Analysis of Litigation and Settlement at the World Trade Organization*, 31 J. Leg. Stud. S205 (2002)

Mary Hallward-Driemeier, Do Bilateral Investment Treaties Attract FDI? Only a Bit and They Could Bite

America and the World – A Conversation with Jürgen Habermas, with Eduardo Mendieta, LOGOS: A JOURNAL OF MODERN SOCIETY & CULTURE 3.3 (SUMMER 2004)

Michael Hardt & Antonio Negri, EMPIRE (2000)

Oliver D. Hart & John Moore, Property Rights and the Nature of the Firm, 98 J. POL. ECON. 1119 (1990)

H. L. A. Hart, THE CONCEPT OF LAW (1961)

TREVOR C. HARTLEY, CONSTITUTIONAL PROBLEMS OF THE EUROPEAN UNION (1999)

Oona Hathaway, Do Human Rights Treaties Make a Difference? 111 YALE L. J. 1935 (2002)

Laurence R. Helfer, Overlegalizing Human Rights: International Relations Theory and the Commonwealth Caribbean Backlash Against Human Rights Regimes, 102 COLUM. L. REV. 1832 (2002)

Laurence R. Helfer & Anne-Marie Slaughter, Toward a Theory of Effective Supranational Adjudication, 107 YALE L. J. 272 (1997)

Laurence R. Helfer & Anne-Marie Slaughter, Why States Create International Tribunals: A Response To Professors Posner and Yoo, 93 CALIF. L. REV. 899 (2005)

Elhanan Helpman & Paul R. Krugman, MARKET STRUCTURE AND FOREIGN TRADE – INCREASING RETURNS, IMPERFECT COMPETITION, AND THE INTERNATIONAL ECONOMY (1985)

Kathryn Hendley, Business Litigation in the Transition: A Portrait of Debt Collection in Russia, 38 LAW & SOC'Y REV.305 (2004)

Louis Henkin, HOW NATIONS BEHAVE (2nd ed. 1979)

Louis Henkin, FOREIGN AFFAIRS AND THE CONSTITUTION (1972)

Louis Henkin, U.S. Ratification of Human Rights Treaties: The Ghost of Senator Bricker, 89 AM. J. INT'L L. 341 (1995)

Benjamin Hermalin & Michael Katz, Judicial Modification of Contracts Between Sophisticated Parties: A More Complete View of Incomplete Contracts and Their Breach, 9 J. L. ECON. & ORG. 98 (1993)

Noreena Hertz, THE SILENT TAKEOVER: GLOBAL CAPITALISM AND THE DEATH OF DEMOCRACY (2002)

Robert Hillman, Court Adjustment of Long-Term Contracts: An Analysis Under Modern Contract Law, 1987 DUKE L. J. 1

Albert O. Hirschman, EXIT, VOICE, AND LOYALTY: RESPONSES TO DECLINE IN FIRMS, ORGANIZATIONS, AND STATES (1970)

Thomas Hobbes, LEVIATHAN (1651)

J. A. Hobson, IMPERIALISM: A STUDY (1965) [1902]

Duncan B. Hollis, *Why State Consent Still Matters – Non-State Actors, Treaties, and the Changing Sources of International Law*, 24 BERKELEY J. INT'L L. 137 (2005)

Robert E. Hudec, *The Legal Status of the GATT in the Domestic Law of the United States*, in THE EUROPEAN COMMUNITY AND GATT 187 (Meinhard Hilf, Francis G. Jacobs & Ernst-Ulrich Petersmann eds. 1986)

John H. Jackson, *The General Agreement on Tariffs and Trade in United States Domestic Law*, 66 MICH. L. REV. 260 (1967)

John C. Jeffries, Jr., *The Right-Remedy Gap in Constitutional Law*, 109 YALE L. J. 87 (1999)

John C. Jeffries, Jr., *In Praise of the Eleventh Amendment and Section 1983*, 84 VA. L. REV. 47 (1998)

Michael C. Jensen & William H. Meckling, *Theory of the Firm: Managerial Behavior, Agency Costs and Ownership Structure*, 3 J. FIN. ECON. 305 (1976)

Derek Jinks & David Sloss, *Is the President Bound by the Geneva Conventions?* 90 CORNELL L. REV. 97 (2004)

David Joseph, JURISDICTION AND ARBITRATION AGREEMENTS AND THEIR ENFORCEMENT (2005)

Margaret F. Keck & Kathryn Sikkink, ACTIVISTS BEYOND BORDERS: ADVOCACY NETWORKS IN INTERNATIONAL POLITICS (1998)

David Kennedy, INTERNATIONAL LEGAL STRUCTURES (1987)

Robert O. Keohane, AFTER HEGEMONY: COOPERATION AND DISCORD IN THE WORLD POLITICAL ECONOMY (1984)

Robert O. Keohane, INTERNATIONAL INSTITUTIONS AND STATE POWER: ESSAYS IN INTERNATIONAL RELATIONS THEORY (1989)

Robert O. Keohane, Andrew Moravcsik & Anne-Marie Slaughter, *Legalized Dispute Resolution: Interstate and Transnational*, in LEGALIZATION AND WORLD POLITICS 37 (Judith L. Goldstein, Miles Kahler, Robert O. Keohane & Anne-Marie Slaughter eds. 2001)

Michael J. Klarman, FROM JIM CROW TO CIVIL RIGHTS – THE SUPREME COURT AND THE STRUGGLE FOR RACIAL EQUALITY (2004)

Benjamin Klein, *Why Hold-Ups Occur: The Self-Enforcing Range of Contractual Relationships*, 34 ECON. INQUIRY 444 (1996)

Naomi Klein, NO LOGO: TAKING AIM AT THE BRAND BULLIES (1999)

Harold Hongju Koh, *Is International Law Really State Law?* 111 HARV. L. REV. 1824 (1998)

Harold H. Koh, *Transnational Legal Process*, 75 NEB. L. REV.181 (1996)

Harold H. Koh, *Why Do Nations Obey International Law?* 106 YALE L. J. 2599(1997)

Wilhelm Kohler, *The WTO Dispute Settlement Mechanism: Battlefield or Cooperation?* 5 J. INDUSTRY COMPETITION & TRADE (2005)

S. V. Kortunov, *Basic Principles of Reduction and Limitation of Conventional Forces* in INTERNATIONAL LAW AND INTERNATIONAL SECURITY – MILITARY

John O. McGinnis, *The Decline of the Western Nation State and the Rise of the Regime of International Federalism*, 18 CARDOZO L. REV. 903 (1996)

John J. Mearsheimer, *The False Promise of International Institutions*, 19 INT'L SECURITY 5 (1994–95)

Memorandum for the United States as Amicus Curiae, Filartiga v. Peña-Irala, 630 F.2d 876 (2d Cir. 1980), reprinted in 19 I.L.M. 585 (1980)

Maurice H. Mendelson, *The Formation of Customary International Law*, 272 RECUEIL DES COURS 155 (1998)

Mark L. Movsesian, *Enforcement of WTO Rulings: An Interest Group Analysis*, 32 HOFSTRA L. REV. 1 (2003)

Dennis C. Mueller, PUBLIC CHOICE II (1989)

Makau Mutua, *Savages, Victims, and Saviors: The Metaphor of Human Rights*, 42 HARV. J. INT'L L. 201 (2001)

Gerald Neuman, *Sense and Nonsense About Customary International Law: A Response to Professors Bradley and Goldsmith*, 66 FORDHAM L. REV. 371 (1997)

Eric Neumayer & Laura Spess, Do Bilateral Investment Treaties Increase Foreign Direct Investment to Developing Countries?

William A. Niskanen, Jr., BUREAUCRACY AND PUBLIC ECONOMICS (1994)

William A. Niskanen, *Bureaucrats and Politicians*, 18 J. L. & ECON. 617 (1985)

George Norman & Joel P. Trachtman, *The Customary International Law Game*, 99 AM. J. INT'L L. 541 (2005)

Note, *The United States Participation in the General Agreement on Tariffs and Trade*, 61 COLUM. L. REV. 505 (1961)

Jide Nzelibe, *The Credibility Imperative: The Political Dynamics of Retaliation in the World Trade Organization's Dispute Resolution Mechanism*, 6 THEORETICAL INQUIRIES IN LAW 215 (2005)

Mancur Olson, THE LOGIC OF COLLECTIVE ACTION: PUBLIC GOODS AND THE THEORY OF GROUPS (Rev. ed. 1971)

Diane F. Orentlicher, *Whose Justice? Reconciling Universal Jurisdiction with Democratic Principles*, 92 GEO. L.J. 1057 (2004)

Karthik Panchanathan & Robert Boyd, *A Tale of Two Defectors: The Importance of Standing for Evolution of Indirect Reciprocity*, 224 J. THEORETICAL BIOLOGY 115 (2003)

Vilfredo Pareto, MANUAL OF POLITICAL ECONOMY (Ann S. Schwier & Alfred N. Page, eds. & Ann S. Schwier, trans. 1971) [1927]

Joel R. Paul, *The Geopolitical Constitution: Executive Expediency and Executive Agreements*, 86 CALIF. L. REV. 671 (1998)

Jordan Paust, *Self-Executing Treaties*, 82 AM. J. INT'L L. 760 (1988)

Eric A. Posner, *Arbitration and the Harmonization of International Commercial Law – A Defense of Mitsubishi*, 39 VA. J. INT'L L. 647 (1999)

Eric A. Posner, The Decline of the International Court of Justice

Eric A. Posner, *The Regulation of Groups: The Influence of Legal and Nonlegal Sanctions on Collective Action*, 63 U. CHI. L. REV. 133 (1996)

Eric A. Posner & Miguel F. P. de Figueiredo, *Is the International Court of Justice Biased?* 34 J. LEG. STUD. 599 (2005)

Eric A. Posner & John C. Yoo, *Judicial Independence in International Tribunals*, 93 CALIF. L. REV. 1 (2005)

Eric A. Posner & John C. Yoo, *Reply to Helfer and Slaughter*, 93 CALIF. L. REV. 957 (2005)

Richard A. Posner, *Some Economics of International Law: Comments on Conference Papers*, 31 J. LEG. STUD. S321 (2002)

Thomas A. Pugel & Peter H. Lindert, INTERNATIONAL ECONOMICS (11th ed. 2000)

Matthew Rabin, *Incorporating Fairness into Game Theory and Economics*, 83 AM. ECON. REV. 1281 (1993)

Jeremy Rabkin, *Is EU Policy Eroding the Sovereignty of Non-Member States?* 1 CHI. J. INT'L L. 273 (2000)

Kal Raustiala, *The Architecture of International Cooperation: Transgovernmental Networks and the Future of International Law*, 43 VA. J. INT'L L. 1 (2002)

Eric Reinhardt, Aggressive Multilateralism: The Determinants of GATT/WTO Dispute Initiation, 1948–1998

Peter J. Richerson, ROBERT T. BOYD & JOSEPH HENRICH, *Cultural Evolution of Human Cooperation* in GENETIC AND CULTURAL EVOLUTION OF COOPERATION 357 (2003)

Robert J. S. Ross & Kent C. Trachte, GLOBAL CAPITALISM :THE NEW LEVIATHAN (1990)

Alexander N. Sack, LES EFFETS DES TRANSFORMATIONS DES ÉTATS SUR LEURS DETTES PUBLIQUES ET AUTRES OBLIGATIONS FINANCIÈRES (1927)

Jeswald W. Salacuse & Nicholas P. Sullivan, *Do BITs Really Work?: An Evaluation of Bilateral Investment Treaties and Their Grand Bargain*, 46 HARV. J. INT'L L. 67 (2005)

Saskia Sassen, LOSING CONTROL? SOVEREIGNTY IN AN AGE OF GLOBALIZATION (1999)

Oscar Schachter, *Human Dignity as a Normative Concept*, 77 AM.L. INT'L L. 848 (1983)

Oscar Schachter, *The Invisible College of International Lawyers*, 72 NW. U. L. REV. 217 (1977)

John M. Scheib, *Enforcing Judgments of the European Court of Human Rights: The Conduit Theory*, 19 N.Y. INT'L L.REV. 101 (1997)

Thomas Schelling, *An Essay on Bargaining*, 46 AM. ECON. REV.281 (1956)

Thomas C. Schelling, THE STRATEGY OF CONFLICT (1963)

Constanze Schulte, COMPLIANCE WITH DECISIONS OF THE INTERNATIONAL COURT OF JUSTICE (2004)

Alan Schwartz & Robert E. Scott, *Contract Theory and the Limits of Contract Law*, 113 YALE L.J. 541 (2003)

Alan Schwartz & Robert E. Scott, The Law and Economics of Preliminary Agreements

Warren F. Schwartz & Alan O. Sykes, *The Economic Structure of Renegotiation and Dispute Resolution in the World Trade Organization*, 31 J. LEGAL STUD. S179 (2002)

Robert E. Scott, *A Relational Theory of Default Rules for Commercial Contracts*, 19 J. LEGAL STUD. 597 (1990)

Robert E. Scott, *A Relational Theory of Secured Financing*, 86 COLUM. L. REV.901 (1986)

Robert E. Scott, *A Theory of Self-Enforcing Indefinite Agreements*, 103 COLUM. L. REV. 1641 (2003)

Robert E. Scott, *Conflict and Cooperation in Long-Term Contracts*, 75 CALIF. L. REV. 2000 (1987)

Robert E. Scott, *The Case for Formalism in Relational Contract*, 94 NW. U. L. REV. 847 (2000)

Robert E. Scott, *The Death of Contract Law*, 54 U. TORONTO L.J. 369 (2004)

Robert E. Scott, *The Limits of Behavioral Theories of Law and Social Norms*, 86 VA. L. REV. 1603 (2000)

Robert E. Scott, *The Rise and Fall of Article 2*, 62 LA. L. REV. 1009 (2002)

Robert E. Scott & Jody S. Kraus, CONTRACT LAW AND THEORY (Rev. 3RD ed. 2003)

Robert E. Scott & Paul B. Stephan, *Self-Enforcing International Agreements and The Limits of Coercion*, 2004 WISC. L. REV. 551

Robert E. Scott & George G. Triantis, *Anticipating Litigation by Contract Design*, 115 YALE L. J. 814 (2006)

Robert E. Scott & George G. Triantis, *Embedded Options and the Case Against Compensation in Contract Damages*, 104 COLUM. L. REV. 1428 (2004)

Paul Seabright, THE COMPANY OF STRANGERS: A NATURAL HISTORY OF ECONOMIC LIFE (2004)

John K. Setear, *A Forest with No Trees: The Supreme Court and International Law in the 2003 Term*, 91 VA. L. REV. 579 (2005)

John K. Setear, *Responses to Breach of a Treaty and Rationalist International Relations Theory: The Rules of Release and Remediation in the Law of Treaties and the Law of State Responsibility*, 83 VA. L.REV.1 (1997)

Gregory Shaffer, DEFENDING INTERESTS: PUBLIC-PRIVATE PARTNERSHIPS IN WTO LITIGATION (2003)

Dinah Shelton, REMEDIES ININTERNATIONAL HUMAN RIGHTS LAW (1999)

A. W. B. Simpson, A HISTORY OF THE COMMON LAW OF CONTRACT(1986)

John Cary Sims, *Compliance Without Remand: The Experience under the European Convention on Human Rights*, 36 ARIZ. ST. L.J.639 (2004)

Anne-Marie Slaughter, A NEW WORLD ORDER (2004)

Anne-Marie Slaughter Burley, *International Law and International Relations Theory: A Dual Agenda*, 87 AM. J. INT'LL. 205 (1993)

Anne-Marie [Slaughter] Burley, *Law Among Liberal States: Liberal Internationalism and the Act of State Doctrine*, 92 COLUM. L. REV. 1978 (1992)

Anne-Marie Slaughter, *Andrew S. Tulumello & Stepan Wood,International Law and International Relations Theory: A New Generation of Interdisciplinary Scholarship*, 92 AM. J. INT'L L. 367 (1998)

David Sloss, *Non-Self-Executing Treaties: Exposing A Constitutional Fallacy*, 36 U.C. DAVIS L. REV. 1 (2002)

Adam Smith, THE THEORY OF MORAL SENTIMENTS (1790)

Duncan Snidal, *Coordination versus Prisoners' Dilemma: Implications for International Cooperation and Regimes*, 79 AM. POL. SCI. REV. 923 (1985)

Sylvia Snowis, JUDICIAL REVIEW AND THE LAW OF THE CONSTITUTION (1990)

Paul B. Stephan, *Accountability and International Lawmaking: Rules, Rents and Legitimacy*, 17 NW.J.INT'L L.& BUS. 681 (1996–97)

Paul B. Stephan, *Constitutional Limits on the Struggle Against International Terrorism: Revisiting the Rights of Overseas Aliens*, 19 CONN. L. REV. 831 (1987)

Paul B. Stephan,*Courts, the Constitution, and Customary International Law – The Intellectual Origins of the Restatement (Third) of the Foreign Relations Law of the United States*, 43 VA. J. INT'L L.33 (2003)

Paul B. Stephan, Courts, *Tribunals and Legal Unification – The Agency Problem*, 3 CHI. J. INT'L L. 333 (2002)

Paul B. Stephan, *International Law in the Supreme Court*, 1990 SUP. CT. REV. 133

Paul B. Stephan, *Process Values, International Law, and Justice*, 23 SOCIAL PHIL. & POL'Y 132 (2006)

Paul B. Stephan, *Redistributive Litigation – Judicial Innovation, Private Expectations and the Shadow of International Law*, 88 VAL. REV. 789 (2002)

Paul B. Stephan, *Sheriff or Prisoner? The United States and the World Trade Organization*, 1 CHI. J. INT'L L. 49 (2000)

Paul B. Stephan, *The Futility of Unification and Harmonization in International Commercial Law*, 39 VA. J. INT'L L. 743 (1999)

Beth Stephens, *The Law of Our Land: Customary International Law as Federal Law After Erie*, 66 FORDHAM L. REV. 393 (1997)

Beth Stephens,*Translating Filártiga: A Comparative and International Law Analysis of Domestic Remedies for International Human Rights Violations*, 27 YALE J. INT'L L.1 (2002)

Susan Strange, THE RETREAT OF THE STATE –THE DIFFUSION OF POWER IN THE WORLD ECONOMY (1996)

Edward T. Swaine, *Rational Custom*, 52 DUKE L.J. 559 (2002)

Alan O. Sykes, *Public versus Private Enforcement of International Economic Law: Standing and Remedy*, 34 J. LEG. STUD. 631 (2005)

Alan O. Sykes, *International Law*, in HANDBOOK OF LAW AND ECONOMICS (Mitchell Polinsky & Steven Shavell eds. 2006)

Wendy Tacaks, *Pressures for Protectionism: An Empirical Analysis*, 19 ECON. INQUIRY 687 (1981)

Duane Tananbaum, THE BRICKER AMENDMENT CONTROVERSY – A TEST OF EISENHOWER'S POLITICAL LEADERSHIP (1988)

Daniel K. Tarullo, *Norms and Institutions in Global Competition Policy*, 94 AM. J. INT'L L. 478 (2000)

Maria A. Theodossiou, *An Analysis of the Recent Response of the Community to Non Compliance with Court of Justice Judgments: Article 228(2) E.C.*, 27 EUR. L. REV. 25 (2002)

Chantal Thomas, *Globalization and the Reproduction of Hierarchy*, 33 U.C. DAVIS L. REV. 1451 (2000)

Jean Tirole, *Incomplete Contracts: Where Do We Stand?*, 67 ECONOMETRICA 741 (1999)

Jennifer Tobin & Susan Rose-Ackerman, FOREIGN DIRECT INVESTMENT AND THE BUSINESS ENVIRONMENT IN DEVELOPING COUNTRIES: THE IMPACT OF BILATERAL INVESTMENT TREATIES (2005)

Joel P. Trachtman, *The Theory of the Firm and the Theory of International Economic Organization: Toward Comparative Institutional Analysis*, 17 NW. J. INT'L L. & BUS. 470 (1996–97)

Joel P. Trachtman & Philip M. Moremen, *Costs and Benefits of Private Participation in WTO Dispute Settlement: Whose Right Is It Anyway?* 44 HARV. INT'L L. J.221 (2003)

Laurence H. Tribe, *Taking Text and Structure Seriously: Reflections on Free-Form Method in Constitutional Interpretation*, 108 HARV. L. REV.1221 (1995)

Bakhtiyar Tuzmukhamedov, *The ICC and Russian Constitutional Problems*, 3 J. INT'L CRIM. JUSTICE 621 (2005)

U.N. Conf. on Trade and Dev, Bilateral Investment Treaties in the Mid-1990s, U.N. Doc. UNCTAD/ITE/IIT/7 (1998)

Michael P. Van Alstine, *The Costs of Legal Change*, 49 U.C.L.A. L. REV. 789 (2002)

Carlos Manuel Vázquez, *The Four Doctrines of Self-Executing Treaties*, 89 AM. J. INT'L L. 695 (1995)

Pierre-Hugues Verdier, *Cooperative States: International Relations, State Responsibility and the Problem of Custom*, 42 VA. J. INT'L. L. 839 (2002)

Max Weber, THE THEORY OF SOCIAL AND ECONOMIC ORGANIZATION (A.M. Henderson & Talcott Parsons trans. 1947)

J. H. H. Weiler, *The Transformation of Europe*, 100 YALE L.J. 2403 (1991)

Mark Weisburd, *International Courts and American Courts*, 21 MICH. J. INT'L L. 877 (2000)

Oliver E. Williamson, *Credible Commitments: Using Hostages to Support Exchange*, 73 AM. ECON. REV. 519 (1983)

Oliver E. Williamson, THE ECONOMIC INSTITUTIONS OF CAPITALISM : FIRMS, MARKETS, AND RELATIONAL CONTRACTING (1985)

Samuel Williston, A TREATISE ON THE LAW OF CONTRACTS, VOL. I (1990)

Karol Wolke, CUSTOM IN PRESENT INTERNATIONAL LAW (2ND rev. ed. 1993)

Tim Wu, *When D. American Judges Enforce Treaties?* 93 VA. L. REV. (2007)

Henry R. Zheng, *Defining Relationships and Resolving Conflicts Between Interrelated Multinational Trade Agreements: The Experience of the MFA and the GATT*, 25 STAN. J. INT'L L. 45 (1988)

# INDEX